Architectural Detailing Simplified

Architectural Detailing Simplified

CALEB HORNBOSTEL, ARCHITECT

Temple University, Philadelphia
School of Engineering and Architecture

PRENTICE-HALL, INC., Englewood Cliffs, NJ 07632

Library of Congress Cataloging in Publication Data

Hornbostel, Caleb.
   Architectural detailing simplified.

   Includes index.
   1. Architectural drawing—Detailing. I. Title.
NA2718.H67 1985   720'.28'4   84-9973
ISBN 0-13-044173-2

Editorial/production supervision
  and interior design: *Mary Carnis*
Cover design: *20/20 Services, Inc.*
Manufacturing buyer: *Anthony Caruso*
Delineator of details: *Carolyn E. Meyer*

Printed in the United States of America

10 9 8 7 6 5 4 3 2 1

ISBN 0-13-044173-2 01

Prentice-Hall International, Inc., *London*
Prentice-Hall of Australia Pty. Limited, *Sydney*
Editora Prentice-Hall do Brasil, Ltda., *Rio de Janeiro*
Prentice-Hall Canada Inc., *Toronto*
Prentice-Hall of India Private Limited, *New Delhi*
Prentice-Hall of Japan, Inc., *Tokyo*
Prentice-Hall of Southeast Asia Pte. Ltd., *Singapore*
Whitehall Books Limited, *Wellington, New Zealand*

Dedicated to the
National Institute for Architectural Education
to honor their unwavering devotion
to helping gifted and creative
architectural students

Contents

Contents

Preface

After many years of teaching in technical institutions, colleges, and universities, I slowly became aware of a continuing lack of down-to-earth, professional, architectural detailing books that presented working drawing details in such a way that students and young architects could easily understand what the basic design problem was and how it was answered. It was during the teaching of courses on working drawings and the use of materials to second, third, and fourth year students in Temple University that I compiled this group of details and developed the format of this book. My specific goal was to prepare aspiring architects-to-be in general with hands-on knowledge of how to combine theory, design and reality.

In addition, the format of this book was developed to show the *wide scope* of architectural details. It is hoped that through such a selective, qualitative approach, the book can become a valuable tool and reference source for practicing architects, draftpersons, contractors, and others in the construction field.

All the principles and details of this book are based on the realities of practice. All of the details have been built and in use for long enough periods of time to prove their effectiveness and practicality. These architectural details, taken from actual working drawings, have been carefully organized in single and double page layouts in such a manner so as to include all pertinent information related both to the basic problem and the resultant detail.

Where extra dimensions, explanatory notes, or descriptions of materials were felt to be necessary, they were incorporated either in the drawing itself or in the text, to clarify the detail. To make it even more easily understood, a general description of the detail problem and its solution was incorporated in chapter text and amplified in the text that accompanies and is part of the illustration.

As a textbook for architectural, structural engineering, and technical students, it is organized into 16 chapters that include a discussion of the general problems inherent in the designing of the details in that chapter. Each general discussion is followed by notes on every detail, including pertinent data not covered in the text that accompanies the illustrated detail itself. Thus each detail is further annotated to explain design, construction, and function, so that it can be fully understood and adapted for similar situations.

It is hoped that the book will serve as a guide for further development of an individual solution to problems of the same nature and not just as a copy source; that students and practicing professionals will be stimulated into analyzing basic problems and possible solutions in an innovative, creative way for both conventional and new materials and structural systems.

ACKNOWLEDGMENTS

To the many architects whose contribution of details to this book enriched the design concepts and realities it offers, I wish to express my deepest appreciation. Their names are listed alphabetically at the end of this section. I especially want to thank Carolyn E. Meyer, who was responsible for the delineation of the details, transforming my rough sketches into clear, crisp finished drawings. Next, my thanks to Sydnie Simone, who patiently typed the first rough drafts of text, then the final manuscript.

One of the pleasures of transforming an idea into a manuscript and then into its final book form was working first with Dennis Hogan, who encouraged me to produce the book, and then with Marcia J. Horton and the editorial staff at Prentice-Hall, Inc., who saw it through the various phases of production. All of them, especially Mary Carnis, were encouraging, cooperative, and creative at every step of the way.

Caleb Hornbostel

LIST OF CONTRIBUTING ARCHITECTS

1. Alley Friends Architects
   Front and Vine Streets
   Philadelphia, PA 19106

2. CRS/Caudill Rowlett Scott
   Architects Planners Engineers
   1111 West Loop South
   Houston, TX 70727

3. Collins and Associates
   Architects & Planners
   11 West 23rd Street
   Panama City, FL 32405

4. Gruen & Krummeck, Architects
   (No current address available)

5. Gwathmay Siegel & Associates,
   Architects
   475 Tenth Avenue
   New York, NY 10018

6. Caleb Hornbostel, Architect,
   F.N.I.A.E.
   515 West Chelten Avenue
   Philadelphia, PA 19144

7. Hugh Newell Jacobsen,
   F.A.I.A. Architect
   2529 P Street, N.W.
   Washington, D.C. 20007

8. David Hodges Karp, Architect
   5321 Knox Street
   Philadelphia, PA 19144

9. BJC/Knowles Architects, Associates,
   AIA/ARIBA
   419 S. Third Street, Society Hill
   Philadelphia, PA 19147

10. Robert D. Lynn Associates
    1501 Walnut Street
    Philadelphia, PA 19102

11. Don Metz, Architect
    Pinnacle Road, Box 52
    Lyme, NH 03768

12. Hugh H. Stubbins, Jr.
    and Associates, Inc.
    1033 Massachusetts Avenue
    Cambridge, MA 02138

13. Harry Teague, Architect
    P.O. Box 4684
    Aspen, CO 81611

Getting the Most Out of This Book

This book has been meticulously cross-indexed so that for any given chapter, with its topic introduction and individual general descriptions of each detail followed by full-page drawings of the details included in that chapter, there is also a thorough cross-reference section. This section lists the title and page number of all other drawings in the book where one can find similar detail features which relate to that particular chapter subject.

To take full advantage of the book's contents, one should start with the table of contents and select the chapter that covers the type of detail being researched. Then, after reading the text and studying the drawings with their explanatory text, one should turn to the cross-reference section and examine the details in other chapters which have within them alternative solutions to this specific detail problem. By using this approach, almost any problem in detailing can be studied in depth to find solutions upon which to build an individualized creative solution to a particular problem. The index was compiled to be as complete as possible and should add to the usefulness of this book.

Almost every detail in this book was actually built as designed and shown here. Most of them are still around for one to examine to see if they perform the function for which they were developed. They have withstood the test of time and thus met the criteria for selection and inclusion in this book.

Architectural Detailing Simplified

1

Historical Introduction to Detailing

INTRODUCTION

Putting materials together in a trouble-free manner has been a constant struggle in the construction of buildings for over four thousand years. The results of this struggle comprise what professionals term *architectural detailing*. Formats and handbooks for detailing were developed from the earliest times to approximately 1800, through the on-site experience of putting together buildings made of stone, brick, wood and cast iron. These time-hallowed handbooks based on materials and styles of various former periods of history, unfortunately for today's purposes, gradually became useless and now are practically obsolete.

Historically, there are several reasons. First, the Industrial Revolution created changes in the techniques of construction. Simultaneously, the philosophical roots of architecture were reexamined and new "contemporary" approaches were formulated in both thinking and design. None of these changes remained static for any length of time either in Europe or in the Western world in general. In the years following the early 1800s, acceleration in the development of new materials—the various types of steel; concrete that could be reinforced, prestressed, poststressed, precast, poured as shells; wood lamination; new paints, glass, adhesives, and synthetics—plus the new aesthetic and design philosophies created an illusionary outlook that human beings were beyond nature and could completely ignore it and its physical laws.

As a result, many buildings failed, some in a multitude of small ways and others spectacularly. Some of these failings can be attributed to detailing that was inadequately studied or, worse, that was not studied at all. Because of an overemphasis on theoretical design and aesthetic philosophies, intelligent thinking on how to put materials together was largely disregarded or even ignored entirely. How often has one heard, "Details are so tedious and difficult."

So we come to a conundrum for the architects of today and tomorrow: *design* and *details*, what is the interrelationship? Is it a case of the chicken and the egg? Which is first? Which is primary? Can either be primary?

The best overall design may be impossible or, worse, may prove defective when constructed and put to its intended use. After all the talk and graphics are done, any building, however grandiose and seemingly perfect in its philosophical and design concepts, is in reality the sum of its parts. Details therefore can be and often are determinants rather than chores in the execution of design abstractions. In many cases the overall concept was stimulated, changed, and improved by an architectural detail. The trigger effect or thought release in the working out of a detail should never be underestimated. Without details that are clearly thought out, correctly designed, and coordinated into a three-dimensional reality, no building can be truly successful.

Lately the architectural profession has followed the trend toward specialization that has occurred in other areas, and one finds that in today's and tomorrow's world the entire field of detailing has taken on a completely new significance. It has become a "speciality" unto itself within the overall field of architecture, a specialty now designated as *Technology*.

CROSS-REFERENCES TO *HISTORICAL INTRODUCTION TO DETAILING*
IN OTHER CHAPTERS

Chapter Number	Drawing Number	Drawing Title	Described on Page	Drawing on Page
2	2–3	Residential wall sections	7	11
	2–5	Exterior skin curtain wall	8	13
11	11–2	Sloping window with sill ventilation	99	102
12	12–1	Solar residence	109	110, 111
	12–2	Underground house	109	112, 113
14	14–9	Reception desk	128	140, 141

Note: Cross references are given in this introductory chapter merely to emphasize how answers are constantly emerging with regard to new techniques, materials and architectural design concepts.

2

Walls and Skins

INTRODUCTION

In this chapter a sampling of various types of walls and skins has been included, ranging from simple wood stud wall partitions and masonry bearing walls to various combinations of veneers, plastics, and metals and other materials to form skins, walls covered with earth, and other types seen in today's architecture.

With regard to "skin" walls, a word of caution is appropriate in view of all the complications of designing the entire surface skin of a building, which incorporates a grid system for windows, spandrel panels, the attachment of these elements to the grid system, the provision for expansion both vertically and horizontally, and finally the method of securing the skin with all its parts to the building structure proper. It is necessary to specify that a full-scale mock-up be made and tested for all environmental conditions of the area and site where the building is to be constructed.

The variety of treatments of the exterior walls has grown in scope to such an extent that there is tremendous opportunity for creative design and detailing in this area. It is hoped that examining some of the details here and those listed in the cross-references will stimulate innovative approaches to materials, old and new, and to designs ranging from the starkly simple to the decorative and complex.

CHAPTER DETAIL TEXT

2-1 Reinforced Concrete Structure with Cavity Wall

This detail from a multistory elementary school shows the use of vertical brick coursing in a reinforced concrete structure with cavity walls. The emphasis here is on the importance of correct detailing for vertical brick coursing in a cavity wall resting on a spandrel beam projection. The plan here shows two alternative treatments, one using continuous windows, and the other a 1' brick pier at the columns.

A very high R value is obtained for the exterior wall by the use of 2" foam (R-12.50), glazed masonry units with voids filled with foam insulation (R-16.20), brick (R-0.40), and 1" air space (R-0.92). Thus an R value of 30.02 is obtained.

Note that the concrete projection has a 1" vertical recess at the 4" brick depth dimension. This is done so that the windows can be installed from the inside of the building.

2-2 Curtain Wall This detail of a 6" limestone-faced curtain wall by Collins and Associates, Architects and Planners, Panama City, Florida, shows that the many difficult problems of designing the exterior skin of a building can be made very simple by good architectural detailing.

The 9'-0" floor-to-ceiling height with the hung lay-in acoustical tile allows sufficient space for the air-conditioning supply and return ducts. Note how simply the low parapet wall is treated: a wood nailer, a continuous metal clip on the exterior face, and a metal cap merely nailed to the wood nailer on the roof side.

2-3 Residential Wall Sections Various wall sections of the Viereck residence in Amagansett, New York, by Gwathmey Siegel, Architects, show a wide variety of simple detail solutions for roofs, decks, walls, windows, and insulation. Each detail has been carefully thought out to find a simple, direct answer to a problem and keep the design clean, crisp, and elegant.

Note the simple design detailing at the sills of the glass sliding doors, where the sill flashing, 2" × 4" sleepers, and the ¾" × 4" redwood decking allow the deck floor to be at the same elevation as the inside carpet.

The termination of the ½" gypsum board at the heads, sills, and jambs, with a painted ½" × 2⅞" hardwood trim, gives a simple answer to this normally difficult design detail.

2-4 Simple Exterior and Interior Load-Bearing Walls These wall details are from an elementary school and a junior high school designed by the author's office. The wall details are of simple wall-bearing structures in which the exterior walls were made waterproof by overlapping membranes and the inside walls were treated to match the purpose for which the area was to be used. Thus it was acoustically treated for multipurpose rooms, finished with birch plywood with bronze channels for all horizontal and vertical joints in the library, and in the corridors. Selected colors of glazed masonry units were used.

The ½" × ½" bronze channels are secured to the wood furring strips with ⅛" × 1" round-head bronze wood-type Phillips Screws ® 2'-0" apart both vertically and horizontally.

Note that the lintel over the windows is a heavy I-beam with a welded plate on the bottom. The small angle to support the brick is on an extension so that a small ⅛" slot remains between the plate and the angle, and the window head piece can then be inserted in the slot.

The floor of the multipurpose room consists of a 5" reinforced concrete slab, a heavy asphaltic two-ply waterproof membrane, and then 2" × 6" by 2'-0"s staggered and placed flatwise directly on the asphaltic membrane 16" apart. Then the 1¼″ T & G maple flooring was installed, leaving a 1″ expansion void on all four sides. A simple steel angle was installed to cover this open joint.

2-5 Exterior Skin Curtain Wall

This detail is a true expression of the term "skin" for the exterior surface of a building. The Herman Miller Seating Plant, Holland, Michigan, was designed by CRS/Caudill Rowlett Scott, Architects, Planners, Engineers; Paul Kennon FAIA, design principal; and Jay Bauer AIA, project architect. The ingenious use of bent 2½″ structural steel pipes applied to the exterior of the basic steel structure provide clerestory light, metal insulated panels, and fixed and sliding windows that are in-sloping for sun control. This simple skin results in an extremely simple, well-proportioned, and handsome building.

Note the careful detailing of the juncture of the double acrylic clerestory and roof. The method of attaching the 4″ insulated panels to the 2½″ structural steel pipe and the use of a continuous extruded black silicone gasket at the joints indicate detailing which not only answers a joining problem but also creates an important imaginative design element for the entire building.

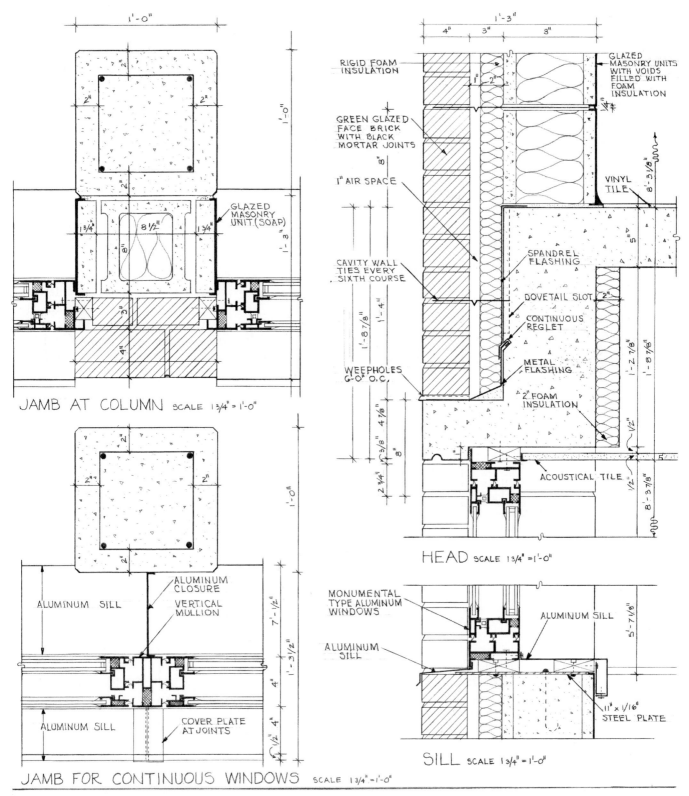

JAMB AT COLUMN SCALE 1 3/4" = 1'-0"

GLAZED MASONRY UNIT (SOAP)

JAMB FOR CONTINUOUS WINDOWS SCALE 1 3/4" = 1'-0"

ALUMINUM CLOSURE
VERTICAL MULLION
ALUMINUM SILL
ALUMINUM SILL
COVER PLATE AT JOINTS

RIGID FOAM INSULATION
GREEN GLAZED FACE BRICK WITH BLACK MORTAR JOINTS
1" AIR SPACE
CAVITY WALL TIES EVERY SIXTH COURSE
WEEPHOLES 6'-0" O.C.
GLAZED MASONRY UNITS WITH VOIDS FILLED WITH FOAM INSULATION
VINYL TILE
SPANDREL FLASHING
DOVETAIL SLOT 2"
CONTINUOUS REGLET
METAL FLASHING
2" FOAM INSULATION
ACOUSTICAL TILE

HEAD SCALE 1 3/4" = 1'-0"

MONUMENTAL TYPE ALUMINUM WINDOWS
ALUMINUM SILL
ALUMINUM SILL
11" x 1/16" STEEL PLATE

SILL SCALE 1 3/4" = 1'-0"

REINFORCED CONCRETE STRUCTURE WITH CAVITY WALL

2–1

The concrete spandrel beams have a concrete projection 7" X 5¼" which is 1'-4" below the top of the spandrel beams. This projection was designed to support the exterior brick facing, including a 3" cavity consisting of a 1" air space and 2" of rigid foam insulation. The rigid foam insulation in 16" heights (to fit between the cavity wall ties) is applied with adhesive to the spandrel and the back face of the glazed masonry units. Voids in the glazed masonry units are filled with field-applied foam insulation to increase the *R* factor of the exterior wall. Note the continuous reglet in the spandrel beams, designed to take the continuous metal flashing, which directs any water from the cavity to the weepholes. Dovetail slots are installed in the outside face of the spandrel beams 2'-8" o.c. for the cavity wall ties, which are installed every six brick courses.

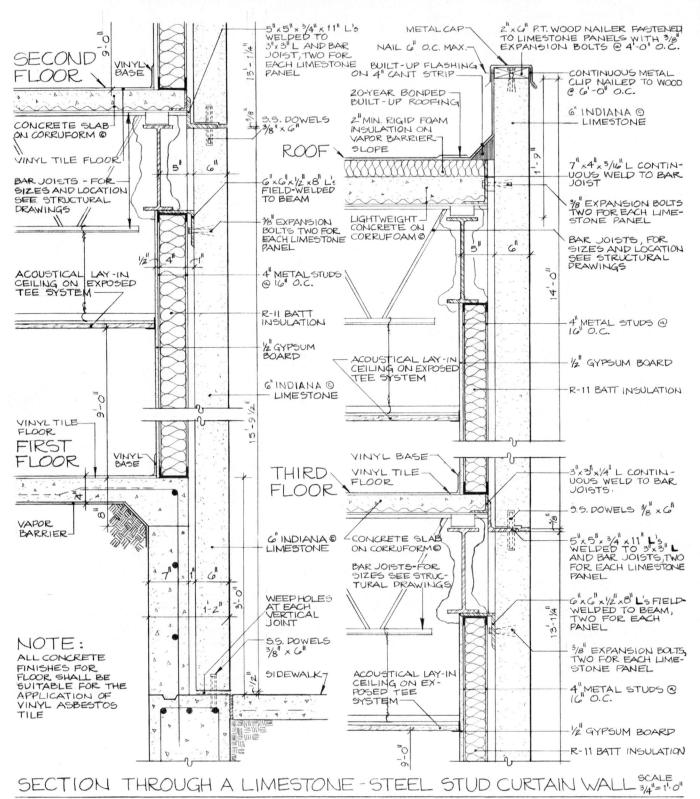

SECTION THROUGH A LIMESTONE-STEEL STUD CURTAIN WALL
SCALE ¾"=1'-0"

2-2 **CURTAIN WALL**

Collins and Associates, architects and planners for the three-story addition to the Bay County Courthouse in Florida, were faced with the design problem of how to remain in the same architectural character as the existing structure. Their solution was extremely simple: they designed a steel frame building using open web joists, with concrete slabs on Corroform® spanning between the joists. They faced the building with a 6" veneer of Indiana limestone, backed up with 4" steel studs, R-11 batt-type insulation, and enclosed with ½" gypsum board for the interior surface. The top 14'-0" high limestone panels are designed to extend 1'-9" above the top of the roof structural steel, creating by this means a low parapet wall. Note the use of Indiana limestone here to tie in designwise to the existing courthouse.

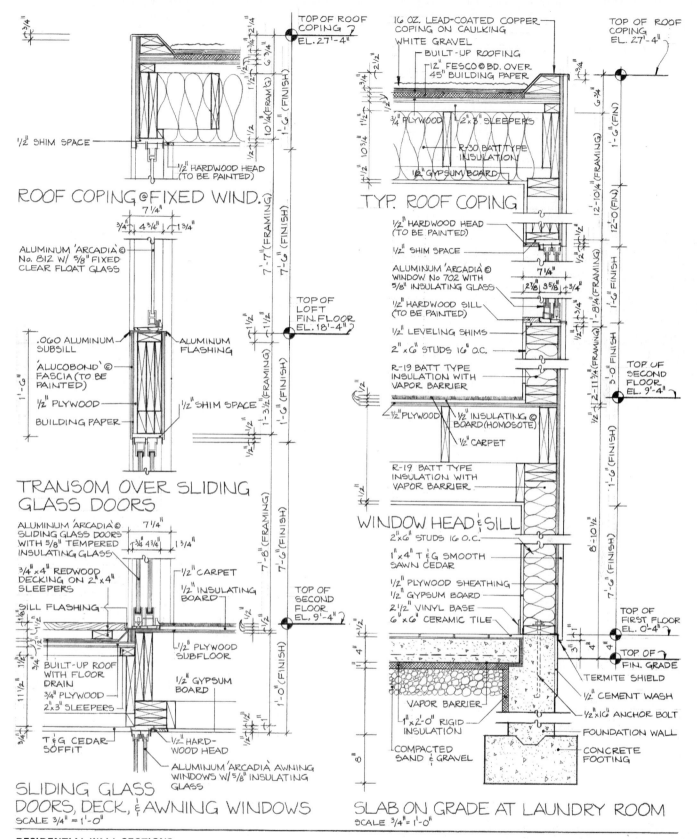

ROOF COPING @ FIXED WIND.

- ½" SHIM SPACE
- ½" HARDWOOD HEAD (TO BE PAINTED)
- TOP OF ROOF COPING EL. 27'-4"

TRANSOM OVER SLIDING GLASS DOORS

- ALUMINUM 'ARCADIA'© No. 812 W/ ⅝" FIXED CLEAR FLOAT GLASS
- .060 ALUMINUM SUBSILL
- 'ALUCOBOND'© FASCIA (TO BE PAINTED)
- ½" PLYWOOD
- BUILDING PAPER
- ALUMINUM FLASHING
- ½" SHIM SPACE
- TOP OF LOFT FIN. FLOOR EL. 18'-4"

SLIDING GLASS DOORS, DECK, & AWNING WINDOWS
SCALE ¾" = 1'-0"

- ALUMINUM 'ARCADIA'© SLIDING GLASS DOORS WITH ⅝" TEMPERED INSULATING GLASS
- ¾" x 4" REDWOOD DECKING ON 2" x 4" SLEEPERS
- SILL FLASHING
- BUILT-UP ROOF WITH FLOOR DRAIN
- ¾" PLYWOOD
- 2" x 3" SLEEPERS
- T & G CEDAR SOFFIT
- ½" CARPET
- ½" INSULATING BOARD
- ½" PLYWOOD SUBFLOOR
- ½" GYPSUM BOARD
- ½" HARDWOOD HEAD
- ALUMINUM 'ARCADIA' AWNING WINDOWS W/ ⅝" INSULATING GLASS
- TOP OF SECOND FLOOR EL. 9'-4"

TYP. ROOF COPING

- 16 OZ. LEAD-COATED COPPER COPING ON CAULKING
- WHITE GRAVEL
- BUILT-UP ROOFING
- ½" FESCO© BD. OVER 45# BUILDING PAPER
- ¾" PLYWOOD
- 2" x 8" SLEEPERS
- R-30 BATT TYPE INSULATION
- ½" GYPSUM BOARD
- TOP OF ROOF COPING EL. 27'-4"

WINDOW HEAD & SILL

- ½" HARDWOOD HEAD (TO BE PAINTED)
- ½" SHIM SPACE
- ALUMINUM 'ARCADIA'© WINDOW No. 702 WITH ⅝" INSULATING GLASS
- ½" HARDWOOD SILL (TO BE PAINTED)
- ½" LEVELING SHIMS
- 2" x 6" STUDS 16" O.C.
- R-19 BATT TYPE INSULATION WITH VAPOR BARRIER
- ½" PLYWOOD
- ½" INSULATING @ BOARD (HOMOSOTE)
- ½" CARPET
- R-19 BATT TYPE INSULATION WITH VAPOR BARRIER
- 2" x 6" STUDS 16" O.C.
- 1" x 4" T & G SMOOTH SAWN CEDAR
- ½" PLYWOOD SHEATHING
- ½" GYPSUM BOARD
- 2½" VINYL BASE
- 6" x 6" CERAMIC TILE
- TOP OF SECOND FLOOR EL. 9'-4"

SLAB ON GRADE AT LAUNDRY ROOM
SCALE ¾" = 1'-0"

- VAPOR BARRIER
- 4" x 2'-0" RIGID INSULATION
- COMPACTED SAND & GRAVEL
- TOP OF FIRST FLOOR EL. 0'-4"
- TOP OF FIN. GRADE
- TERMITE SHIELD
- ½" CEMENT WASH
- ½" x 10" ANCHOR BOLT
- FOUNDATION WALL
- CONCRETE FOOTING

RESIDENTIAL WALL SECTIONS

These details by Gwathmey Siegel, Architects, of the Viereck residence in Amagamsett, New York, include a series of wall sections. These sections show simple answers to many of the contemporary detail problems, such as roof copings, flat roof insulation, window heads and sills, roof decking, sliding glass doors, and insulation of exterior walls and slab on grade. Note careful acoustical treatment of floors by using ½" plywood subflooring, ½" Homosote® as a sound deadener, and ½" carpet. Note the careful treatment at grade by offsetting the 2" × 6" sill ½", thereby allowing a ½" cement wash to be applied to the foundation wall at grade. Termite control is achieved by a small shield on the exterior, and the fact that the vapor barrier and rigid insulation on the inside and underside of the slab automatically become a shield.

2—3

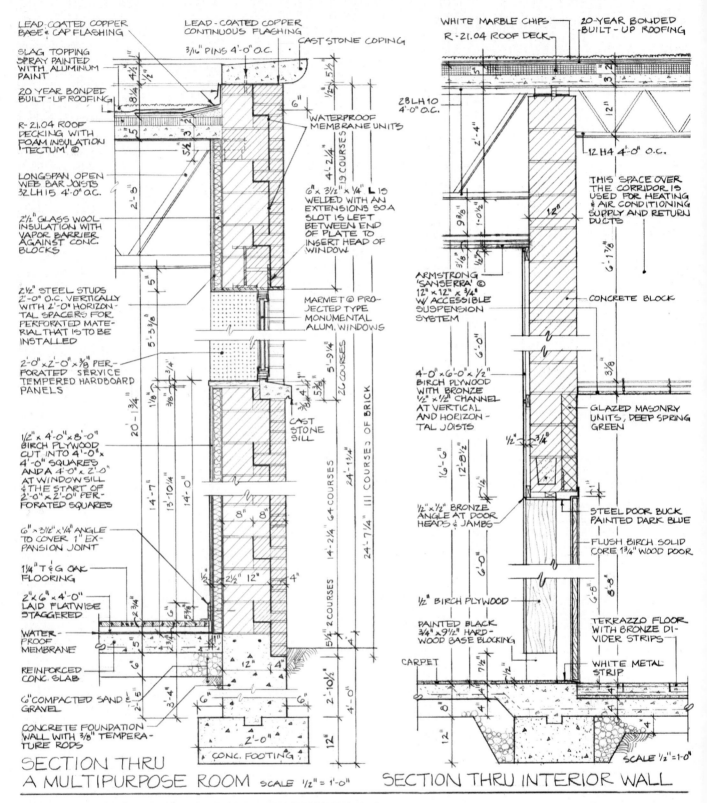

LEAD-COATED COPPER BASE & CAP FLASHING

LEAD-COATED COPPER CONTINUOUS FLASHING

CAST STONE COPING

WHITE MARBLE CHIPS

20-YEAR BONDED BUILT-UP ROOFING

R-21.04 ROOF DECK

3/16" PINS 4'-0" O.C.

SLAG TOPPING SPRAY PAINTED WITH ALUMINUM PAINT

WATERPROOF MEMBRANE UNITS

20 YEAR BONDED BUILT-UP ROOFING

2 BLH 10 4'-0" O.C.

R-21.04 ROOF DECKING WITH FOAM INSULATION 'TECTUM' ©

6" x 3½" x ¼" L 15 WELDED WITH AN EXTENSIONS SO A SLOT IS LEFT BETWEEN END OF PLATE TO INSERT HEAD OF WINDOW

12 H4 4'-0" O.C.

LONGSPAN OPEN WEB BAR JOISTS 32LH15 4'-0" O.C.

THIS SPACE OVER THE CORRIDOR IS USED FOR HEATING & AIR CONDITIONING SUPPLY AND RETURN DUCTS

2½" GLASS WOOL INSULATION WITH VAPOR BARRIER AGAINST CONC. BLOCKS

MARMET © PROJECTED TYPE MONUMENTAL ALUM. WINDOWS

CONCRETE BLOCK

2½" STEEL STUDS 2'-0" O.C. VERTICALLY WITH 2'-0" HORIZONTAL SPACERS FOR PERFORATED MATERIAL THAT IS TO BE INSTALLED

ARMSTRONG 'SANSERRA' © 12" x 12" x ¾" W/ ACCESSIBLE SUSPENSION SYSTEM

2'-0" x 2'-0" x 3/8" PERFORATED SERVICE TEMPERED HARDBOARD PANELS

4'-0" x 6'-0" x ½" BIRCH PLYWOOD WITH BRONZE ½" x ½" CHANNEL AT VERTICAL AND HORIZONTAL JOISTS

GLAZED MASONRY UNITS, DEEP SPRING GREEN

½" x 4'-0" x 8'-0" BIRCH PLYWOOD CUT INTO 4'-0" x 4'-0" SQUARES AND A 4'-0" x 2'-0" AT WINDOW SILL & THE START OF 2'-0" x 2'-0" PERFORATED SQUARES

CAST STONE SILL

6" x 3½" x ¼" ANGLE TO COVER 1" EXPANSION JOINT

½" x ½" BRONZE ANGLE AT DOOR HEADS & JAMBS

STEEL DOOR BUCK PAINTED DARK BLUE

1¼" T & G OAK FLOORING

FLUSH BIRCH SOLID CORE 1¾" WOOD DOOR

2" x 6" x 4'-0" LAID FLATWISE STAGGERED

WATERPROOF MEMBRANE

½" BIRCH PLYWOOD

TERRAZZO FLOOR WITH BRONZE DIVIDER STRIPS

REINFORCED CONC. SLAB

PAINTED BLACK ¾" x 9½" HARDWOOD BASE BLOCKING

WHITE METAL STRIP

6" COMPACTED SAND & GRAVEL

CARPET

CONCRETE FOUNDATION WALL WITH 3/8" TEMPERATURE RODS

CONC. FOOTING

SCALE ½" = 1'-0"

SECTION THRU A MULTIPURPOSE ROOM SCALE ½" = 1'-0"

SECTION THRU INTERIOR WALL

2–4 SIMPLE EXTERIOR AND INTERIOR LOAD-BEARING WALLS

This multipurpose wall is made completely waterproof by using overlapping waterproof membrane units. The interior of the wall is treated with ½" X 4'-0" squares of birch plywood with 2½" of glass wool insulation up to the sills of the clerestory windows. From the window sill up to the underside of the decking are installed 3/8" X 2'-0" squares of service-grade perforated tempered hardboard panels backed by 2½" of glass wool with vapor barrier against the concrete block. The Tectum® decking has a surface with good acoustical characteristics. The interior concrete block bearing wall is faced with glazed masonry units on the corridor side and treated on the library side with ½" birch plywood with ½" X ½" bronze channels for all horizontal and vertical joints.

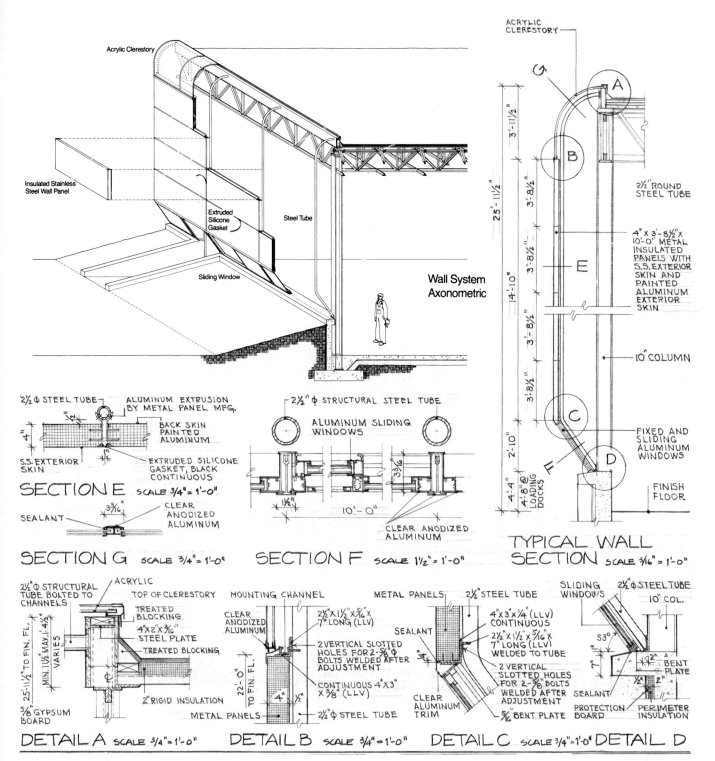

Acrylic Clerestory

Insulated Stainless Steel Wall Panel

Extruded Silicone Gasket

Steel Tube

Sliding Window

Wall System Axonometric

ACRYLIC CLERESTORY

2½" ROUND STEEL TUBE

4" X 3'-8½" X 10'-0" METAL INSULATED PANELS WITH S.S. EXTERIOR SKIN AND PAINTED ALUMINUM EXTERIOR SKIN

10" COLUMN

FIXED AND SLIDING ALUMINUM WINDOWS

FINISH FLOOR

25'-11½"

3'-11½"

3'-8½"

3'-8½"

14'-10"

3'-8½"

3'-8½"

2'-10"

4'-4"

4'-8" @ LOADING DOCKS

2½" Φ STEEL TUBE

ALUMINUM EXTRUSION BY METAL PANEL MFG.

BACK SKIN PAINTED ALUMINUM

S.S. EXTERIOR SKIN

EXTRUDED SILICONE GASKET, BLACK CONTINUOUS

4"

SECTION E   SCALE ¾"= 1'-0"

SEALANT

3³⁄₁₆"

CLEAR ANODIZED ALUMINUM

SECTION G   SCALE ¾"= 1'-0"

2½" Φ STRUCTURAL STEEL TUBE

ALUMINUM SLIDING WINDOWS

CLEAR ANODIZED ALUMINUM

1½"

10'-0"

3³⁄₁₆"

SECTION F   SCALE 1½"= 1'-0"

TYPICAL WALL SECTION   SCALE 3⁄₁₆"= 1'-0"

2½" Φ STRUCTURAL TUBE BOLTED TO CHANNELS

ACRYLIC

TOP OF CLERESTORY

TREATED BLOCKING

4"x2"x⁵⁄₁₆" STEEL PLATE

TREATED BLOCKING

25'-11½" TO FIN. FL.

MIN. 1½" MAY. 4½" VARIES

5⁄₈" GYPSUM BOARD

2" RIGID INSULATION

DETAIL A   SCALE ¾"= 1'-0"

MOUNTING CHANNEL

CLEAR ANODIZED ALUMINUM

2½"x1½"x⁵⁄₁₆"x 7" LONG (LLV)

2 VERTICAL SLOTTED HOLES FOR 2-⁵⁄₈" Φ BOLTS WELDED AFTER ADJUSTMENT

CONTINUOUS 4"X3" X ⅜" (LLV)

22'-0" TO FIN. FL.

4"

½"

METAL PANELS

2½" Φ STEEL TUBE

DETAIL B   SCALE ¾"= 1'-0"

METAL PANELS

SEALANT

2½" STEEL TUBE

4"x3"x¼" (LLV) CONTINUOUS

2½"x1½"x⁵⁄₁₆"x 7" LONG (LLV) WELDED TO TUBE

2 VERTICAL SLOTTED HOLES FOR 2-⁵⁄₈" BOLTS WELDED AFTER ADJUSTMENT

CLEAR ALUMINUM TRIM

⁵⁄₁₆" BENT PLATE

DETAIL C   SCALE ¾"= 1'-0"

SLIDING WINDOWS

2½" Φ STEEL TUBE

10" COL.

53°

7"

2" BENT PLATE

½"   2"

SEALANT

PROTECTION BOARD

PERIMETER INSULATION

DETAIL D

EXTERIOR SKIN CURTAIN WALL

2–5

The curtain wall details in this illustration are of the Herman Miller Seating Plant, Holland, Michigan, created by CRS/Caudill Rowlett Scott, Architects, Planners, Engineers of Houston, Texas; Paul Kennon FAIA, design principal; and Jay Bauer AIA, project engineer. This creative treatment of the exterior skin of a factory is handsome, simple, and efficient. Here top light is supplied by a double acrylic clerestory which is curved, thus letting maximum light into the space. Then a vertical surface (consisting of 4" insulated panels with stainless steel on the exterior and painted aluminum on the interior) has these insulated panels joined by a 1" black silicone joint cover both vertically and horizontally. These black strips are important design accents. At the bottom, fixed and sliding windows set at a 53° angle for sun control are installed. The simple steel structure has bent 2½" structural pipes attached to the top of the structure upon which the entire clerestory, metal panels and windows are supported.

CROSS-REFERENCES TO *WALLS AND SKINS*
IN OTHER CHAPTERS

3

Flashing

INTRODUCTION

Flashing refers to both the material used and the application of that material to weatherproof and waterproof joints wherever different materials are brought together and wherever different parts of a structure meet. Flashing prevents the penetration of water into a building. It is used where a roof meets vertical walls and where a building meets the earth at grade, and it is installed at the head and sill of any and all openings in buildings. In exterior walls, the flashing is installed behind the facing of the building and is known as spandrel flashing. When cavity walls are used, the spandrel flashing and cavity flashing are combined to direct any water within the cavity to the weepholes. Perhaps some of the most difficult flashing problems occur when a roof surface is penetrated by pipes, chimneys, ducts, railings, supports for mechanical units and similar penetrating structures. Flashing also includes the devices and joints that serve as control joints and expansion joints in buildings.

There are two types of flashing, exposed and concealed, and their terminology explains the difference. Exposed flashing can and does affect the design of a building. Since it is exposed, it must withstand this exposure for a long period of time. Most exposed flashing is either metal or plastic, and it must meet the requirements of color, texture, and resistance to the weather and atmospheric conditions that the building must withstand.

With concealed flashing, because it is not visible, the only problems lie in selecting the material that will be correct for the job and then applying it properly. Thin metal sheet or foil, a fabric, a plastic, and various combinations of these materials are used. Papers and fabrics saturated with asphalt or plastics are also used for concealed flashing. The cross-references for this chapter list the many examples to be found throughout the book of the various types of flashing and how they are used.

CHAPTER DETAIL TEXT

3-1 Chimney Flashing at Ridge and Flat Roofs

DETAIL 1. This shows various types of roofing materials with base flashing and chimney cap flashing when a chimney penetrates through a flat roof. The cant strips at the chimney must be of fireproof material if placed against the wall of the chimney.

When a fire is started in a boiler the chimney expands vertically. This expansion in a 30-story building can be considerable and could cause structural damage if the chimney is incorporated with and as part of the building structure. In multistory buildings the chimney cap flashing should overlap the base flashing sufficiently to allow for the vertical expansion of the chimney.

DETAIL 2. This shows all of the required flashing when a chimney penetrates the ridge of a roof. Note the 2″ separation between chimney and wood roof structure as a fireproofing precaution. The base flashing at ridge bends up vertically and goes under the chimney cap flashing.

3-2 Four Common Flashing Conditions

DETAIL 1. This shows how to cap a stone veneer at roof.

DETAIL 2. This shows treatment of a simple low parapet wall with railing by the use of stock aluminum coping and projecting the pipe railing from the parapet wall in order to clear the coping.

DETAILS 3 AND 4. Shown are two methods of installing the cover of an expansion joint, one on built-up roofing, and the other on membrane-type roofing.

3-3 Four Special Flashing Conditions

DETAIL 1. We see here a method of supporting an air-conditioning unit or other heavy equipment to be installed above the roof. Note the use of a neoprene pad and washer plus the water seal membrane to help stop the vibrating of the air-conditioning unit from passing into the structure.

DETAIL 2. Shown is a simple light steel one-story structure with full-height pebble-concrete precast panels on the exterior and a single-ply membrane roofing.

DETAIL 3. Here is a method of installing a stainless pipe railing in which all flashing is of stainless steel to eliminate any possibility of galvanic action. With the use of all aluminum or galvanized steel components, an aluminum or galvanized steel pipe railing could be installed.

DETAIL 4. In the installation of a stainless steel gutter, concrete block is used to enclose the steel beam and allow the brick veneer to extend up and act as a form for the $2\frac{1}{2}$″ reinforced concrete roof slab.

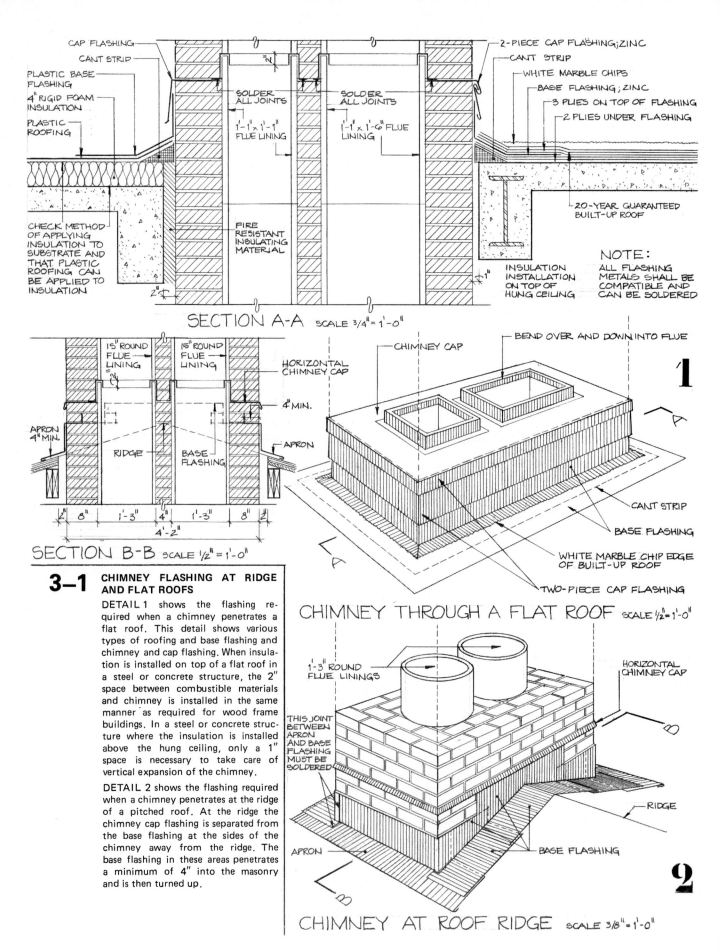

CAP FLASHING

CANT STRIP

PLASTIC BASE FLASHING

4" RIGID FOAM INSULATION

PLASTIC ROOFING

CHECK METHOD OF APPLYING INSULATION TO SUBSTRATE AND THAT PLASTIC ROOFING CAN BE APPLIED TO INSULATION

SOLDER ALL JOINTS

SOLDER ALL JOINTS

1'-1" x 1'-1" FLUE LINING

1'-1" x 1'-6" FLUE LINING

FIRE RESISTANT INSULATING MATERIAL

2" ℄

2-PIECE CAP FLASHING; ZINC

CANT STRIP

WHITE MARBLE CHIPS

BASE FLASHING; ZINC

3 PLIES ON TOP OF FLASHING

2 PLIES UNDER FLASHING

20-YEAR GUARANTEED BUILT-UP ROOF

1"

INSULATION INSTALLATION ON TOP OF HUNG CEILING

NOTE: ALL FLASHING METALS SHALL BE COMPATIBLE AND CAN BE SOLDERED

SECTION A-A SCALE 3/4" = 1'-0"

15" ROUND FLUE LINING

15" ROUND FLUE LINING

HORIZONTAL CHIMNEY CAP

4" MIN.

APRON 4" MIN.

RIDGE

BASE FLASHING

APRON

2" 8" 1'-3" 4" 1'-3" 8" 2"

4'-2"

SECTION B-B SCALE 1/2" = 1'-0"

3–1 CHIMNEY FLASHING AT RIDGE AND FLAT ROOFS

DETAIL 1 shows the flashing required when a chimney penetrates a flat roof. This detail shows various types of roofing and base flashing and chimney and cap flashing. When insulation is installed on top of a flat roof in a steel or concrete structure, the 2" space between combustible materials and chimney is installed in the same manner as required for wood frame buildings. In a steel or concrete structure where the insulation is installed above the hung ceiling, only a 1" space is necessary to take care of vertical expansion of the chimney.

DETAIL 2 shows the flashing required when a chimney penetrates at the ridge of a pitched roof. At the ridge the chimney cap flashing is separated from the base flashing at the sides of the chimney away from the ridge. The base flashing in these areas penetrates a minimum of 4" into the masonry and is then turned up.

CHIMNEY CAP

BEND OVER AND DOWN INTO FLUE

1

A

CANT STRIP

BASE FLASHING

WHITE MARBLE CHIP EDGE OF BUILT-UP ROOF

TWO-PIECE CAP FLASHING

A

CHIMNEY THROUGH A FLAT ROOF SCALE 1/2" = 1'-0"

1'-3" ROUND FLUE LININGS

HORIZONTAL CHIMNEY CAP

THIS JOINT BETWEEN APRON AND BASE FLASHING MUST BE SOLDERED

RIDGE

APRON

BASE FLASHING

B

2

CHIMNEY AT ROOF RIDGE SCALE 3/8" = 1'-0"

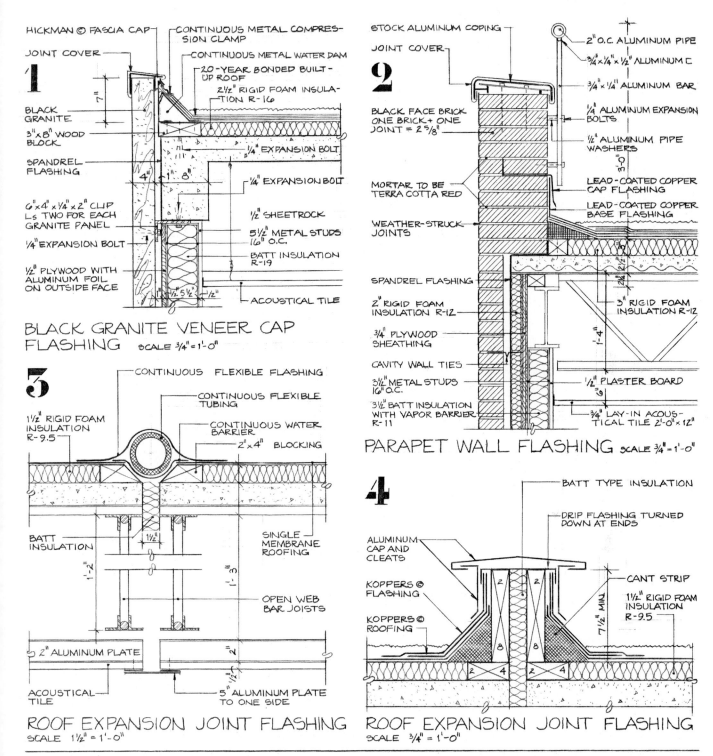

1
BLACK GRANITE VENEER CAP FLASHING SCALE 3/4" = 1'-0"

- HICKMAN © FASCIA CAP
- JOINT COVER
- BLACK GRANITE
- 3"×8" WOOD BLOCK
- SPANDREL FLASHING
- 6"×4"×1/4"×2" CLIP Ls TWO FOR EACH GRANITE PANEL
- 1/4" EXPANSION BOLT
- 1/2" PLYWOOD WITH ALUMINUM FOIL ON OUTSIDE FACE
- CONTINUOUS METAL COMPRESSION CLAMP
- CONTINUOUS METAL WATER DAM
- 20-YEAR BONDED BUILT-UP ROOF
- 2½" RIGID FOAM INSULATION R-16
- 1/4" EXPANSION BOLT
- 1/4" EXPANSION BOLT
- 1/2" SHEETROCK
- 5½" METAL STUDS 16" O.C.
- BATT INSULATION R-19
- ACOUSTICAL TILE

2
PARAPET WALL FLASHING SCALE 3/4" = 1'-0"

- STOCK ALUMINUM COPING
- JOINT COVER
- BLACK FACE BRICK ONE BRICK + ONE JOINT = 2 5/8"
- MORTAR TO BE TERRA COTTA RED
- WEATHER-STRUCK JOINTS
- SPANDREL FLASHING
- 2" RIGID FOAM INSULATION R-12
- 3/4" PLYWOOD SHEATHING
- CAVITY WALL TIES
- 3½" METAL STUDS 16" O.C.
- 3½" BATT INSULATION WITH VAPOR BARRIER R-11
- 2" O.C. ALUMINUM PIPE
- 3/4"×1/4"×1/2" ALUMINUM C
- 3/4"×1/4" ALUMINUM BAR
- 1/4" ALUMINUM EXPANSION BOLTS
- 1/2" ALUMINUM PIPE WASHERS
- LEAD-COATED COPPER CAP FLASHING
- LEAD-COATED COPPER BASE FLASHING
- 3" RIGID FOAM INSULATION R-12
- 1/2" PLASTER BOARD
- 3/4" LAY-IN ACOUSTICAL TILE 2'-0"×12"

3
ROOF EXPANSION JOINT FLASHING SCALE 1½" = 1'-0"

- CONTINUOUS FLEXIBLE FLASHING
- CONTINUOUS FLEXIBLE TUBING
- CONTINUOUS WATER BARRIER
- 2"×4" BLOCKING
- 1½" RIGID FOAM INSULATION R-9.5
- BATT INSULATION
- SINGLE MEMBRANE ROOFING
- OPEN WEB BAR JOISTS
- 5" ALUMINUM PLATE
- ACOUSTICAL TILE
- 5" ALUMINUM PLATE TO ONE SIDE

4
ROOF EXPANSION JOINT FLASHING SCALE 3/4" = 1'-0"

- BATT TYPE INSULATION
- DRIP FLASHING TURNED DOWN AT ENDS
- ALUMINUM CAP AND CLEATS
- KOPPERS © FLASHING
- KOPPERS © ROOFING
- CANT STRIP
- 1½" RIGID FOAM INSULATION R-9.5
- 7½" MIN

FOUR COMMON FLASHING CONDITIONS

3–2

These four details show commonly encountered flashing conditions which must be designed correctly in order to stop any possible roof leakage. DETAIL 1 shows a method of cap-flashing a granite veneer wall. The Hickman® fascia cap, as shown, is one of the many existing stock cap flashings that are manufactured. Note the metal water dam, which not only stops any water from penetrating under the roofing, but also acts to hold the continuous compression clamp that holds roofing plies tight and, finally, holds the fascia cap in place. DETAIL 2 shows a simple brick parapet wall capped with a stock aluminum coping. Note that 2" O.D. pipe railing is supported by aluminum bars and, in order to clear the coping, the 3/4" × 1/4" aluminum bars are held away from the parapet wall by 1½" pipe washers. DETAILS 3 and 4 show two stock methods of installing the cover of an expansion joint. One is for single-membrane type of roofing, whereas the other is for built-up roofing.

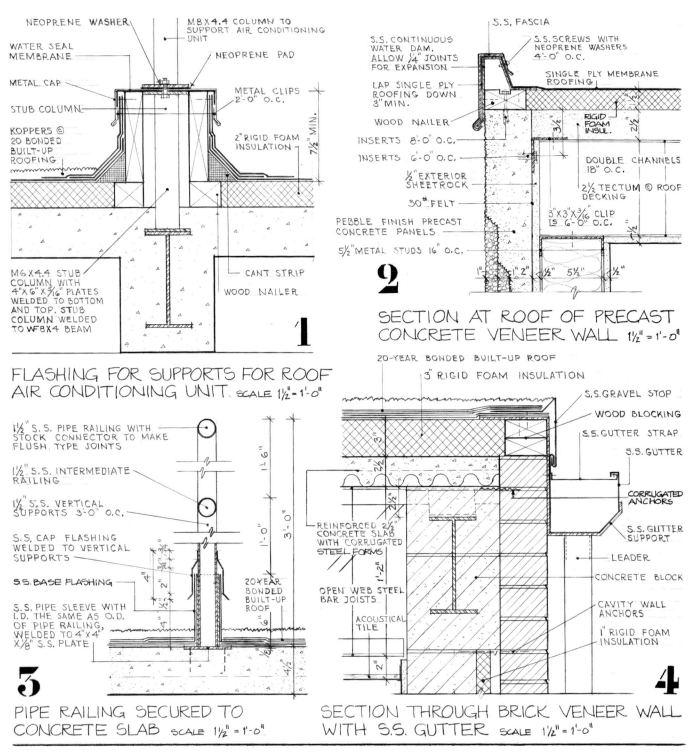

NEOPRENE WASHER
WATER SEAL MEMBRANE
METAL CAP
STUB COLUMN
KOPPERS © 20 BONDED BUILT-UP ROOFING
M6X4.4 STUB COLUMN WITH 4"X6"X5/16" PLATES WELDED TO BOTTOM AND TOP. STUB COLUMN WELDED TO WF8X4 BEAM
M8X4.4 COLUMN TO SUPPORT AIR CONDITIONING UNIT
NEOPRENE PAD
METAL CLIPS 2'-0" O.C.
2" RIGID FOAM INSULATION
7½" MIN.
CANT STRIP
WOOD NAILER

1

FLASHING FOR SUPPORTS FOR ROOF AIR CONDITIONING UNIT. SCALE 1½" = 1'-0"

S.S. FASCIA
S.S. CONTINUOUS WATER DAM. ALLOW ¼" JOINTS FOR EXPANSION
LAP SINGLE PLY ROOFING DOWN 3" MIN.
WOOD NAILER
INSERTS 8'-0" O.C.
INSERTS 6'-0" O.C.
½" EXTERIOR SHEETROCK
30# FELT
PEBBLE FINISH PRECAST CONCRETE PANELS
5½" METAL STUDS 16" O.C.
S.S. SCREWS WITH NEOPRENE WASHERS 4'-0" O.C.
SINGLE PLY MEMBRANE ROOFING
RIGID FOAM INSUL.
DOUBLE CHANNELS 18" O.C.
2½ TECTUM © ROOF DECKING
3"X3"X3/16" CLIP IS 6'-0" O.C.
1" 1" 2" ½" 5½ ½"

2

SECTION AT ROOF OF PRECAST CONCRETE VENEER WALL 1½" = 1'-0"

1½" S.S. PIPE RAILING WITH STOCK CONNECTOR TO MAKE FLUSH, TYPE JOINTS
1½" S.S. INTERMEDIATE RAILING
1½" S.S. VERTICAL SUPPORTS 3'-0" O.C.
S.S. CAP FLASHING WELDED TO VERTICAL SUPPORTS
S.S. BASE FLASHING
S.S. PIPE SLEEVE WITH I.D. THE SAME AS O.D. OF PIPE RAILING, WELDED TO 4"X4"X⅛" S.S. PLATE
1'-6"
3'-0"
1'-0"
20-YEAR BONDED BUILT-UP ROOF

3

PIPE RAILING SECURED TO CONCRETE SLAB SCALE 1½" = 1'-0"

20-YEAR BONDED BUILT-UP ROOF
3" RIGID FOAM INSULATION
REINFORCED 2½" CONCRETE SLAB WITH CORRUGATED STEEL FORMS
OPEN WEB STEEL BAR JOISTS
ACOUSTICAL TILE
S.S. GRAVEL STOP
WOOD BLOCKING
S.S. GUTTER STRAP
S.S. GUTTER
CORRUGATED ANCHORS
S.S. GUTTER SUPPORT
LEADER
CONCRETE BLOCK
CAVITY WALL ANCHORS
1" RIGID FOAM INSULATION

4

SECTION THROUGH BRICK VENEER WALL WITH S.S. GUTTER SCALE 1½" = 1'-0"

3–3 **FOUR SPECIAL FLASHING CONDITIONS**

DETAIL 1 shows all necessary flashing when the air-conditioning unit is installed above the roof and must be supported by the structure below the roof. Other heavy above-roof equipment needs similar flashing.

DETAIL 2 shows treatment of pebble-finish precast concrete panels at roof where a single-ply membrane roofing is used. Note that the continuous water dam also is the member to which the stainless steel fascia is anchored.

DETAIL 3 shows the treatment of a stainless steel pipe railing on a roof. First, pipe sleeves are anchored to the roof structural slab, then roofing and base flashing are installed and, last, pipe railing with integral cap flashing is installed.

DETAIL 4 shows installation of a stainless steel gutter on a simple structural steel building with open web joists and a cavity wall with brick veneer. Note that the stainless steel gutter is supported by stainless steel gutter supports and also interlocks with the stainless steel gravel stop.

CROSS-REFERENCES TO *FLASHING*
IN OTHER CHAPTERS

Chapter Number	Drawing Number	Drawing Title	Described on Page	Drawing on Page
2	2-1	Reinforced concrete structure with cavity wall	6, 7	9
	2-2	Curtain wall	7	10
	2-3	Residential wall sections	7	11
	2-4	Simple exterior and interior load-bearing walls	7	12
4	4-2	Carport storage cabinets	25	28
6	6-1	Section through parapet wall and railing	42	44
	6-2	Parapet and coping	43	45
	6-3	Walls and skins	43	46
7	7-2	Intermediate platform stairs	51	54, 55
9	9-2	Up-sliding doors	79, 80	82
10	10-2	Double fireplaces	89, 90	92, 93
	10-3	Chimney flashing at pitched roof	90	94
11	11-3	Light construction roof details	99, 100	103
12	12-1	Solar residence	109	110, 111
	12-2	Underground house	109	112, 113
13	13-1	Four types of insulated walls	119	121
	13-2	Residential wall sections	119, 120	122
15	15-1	Interior planters for residences	147	149
	15-2	Interior planters for buildings	147	150
	15-3	Exterior planters	147, 148	151

4

Structure

INTRODUCTION

This chapter does not approach structure from an engineering viewpoint but primarily from an innovative, creative approach to simple structural problems. There are many details within the other chapters that show various types and methods of construction, but in no case are the actual engineering design problems dealt with, as this book is limited to architectural detailing.

The architect and the structural engineer must work in harmony as a team on any structure. In situations where there is unlimited money, as a team they can do amazing structural gymnastics. In today's world, however, to create an attractive, well-designed building requires a team effort of not just the architect and structural engineer, but particularly the mechanical and electrical engineers as coworkers, in order to coordinate all the parts of a building into a sound, technically and structurally unified whole.

For large structures or multiple structures entailing site development which includes parking, bridges, roads, ponds, utilities, landscaping, and planting, the working team would require the addition of an urban planner (or site planner, depending on the size of the project) and a landscape architect for optimal results.

CHAPTER DETAIL TEXT

4-1 Plywood Disk Framing

DETAILS 1 AND 2. These details by Harry Teague, Architect, show a method of connecting wood members with plywood disks instead of metal wood hangers. The end result is decorative as well as structural, an example of innovative thinking. Two types of flooring are shown in these details: maple strip finish flooring and vinyl tile finish flooring.

DETAILS 3 AND 4. These are variations based on the same idea of 1″ plywood connectors as shown in DETAILS 1 AND 2. DETAIL 3 shows the three 2″ × 12″ beams covered at the bottom by a ¾″ × 5½″ wood trim to conceal the joints between the 2″ × 12″s. A ¾″ plywood subfloor is used which has one side prepainted before it is installed with the painted side face down on the beams. DETAIL 4 shows a 2″ × 6″ T & G redwood balcony flooring. The railing, balusters, and trim are redwood; the plywood hexagons and rectangles are redwood finished on both sides, with edges painted to match the redwood. Note that a ⅛″ × 1″ continuous aluminum bar is recessed into the redwood railing. The bar is secured to the balusters with aluminum wood screws, and the railing is secured to the bar with aluminum wood screws installed between the balusters.

4-2 Carport Storage Cabinets

An extremely simple system of constructing storage cabinets that can have many applications is shown here. In this detail the carport roof was set at a 1½-to-12 roof pitch, and it was covered with roll roofing installed with a simple gravel stop at the roof edges.

The use of plywood as a structural member has many other applications, as shown in the cross-references of this chapter.

4-3 Supports for Porches and Carports

Five different methods for support of porches and carports are shown on this detail. In DETAIL 1 note that at a 4′-6″ height and at the top, spacers are inserted to stiffen the two 2″ × 4″s. In DETAIL 2 the 3½″ × 3½″ plate is raised or lowered by the first nut and, once all posts are level, the second nut is tightened to become a locknut.

In DETAILS 1 and 2 canvas roofing is shown, and in DETAILS 3, 4, and 5 built-up roofing is shown. Where wood supports are used, two methods are shown to keep the wood from direct contact with the slab so that no rotting can occur. Various treatments for the finish surfaces of the concrete slabs are also shown.

4-4 On-Site Prefabricated Trusses

The designs of two on-site prefabricated wood trusses are shown on this detail. These were developed when the author's office did extensive studies for several summer camps and low-cost housing developments. Worthwhile savings in cost resulted from using exact stock lumber lengths so there is a minimum of cutting (labor costs) and the careful layout of truss gusset plates from stock ½″ × 4′-0″ × 8′-0″ plywood sheets with minimum waste. This can drop building costs by at least 12%. All that is required is a combination of architectural design, a juggling of roof pitches and overhangs, and mainly, imagination and creativity.

4-5 Plywood Truss

The problem here was designing a residence to be located on the crest of a steep hill. The solution to the site problem was to enter at the half-level and go up to a dining-room and kitchen level, and to descend to the living room with a dining-room balcony. To accomplish this, a 32′-0″ truss of some type had to be used. The architect, working with an imaginative structural engineer, designed a plywood truss which answered three design problems: *one,* to support the beams and load of the dining-room balcony; *two,* to create a railing for the balcony; and *three,* to create a library and music area within the two-story living room. Note that the dining-room-balcony face of the finished truss is maple, and the living-room side and the ceiling of the library-music space are of aromatic cedar.

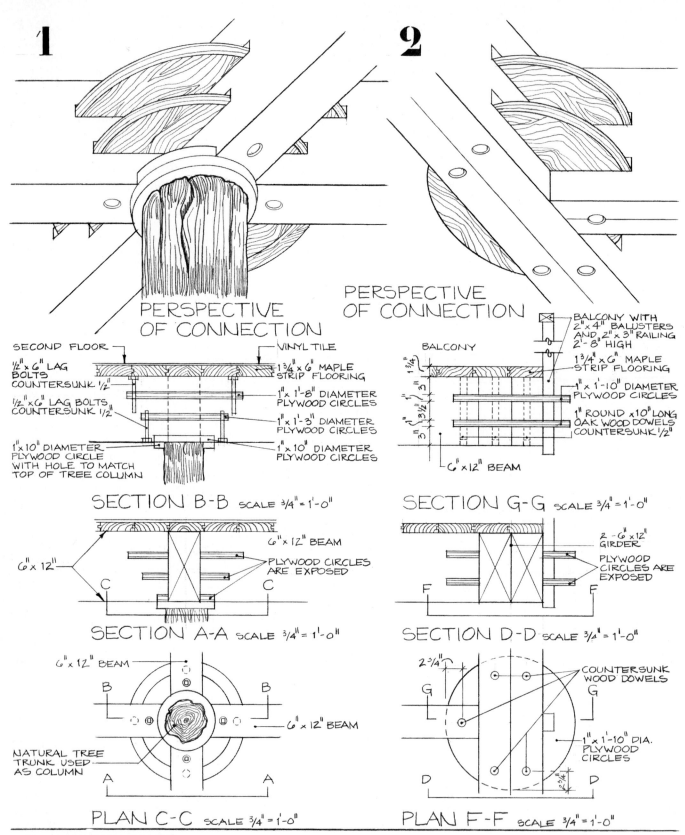

1

PERSPECTIVE OF CONNECTION

2

PERSPECTIVE OF CONNECTION

SECOND FLOOR

½" x 6" LAG BOLTS COUNTERSUNK ½"

½" x 6" LAG BOLTS COUNTERSUNK ½"

1" x 10" DIAMETER PLYWOOD CIRCLE WITH HOLE TO MATCH TOP OF TREE COLUMN

VINYL TILE

1¾" x 6" MAPLE STRIP FLOORING

1" x 1'-8" DIAMETER PLYWOOD CIRCLES

1" x 1'-3" DIAMETER PLYWOOD CIRCLES

1" x 10" DIAMETER PLYWOOD CIRCLES

SECTION B-B SCALE ¾" = 1'-0"

BALCONY

BALCONY WITH 2" x 4" BALUSTERS AND 2" x 3" RAILING 2'-8" HIGH

1¾" x 6" MAPLE STRIP FLOORING

1" x 1'-10" DIAMETER PLYWOOD CIRCLES

1" ROUND x 10" LONG OAK WOOD DOWELS COUNTERSUNK ½"

6" x 12" BEAM

SECTION G-G SCALE ¾" = 1'-0"

6" x 12"

6" x 12" BEAM

PLYWOOD CIRCLES ARE EXPOSED

SECTION A-A SCALE ¾" = 1'-0"

2 - 6" x 12" GIRDER

PLYWOOD CIRCLES ARE EXPOSED

SECTION D-D SCALE ¾" = 1'-0"

6" x 12" BEAM

6" x 12" BEAM

NATURAL TREE TRUNK USED AS COLUMN

PLAN C-C SCALE ¾" = 1'-0"

2¾"

COUNTERSUNK WOOD DOWELS

1" x 1'-10" DIA. PLYWOOD CIRCLES

PLAN F-F SCALE ¾" = 1'-0"

4—1 **PLYWOOD DISK FRAMING**

These details were developed by Harry Teague for the Boyle House in Aspen, Colorado. DETAIL 1 shows how a structural connection can be made by using plywood disks. Here is a contemporary solution to this type of connection which was originally done with mortise and tenon and wooden pins. Architect Teague also used the plywood disks to create a new form of column capital by increasing the diameters of the disks. DETAIL 2 shows the same principle used in the connection between a girder and a beam. In this detail, wooden dowels are suggested instead of lag bolts or a nut-and-bolt system.

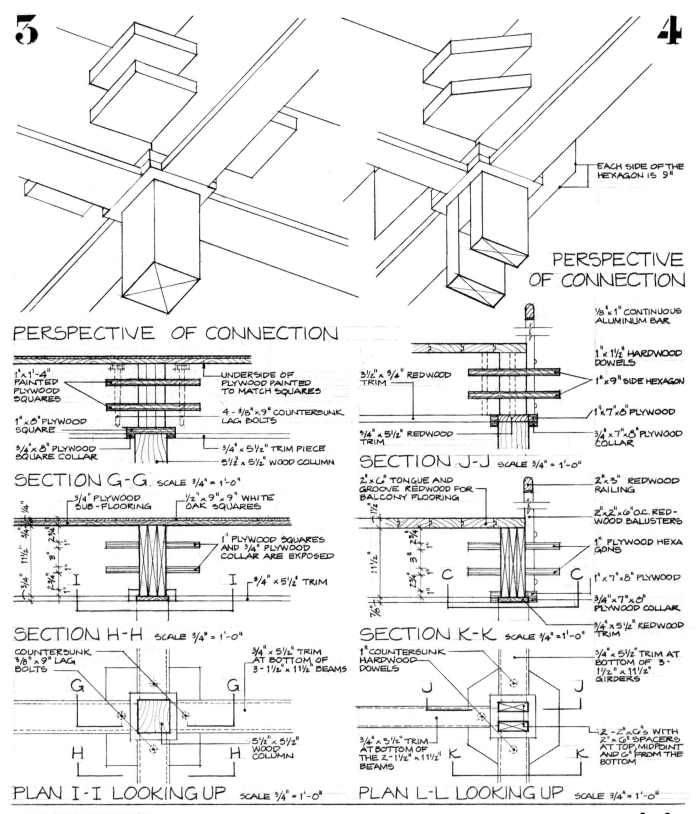

3

4

EACH SIDE OF THE HEXAGON IS 9"

PERSPECTIVE OF CONNECTION

PERSPECTIVE OF CONNECTION

SECTION G-G SCALE 3/4" = 1'-0"

1"×1'-4" PAINTED PLYWOOD SQUARES

UNDERSIDE OF PLYWOOD PAINTED TO MATCH SQUARES

4 - 3/8"×9" COUNTERSUNK LAG BOLTS

1"×8" PLYWOOD SQUARE

3/4"×8" PLYWOOD SQUARE COLLAR

3/4" × 5½" TRIM PIECE

5½"× 5½" WOOD COLUMN

SECTION H-H SCALE 3/4" = 1'-0"

3/4" PLYWOOD SUB-FLOORING

½"×9"×9" WHITE OAK SQUARES

1" PLYWOOD SQUARES AND 3/4" PLYWOOD COLLAR ARE EXPOSED

3/4" × 5½" TRIM

PLAN I-I LOOKING UP SCALE 3/4" = 1'-0"

COUNTERSUNK 3/8" × 9" LAG BOLTS

3/4" × 5½" TRIM AT BOTTOM OF 3 - 1½" × 11½" BEAMS

5½" × 5½" WOOD COLUMN

SECTION J-J SCALE 3/4" = 1'-0"

3½"× 3/4" REDWOOD TRIM

⅛"×1" CONTINUOUS ALUMINUM BAR

1"×1½" HARDWOOD DOWELS

1"×9" SIDE HEXAGON

1"×7"×8" PLYWOOD

3/4"× 7"×8" PLYWOOD COLLAR

3/4" × 5½" REDWOOD TRIM

SECTION K-K SCALE 3/4" = 1'-0"

2"×6" TONGUE AND GROOVE REDWOOD FOR BALCONY FLOORING

2"×3" REDWOOD RAILING

2"×2"×6" O.C. RED-WOOD BALUSTERS

1" PLYWOOD HEXA GONS

1"×7"×8" PLYWOOD

3/4"×7"×8" PLYWOOD COLLAR

3/4"× 5½" REDWOOD TRIM

PLAN L-L LOOKING UP SCALE 3/4" = 1'-0"

1" COUNTERSUNK HARDWOOD DOWELS

3/4" × 5½" TRIM AT BOTTOM OF 3 - 1½" × 11½" GIRDERS

3/4" × 3½" TRIM AT BOTTOM OF THE 2 - 1½" × 11½" BEAMS

2 - 2"×6"S WITH 2"×6" SPACERS AT TOP, MIDPOINT AND 6" FROM THE BOTTOM

PLYWOOD DISK FRAMING

4—1

DETAIL 3 shows a variation of the 1" plywood connectors shown on the opposite page in which a 6" × 6" wood column terminates with a 3/4" × 8" plywood collar with a 1" × 8" plywood square let into the three 2" × 12" beams and acts as a bearing plate for the wood column. Two 1" × 1'-4" squares are let into the beams and the entire assembly is anchored together by four countersunk lag bolts. DETAIL 4 is similar to DETAIL 2 except that a support of two 2" × 6"s is used and the plywood connectors are hexagons. The hand railing is a wood 2" × 3" supported by 2" × 2" balusters spaced 6" o.c.

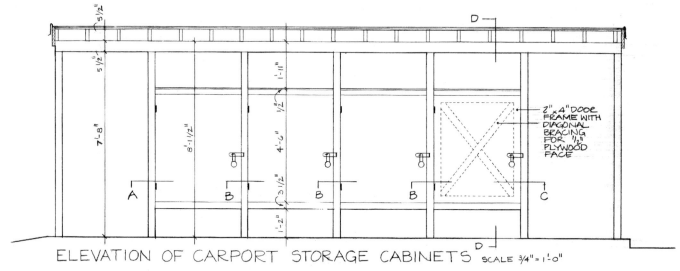

ELEVATION OF CARPORT STORAGE CABINETS SCALE 3/4" = 1'-0"

2" x 4" DOOR FRAME WITH DIAGONAL BRACING FOR 1/2" PLYWOOD FACE

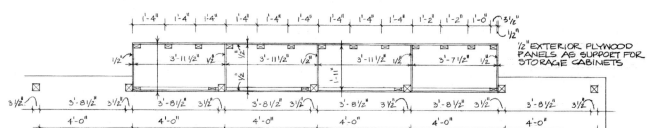

PLAN OF CARPORT STORAGE CABINETS SCALE 1/4" = 1'-0"

1/2" EXTERIOR PLYWOOD PANELS AS SUPPORT FOR STORAGE CABINETS

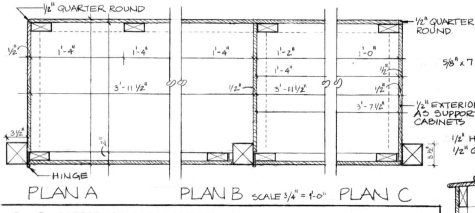

1/2" QUARTER ROUND

1/2" QUARTER ROUND

HINGE

PLAN A   PLAN B SCALE 3/4" = 1'-0"   PLAN C

1/2" EXTERIOR PLYWOOD AS SUPPORT OF STORAGE CABINETS

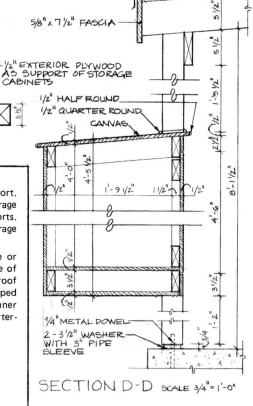

1/2" PLYWOOD
ROLL ROOFING
5/8" x 7 1/2" FASCIA
1/2" HALF ROUND
1/2" QUARTER ROUND
CANVAS
3/4" METAL DOWEL
2 - 3 1/2" WASHER WITH 3" PIPE SLEEVE

SECTION D-D SCALE 3/4" = 1'-0"

4–2 CARPORT STORAGE CABINETS

This detail shows a simple system of installing storage cabinets onto a carport. In like manner the same principle could be used for adding cabinets to a garage or studio-work area. The principle is to use plywood panels as cantilever supports. By this method, with the use of simple 2" X 4" framing, large deep strong storage cabinets can be constructed.

The doors are constructed from 1/2" plywood which can be exterior grade or interior plain or decorative type, each mounted on a diagonally braced frame of 2" X 4"s which is hinged to the carport 4" X 4" supports. In this detail the roof of the storage cabinets is slightly pitched and covered with canvas which is lapped over the 1/2" plywood and covered with a 1/2" half-round moulding. In like manner the canvas is turned up at the carport supports and covered with a 1/4" quarter-round moulding.

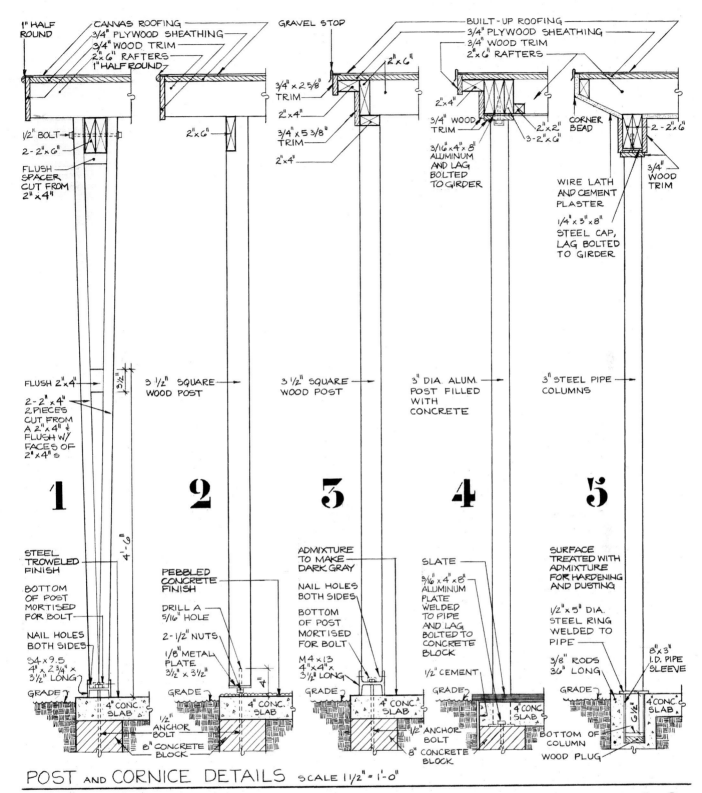

Detail 1 labels: 1" HALF ROUND · CANVAS ROOFING · 3/4" PLYWOOD SHEATHING · 3/4" WOOD TRIM · 2"x6" RAFTERS · 1" HALF ROUND · 1/2" BOLT · 2-2"x6" · FLUSH SPACER CUT FROM 2"x4" · FLUSH 2"x4" · 2-2"x4" 2 PIECES CUT FROM A 2"x4" & FLUSH W/ FACES OF 2"x4"s · 3 1/2" · 4'-6" · STEEL TROWELED FINISH · BOTTOM OF POST MORTISED FOR BOLT · NAIL HOLES BOTH SIDES · S4x9.5 4" x 2 3/4" x 3 1/2" LONG · GRADE · 4" CONC. SLAB · 1/2" ANCHOR BOLT · 8" CONCRETE BLOCK

Detail 2 labels: 2"x6" · GRAVEL STOP · 2"x6" · 3/4" x 2 5/8" TRIM · 2"x4" · 3/4" x 5 3/8" TRIM · 2"x4" · 3 1/2" SQUARE WOOD POST · PEBBLED CONCRETE FINISH · DRILL A 5/16" HOLE · 2-1/2" NUTS · 1/8" METAL PLATE 3 1/2" x 3 1/2" · GRADE · 4" CONC. SLAB

Detail 3 labels: 3 1/2" SQUARE WOOD POST · ADMIXTURE TO MAKE DARK GRAY · NAIL HOLES BOTH SIDES · BOTTOM OF POST MORTISED FOR BOLT · M4x13 4"x4" x 3 1/2" LONG · GRADE · 4" CONC. SLAB · 1/2" ANCHOR BOLT · 8" CONCRETE BLOCK

Detail 4 labels: BUILT-UP ROOFING · 3/4" PLYWOOD SHEATHING · 3/4" WOOD TRIM · 2"x6" RAFTERS · 2"x4" · 3/4" WOOD TRIM · 3/16"x4"x 8" ALUMINUM AND LAG BOLTED TO GIRDER · 2"x2" · 3-2"x6" · 3" DIA. ALUM. POST FILLED WITH CONCRETE · SLATE · 3/16"x4"x8" ALUMINUM PLATE WELDED TO PIPE AND LAG BOLTED TO CONCRETE BLOCK · 1/2" CEMENT · GRADE · 4" CONC. SLAB

Detail 5 labels: CORNER BEAD · 2-2"x6" · 3/4" WOOD TRIM · WIRE LATH AND CEMENT PLASTER · 1/4"x3"x8" STEEL CAP, LAG BOLTED TO GIRDER · 3" STEEL PIPE COLUMNS · SURFACE TREATED WITH ADMIXTURE FOR HARDENING AND DUSTING · 1/2"x5" DIA. STEEL RING WELDED TO PIPE · 3/8" RODS 36" LONG · 8"x3" I.D. PIPE SLEEVE · GRADE · 4" CONC. SLAB · BOTTOM OF COLUMN · WOOD PLUG

POST and CORNICE DETAILS SCALE 1 1/2" = 1'-0"

SUPPORTS FOR PORCHES AND CARPORTS

DETAIL 1: Two 2" × 4"s are bolted to the roof beam and brought together at the bottom and nailed to a piece of steel I-beam bolted to an anchor bolt. DETAIL 2: A 7'-10 1/2" long wood post has the roof beam let in at the top, and at the bottom there is a threaded anchor bolt extending up 4" above the slab with a 3 1/2" × 3 1/2" × 1/8" thick plate plus two nuts for leveling. DETAIL 3: A 7'-9" wood post is secured at the top to a 2" × 4" and nailed to a small piece of an I-beam anchored to the slab at the bottom. DETAIL 4: An 8'-4 1/2" concrete-filled aluminum pipe with 3/8" thick 4" × 8" plates welded to top and bottom is lag-bolted to the wood girder and the concrete block. DETAIL 5: An 8'-0" steel pipe column with a 3" × 8" × 1/4" plate at top and a 1/2" × 5" diameter ring 6 1/2" up from the bottom are welded to the pipe. An 8" long × 3" I.D. pipe sleeve is inserted in the slab.

4—3

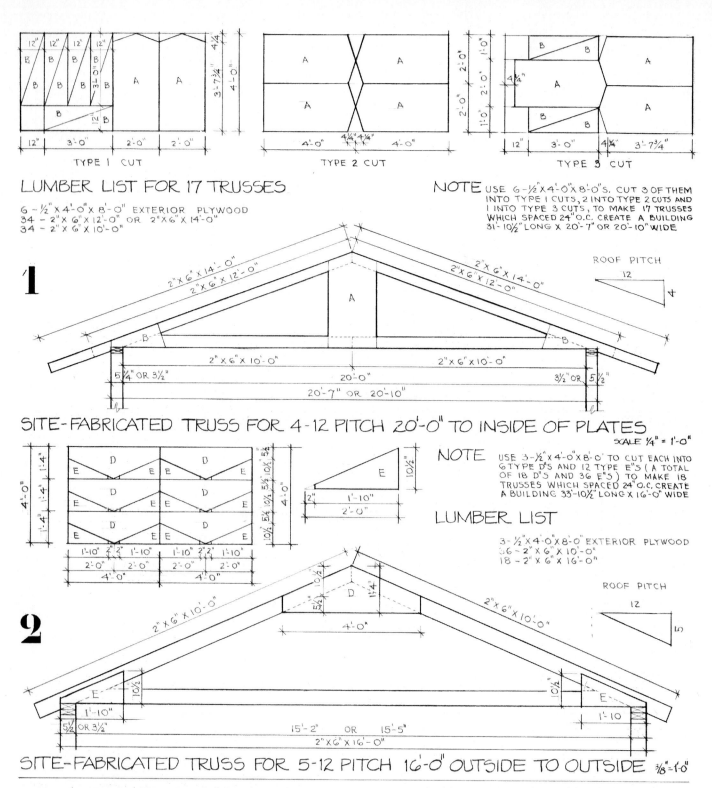

TYPE 1 CUT

TYPE 2 CUT

TYPE 3 CUT

LUMBER LIST FOR 17 TRUSSES

6 – ½" X 4'-0" X 8'-0" EXTERIOR PLYWOOD
34 – 2" X 6" X 12'-0" OR 2" X 6" X 14'-0"
34 – 2" X 6" X 10'-0"

NOTE USE 6-½"X4'-0"X8'-0"S. CUT 3 OF THEM INTO TYPE 1 CUTS, 2 INTO TYPE 2 CUTS AND 1 INTO TYPE 3 CUTS, TO MAKE 17 TRUSSES WHICH SPACED 24" O.C. CREATE A BUILDING 31'-10½" LONG X 20'-7" OR 20'-10" WIDE

1

ROOF PITCH

SITE-FABRICATED TRUSS FOR 4-12 PITCH 20'-0" TO INSIDE OF PLATES

SCALE ¼" = 1'-0"

NOTE USE 3-½"X4'-0"X8'-0" TO CUT EACH INTO 6 TYPE D'S AND 12 TYPE E'S (A TOTAL OF 18 D'S AND 36 E'S) TO MAKE 18 TRUSSES WHICH SPACED 24" O.C. CREATE A BUILDING 33'-10½" LONG X 16'-0" WIDE

LUMBER LIST

3- ½"X4'-0"X8'-0" EXTERIOR PLYWOOD
36 – 2" X 6" X 10'-0"
18 – 2" X 6" X 16'-0"

ROOF PITCH

2

SITE-FABRICATED TRUSS FOR 5-12 PITCH 16'-0" OUTSIDE TO OUTSIDE ⅜"=1'-0"

4–4 ON-SITE PREFABRICATED TRUSSES

The author's office was commissioned to make studies for various types of camp buildings. DETAIL 1 shows an on-site prefabricated truss for which ½" plywood was cut into assorted gusset plates to make roof trusses for a building of a certain width. By carefully selecting the roof pitch, two things were accomplished. First, stock lengths of timber could be used without cutting, and second, a maximum of plywood gusset plates could be made with a minimum of waste. DETAIL 2 also is of an on-site prefabricated truss for a 16'-0" wide cabin, where only stock lumber lengths were used and minimum waste of plywood was accomplished. These types of trusses can be designed if care is taken to determine what roof pitch will permit use of only stock lengths of lumber and yield maximum use of stock 4'-0" X 8'-0" X ½" plywood for gussets.

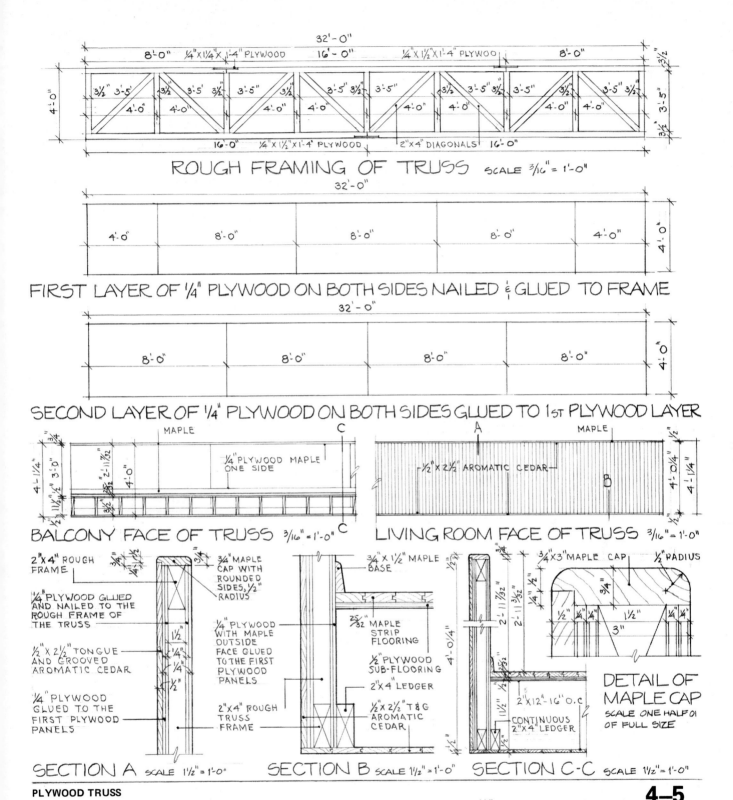

ROUGH FRAMING OF TRUSS SCALE 3/16" = 1'-0"

FIRST LAYER OF 1/4" PLYWOOD ON BOTH SIDES NAILED & GLUED TO FRAME

SECOND LAYER OF 1/4" PLYWOOD ON BOTH SIDES GLUED TO 1st PLYWOOD LAYER

BALCONY FACE OF TRUSS 3/16" = 1'-0"   LIVING ROOM FACE OF TRUSS 3/16" = 1'-0"

SECTION A SCALE 1 1/2" = 1'-0"   SECTION B SCALE 1 1/2" = 1'-0"   SECTION C-C SCALE 1 1/2" = 1'-0"

PLYWOOD TRUSS

The top and bottom 2″ × 4″ members of the rough framing of the truss are tied together with 1/4″ horizontal plywood gussets let into the 2″ × 4″ members. The first layer of plywood on both sides is applied and nailed after the entire faces of the rough frame have been coated with adhesive. Note that the 8′-0″ lengths of plywood are installed in such a way that the joints of the top and bottom 2″ × 4″ members are within an 8′-0″ length. The last layer on both sides is job-laminated to the first layers. Note that the joints of the plywood layers lap by 4′-0″.

4–5

CROSS-REFERENCES TO *STRUCTURE*
IN OTHER CHAPTERS

5

Plywood and Wood Joints and Connections

INTRODUCTION

The joining of plywood and solid wood can be broken into two distinct categories: exterior and interior joints. Plywood is available in two major types, one for exterior use and the other for the interior. Exterior joints for plywood must be made using exterior-type plywood and waterproof adhesives or other compounds if these are part of the joint. In like manner, on the interior, unless moisture or water is present, interior-type plywood is used.

On the exterior, when either plywood or wood is used, fabrication is generally produced on site, except when prefabricated units need only to be assembled. Therefore, the detailing of all exterior joints must be carefully designed and detailed as part of the overall design concept for the building.

When we consider the treatment of plywood on the interior, we face two completely different problems. One consists of built-ins, furniture, prefabricated partitions, cabinets, shelving, and the like, which are considered cabinetwork and millwork, and in many instances are manufactured in a shop where this type of special work is produced, then brought to the site for installation.

The other problem is in alteration work, residential construction, and office planning, where any plywood or wood paneling, shelving, and simple cabinets are produced on site. In all cases, the joints must be carefully considered and detailed. One of the most difficult detailing problems with plywood is how to treat the end grain of the plywood wherever it is entirely or even partially exposed.

The illustrations in this chapter show the various standard methods of joining wood and plywood, and the cross-references to other chapters cover a much larger variety of treatments of wood and plywood joints.

CHAPTER DETAIL TEXT

5-1 Exterior Vertical and Horizontal Joints for Plywood

Plywood as an exterior finish material for buildings has increased steadily, and the design problems of treating the joints causes many detail problems. This illustration shows all the standard and workable joint treatments for horizontal and vertical joints. The horizontal joint is difficult from a design viewpoint because it makes a distinct noticeable line. Detailing to minimize this joint or to increase its importance is one of the design choices that one has to make. When using plywood on the exterior, one assumes that a correct exterior grade will be selected.

When using plywood for the exterior, one must always order the exterior grade and in thicknesses of $1''$, $7/8''$, or $3/4''$. The final finish can be either a colored stain or a clear or opaque organic coating (paint).

5-2 Exterior Internal and External Corners for Plywood

The details shown on the illustration are the tried-and-true methods for treating exterior internal and external corners of plywood. From a design viewpoint, the vertical and horizontal joints selected, in many cases, determined or limited the choice of treatment of the joints of the external and internal corners. The entire design of a building using plywood as the exterior facing demands a very careful integration of *all* the various treatments of the plywood joints for satisfactory overall results.

5-3 Interior Joints for Quarter-Inch Plywood

The treatment of $1/4''$ plywood for furniture, built-ins, wall paneling, cabinets, and the like, requires careful detailing of joints, particularly when using plywood with a distinct grain pattern. This illustration is divided into three parts: (1) the largest portion of the illustration shows the variety of treatments for vertical and horizontal joints, some of which can be used for thicker plywood, particularly on paneling; (2) methods for treating external corners; and (3) treatment of internal corners.

All these interior joints can be used for plywood thicker than $1/4''$. In like manner all the metal accessories are obtainable for various thicknesses of plywood.

5-4 Cabinet and Millwork Joints for Plywood and Solid Wood

This illustration has seven different categories of plywood and solid wood joints for cabinet and millwork. The part labeled No. 1 shows common treatments for plywood end grains. These are used for doors, table and desk edges, shelves, and any other area where plywood end grain becomes visible. No. 2 shows external corner joints for plywood. No. 3 shows internal corner joints for both plywood and solid wood. No. 4 shows treatment of vertical and horizontal joints for plywood. No. 5 shows various treatments of perpendicular joints for both plywood and solid wood. No. 6 shows treatment of solid wood miter joints. No. 7 shows treatment of both horizontal and vertical joints for solid wood.

With poor adhesives many types of joints eventually come apart, but with the correct type of synthetic adhesive, a permanent bond is developed between the materials to be joined.

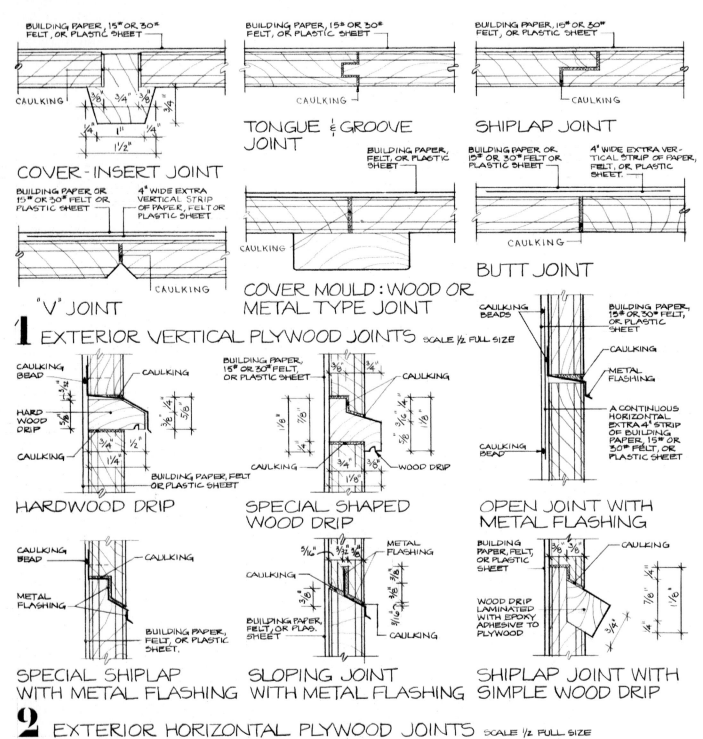

COVER-INSERT JOINT

BUILDING PAPER, 15# OR 30# FELT, OR PLASTIC SHEET

CAULKING

3/8" · 3/4" · 3/8" · 3/4"

1/4" · 1" · 1/4"

1 1/2"

TONGUE & GROOVE JOINT

BUILDING PAPER, 15# OR 30# FELT, OR PLASTIC SHEET

CAULKING

SHIPLAP JOINT

BUILDING PAPER, 15# OR 30# FELT, OR PLASTIC SHEET

CAULKING

"V" JOINT

BUILDING PAPER OR 15# OR 30# FELT OR PLASTIC SHEET

4" WIDE EXTRA VERTICAL STRIP OF PAPER, FELT OR PLASTIC SHEET

CAULKING

COVER MOULD: WOOD OR METAL TYPE JOINT

BUILDING PAPER, FELT, OR PLASTIC SHEET

CAULKING

BUTT JOINT

BUILDING PAPER OR 15# OR 30# FELT OR PLASTIC SHEET

4" WIDE EXTRA VERTICAL STRIP OF PAPER, FELT, OR PLASTIC SHEET.

CAULKING

1 EXTERIOR VERTICAL PLYWOOD JOINTS SCALE 1/2 FULL SIZE

HARDWOOD DRIP

CAULKING BEAD

CAULKING

HARD WOOD DRIP

CAULKING

BUILDING PAPER, FELT, OR PLASTIC SHEET

SPECIAL SHAPED WOOD DRIP

BUILDING PAPER, 15# OR 30# FELT, OR PLASTIC SHEET

CAULKING

WOOD DRIP

OPEN JOINT WITH METAL FLASHING

CAULKING BEADS

BUILDING PAPER, 15# OR 30# FELT, OR PLASTIC SHEET

CAULKING

METAL FLASHING

A CONTINUOUS HORIZONTAL EXTRA 4" STRIP OF BUILDING PAPER, 15# OR 30# FELT, OR PLASTIC SHEET

CAULKING BEAD

SPECIAL SHIPLAP WITH METAL FLASHING

CAULKING BEAD

CAULKING

METAL FLASHING

BUILDING PAPER, FELT, OR PLASTIC SHEET.

SLOPING JOINT WITH METAL FLASHING

METAL FLASHING

CAULKING

BUILDING PAPER, FELT, OR PLAS. SHEET

CAULKING

SHIPLAP JOINT WITH SIMPLE WOOD DRIP

BUILDING PAPER, FELT, OR PLASTIC SHEET

CAULKING

WOOD DRIP LAMINATED WITH EPOXY ADHESIVE TO PLYWOOD

2 EXTERIOR HORIZONTAL PLYWOOD JOINTS SCALE 1/2 FULL SIZE

5—1 EXTERIOR VERTICAL AND HORIZONTAL JOINTS FOR PLYWOOD

The extensive use of plywood on the exterior of buildings has developed many joint problems. These details of joints for exterior plywood show a number of truly time-proved successful methods used for both vertical and horizontal joints on the exterior. The horizontal joint is the more difficult because it cannot avoid creating some sort of a marked horizontal line which affects the design of a building. The architect or designer must accept this horizontal joint and incorporate it somewhere, somehow, in the design satisfactorily for all concerned. Unfortunately, plywood is limited in size to 8'-0" and 10'-0" or 12'-0" in length and 4'-0" in width. The 10'-0" and 12'-0" lengths generally are by special order from the manufacturer, whereas the 8'-0" X 4'-0" size is readily available.

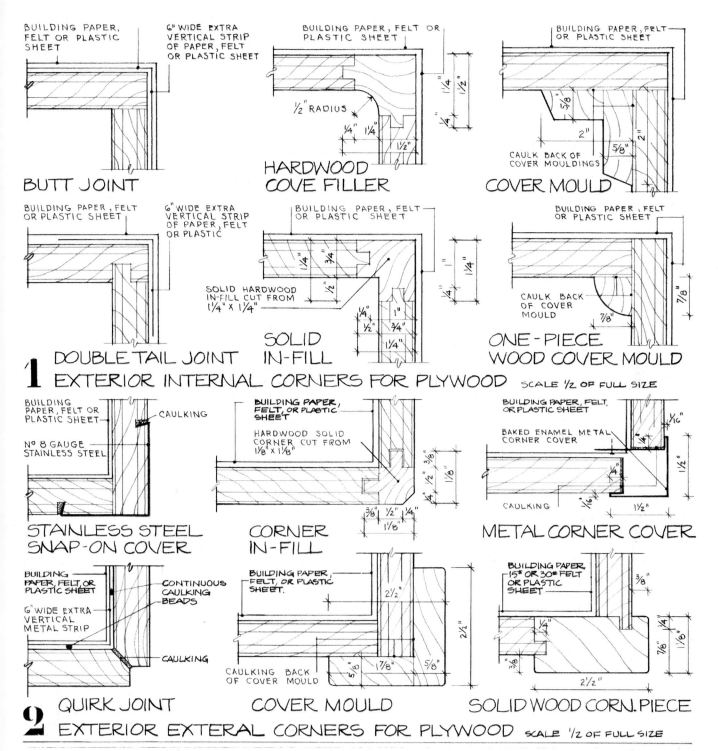

BUTT JOINT

HARDWOOD COVE FILLER

COVER MOULD

DOUBLE TAIL JOINT

SOLID IN-FILL

ONE-PIECE WOOD COVER MOULD

1 EXTERIOR INTERNAL CORNERS FOR PLYWOOD SCALE ½ OF FULL SIZE

STAINLESS STEEL SNAP-ON COVER

CORNER IN-FILL

METAL CORNER COVER

QUIRK JOINT

COVER MOULD

SOLID WOOD CORN. PIECE

2 EXTERIOR EXTERNAL CORNERS FOR PLYWOOD SCALE ½ OF FULL SIZE

EXTERIOR INTERNAL AND EXTERNAL CORNERS FOR PLYWOOD

5–2

This illustration shows current field-tried methods for treating plywood at external and internal corners. Internal corners are relatively simple, as the end grain of the plywood is not exposed and a simple butt joint with a bead of caulking before the edges are brought tight together answers the problem. External corners always have some of the plywood end grain visible. The details shown cover current methods of treating external corners. Perhaps the most common method is use of a cover moulding, as this to a great extent has been the method used for solid wood cabinet and millwork, as well as construction in general.

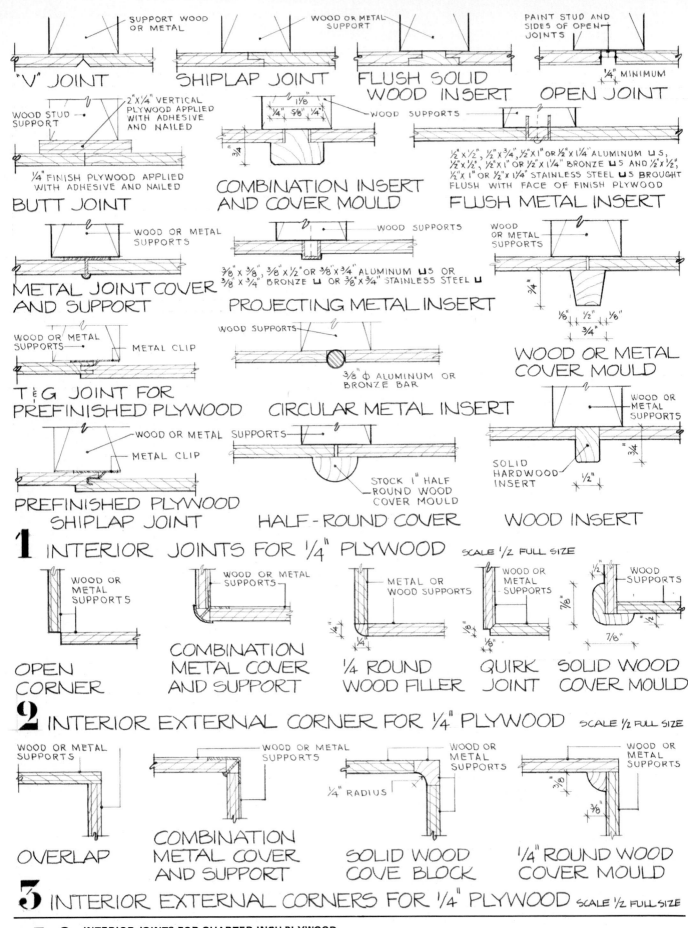

SUPPORT WOOD OR METAL

WOOD OR METAL SUPPORT

PAINT STUD AND SIDES OF OPEN JOINTS

"V" JOINT

SHIPLAP JOINT

FLUSH SOLID WOOD INSERT

OPEN JOINT

¼" MINIMUM

WOOD STUD SUPPORT

2"x¼" VERTICAL PLYWOOD APPLIED WITH ADHESIVE AND NAILED

¼" ⅝" ¼"

1⅛"

¾"

WOOD SUPPORTS

½" x ½", ½" x ¾", ½" x 1" OR ½" x ¼" ALUMINUM ⊔S, ½" x ½", ½" x 1" OR ½" x ¼" BRONZE ⊔S AND ½" x ½", ½" x 1" OR ½" x ¼" STAINLESS STEEL ⊔S BROUGHT FLUSH WITH FACE OF FINISH PLYWOOD

¼" FINISH PLYWOOD APPLIED WITH ADHESIVE AND NAILED

BUTT JOINT

COMBINATION INSERT AND COVER MOULD

FLUSH METAL INSERT

WOOD OR METAL SUPPORTS

WOOD SUPPORTS

WOOD OR METAL SUPPORTS

¾"

METAL JOINT COVER AND SUPPORT

⅜" x ⅜", ⅜" x ½" OR ⅜" x ¾" ALUMINUM ⊔S OR ⅜" x ¾" BRONZE ⊔ OR ⅜" x ¾" STAINLESS STEEL ⊔

PROJECTING METAL INSERT

⅛" ½" ⅛"
¾"

WOOD OR METAL SUPPORTS

METAL CLIP

WOOD SUPPORTS

WOOD OR METAL COVER MOULD

WOOD OR METAL SUPPORTS

T & G JOINT FOR PREFINISHED PLYWOOD

⅜" ⌀ ALUMINUM OR BRONZE BAR

CIRCULAR METAL INSERT

WOOD OR METAL SUPPORTS

METAL CLIP

¾"

SOLID HARDWOOD INSERT

½"

PREFINISHED PLYWOOD SHIPLAP JOINT

STOCK 1" HALF ROUND WOOD COVER MOULD

HALF-ROUND COVER

WOOD INSERT

1 INTERIOR JOINTS FOR ¼" PLYWOOD SCALE ½ FULL SIZE

WOOD OR METAL SUPPORTS

WOOD OR METAL SUPPORTS

METAL OR WOOD SUPPORTS

WOOD OR METAL SUPPORTS

WOOD SUPPORTS

¼"

⅛"

½"

⅞"

⅛"

½"

⁷⁄₈"

OPEN CORNER

COMBINATION METAL COVER AND SUPPORT

¼ ROUND WOOD FILLER

QUIRK JOINT

SOLID WOOD COVER MOULD

2 INTERIOR EXTERNAL CORNER FOR ¼" PLYWOOD SCALE ½ FULL SIZE

WOOD OR METAL SUPPORTS

WOOD OR METAL SUPPORTS

WOOD OR METAL SUPPORTS

WOOD OR METAL SUPPORTS

¼" RADIUS

⅜"

⅜"

OVERLAP

COMBINATION METAL COVER AND SUPPORT

SOLID WOOD COVE BLOCK

¼" ROUND WOOD COVER MOULD

3 INTERIOR EXTERNAL CORNERS FOR ¼" PLYWOOD SCALE ½ FULL SIZE

5–3 INTERIOR JOINTS FOR QUARTER-INCH PLYWOOD

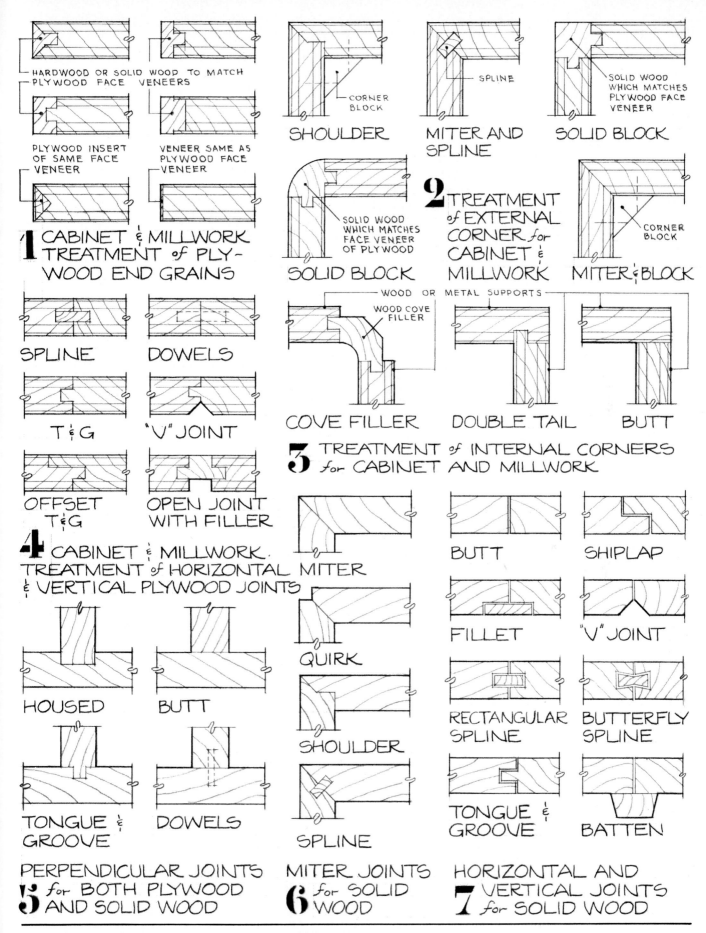

1 CABINET & MILLWORK TREATMENT of PLYWOOD END GRAINS

HARDWOOD OR SOLID WOOD TO MATCH PLYWOOD FACE VENEERS

PLYWOOD INSERT OF SAME FACE VENEER

VENEER SAME AS PLYWOOD FACE VENEER

SHOULDER

MITER AND SPLINE

SPLINE

SOLID WOOD WHICH MATCHES PLYWOOD FACE VENEER

SOLID BLOCK

SOLID BLOCK

SOLID WOOD WHICH MATCHES FACE VENEER OF PLYWOOD

2 TREATMENT of EXTERNAL CORNER for CABINET & MILLWORK

CORNER BLOCK

MITER & BLOCK

SPLINE

DOWELS

T & G

"V" JOINT

OFFSET T & G

OPEN JOINT WITH FILLER

WOOD OR METAL SUPPORTS

WOOD COVE FILLER

COVE FILLER

DOUBLE TAIL

BUTT

3 TREATMENT of INTERNAL CORNERS for CABINET AND MILLWORK

4 CABINET & MILLWORK. TREATMENT of HORIZONTAL & VERTICAL PLYWOOD JOINTS

MITER

QUIRK

SHOULDER

BUTT

SHIPLAP

FILLET

"V" JOINT

RECTANGULAR SPLINE

BUTTERFLY SPLINE

HOUSED

BUTT

TONGUE & GROOVE

DOWELS

SPLINE

TONGUE & GROOVE

BATTEN

5 PERPENDICULAR JOINTS for BOTH PLYWOOD AND SOLID WOOD

6 MITER JOINTS for SOLID WOOD

7 HORIZONTAL AND VERTICAL JOINTS for SOLID WOOD

CABINET AND MILLWORK JOINTS FOR PLYWOOD AND SOLID WOOD

5–4

CROSS-REFERENCES TO *PLYWOOD AND WOOD JOINTS AND CONNECTIONS* IN OTHER CHAPTERS

6 | Parapets

INTRODUCTION

The termination of vertical or curved walls of any building where they meet the roof creates a connection known generally as a parapet. The parapet in today's architecture is relatively simple, certainly when compared to those in Greek, Roman, and Renaissance architecture, yet simple as it is now, it is one of the more important detailing elements in a structure.

Many city building codes require the construction of a 3'-0" high barrier such as a railing at the edge of the roof, or else the exterior wall must extend 3'-0" above the roof. In other building codes, only a 3'-0" high railing or a combination of a wall and a railing will suffice. Therefore we can easily understand that the design of the top of a building can become a challenging detail, since it is also an aesthetic problem that can add or detract from the appearance of the building. Thus, creating an attractive termination or cap for a building includes both code and aesthetic considerations.

The details here show a number of methods that answer this design and detail problem, some where codes dictate the end result and others where codes play a very minor part. The cross-references lead to parapet details in other chapters.

CHAPTER DETAIL TEXT

6-1 Section through Parapet Wall and Railing

Parapet wall, railing and deck by Hugh Stubbins and Associates, Inc., for the Rowland Institute for Science, Cambridge, Massachusetts. Here is a complete detail which looks complicated but is rather simple when analyzed. It is interesting to note how the redwood decking is installed on an insulated, minimally sloped flat roof.

6-2 Parapet and Coping

DETAIL 1. This and the other details show how important detailing is in copings and parapets. In the Rowland Institute for Science in Cambridge, Massachusetts, Hugh Stubbins and Associates, Inc., used careful detailing to decrease the visible cap on the top of a building's exterior wall. Note that by stepping back the $6\frac{1}{4}''$ cap from the face of the brick, only a small $2''$ portion of the cap is visible from either street or river. This strong horizontal line is accented by capping the walls with two soldier courses.

DETAIL 2. This shows a simple wall-bearing structure with a cavity wall of brick and glazed masonry units. The roof insulation is located directly above the acoustical ceiling, creating a dead air space which has to be ventilated to stop any condensation. By locating a series of brick vents on both sides of the building, any possible buildup of condensation is eliminated.

6-3 Walls and Skins

These details show three different types of veneer walls and the various methods of attachment, including flashing, insulation, parapets, and a gravel stop.

DETAIL 1. The cramp anchors and pins, including the continuous through-flashing, are all stainless steel, so no galvanic action can occur. The same applies to reglet and cap flashing, both of which are stainless steel.

DETAIL 2. The through-flashing is zinc and placed only under the joints of the ember red granite coping. Therefore the cramp anchors and pins can be galvanized steel, as they do not come in contact with the zinc through-flashing.

The coping has a reglet which receives the lead-coated copper roof flashing which is wedged into the reglet with lead wedges.

DETAIL 3. Note that the carpet has at its edges beveled wood strips with hooks so that carpet can be stretched from wall to wall.

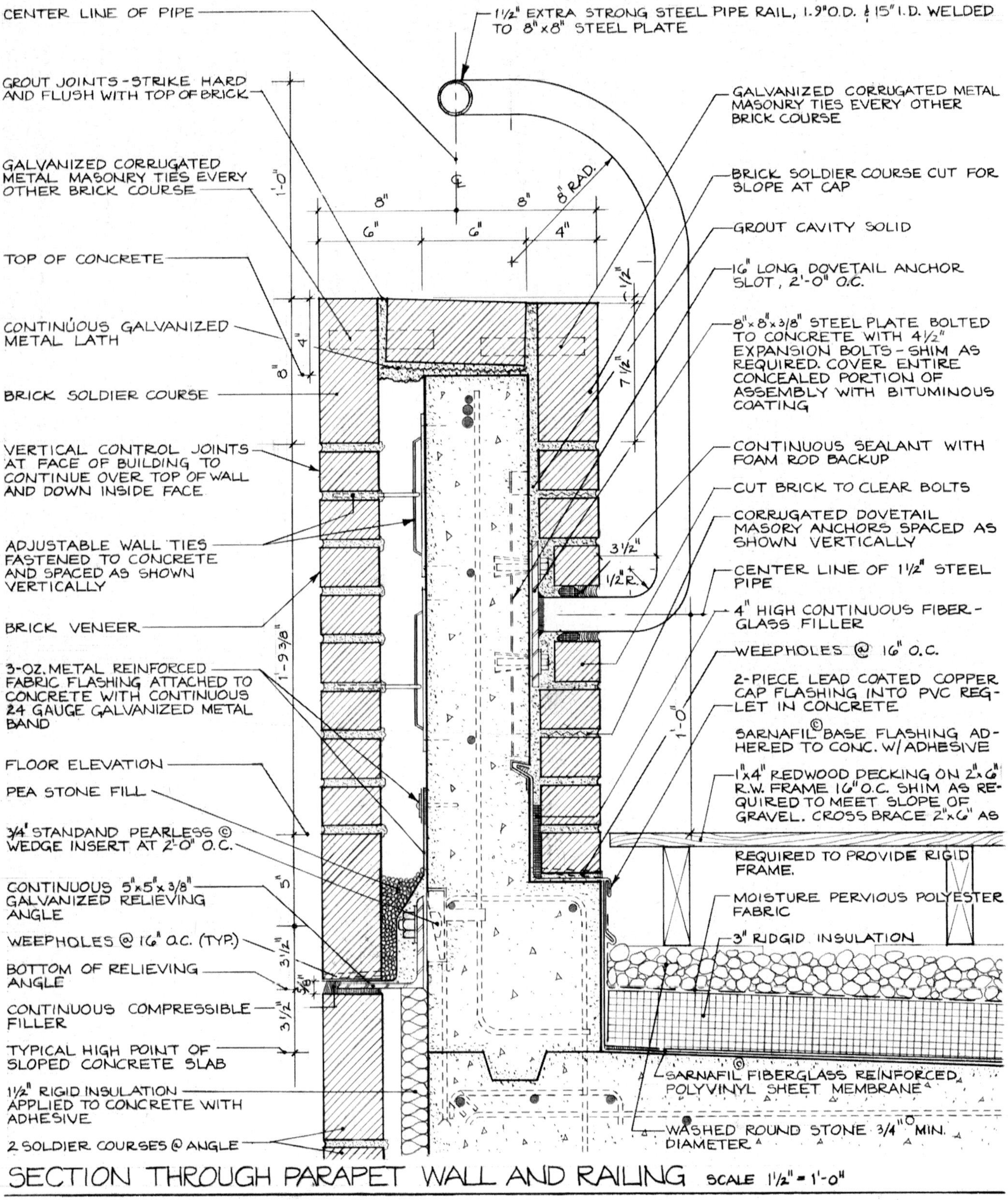

CENTER LINE OF PIPE
1½" EXTRA STRONG STEEL PIPE RAIL, 1.9"O.D. & 15" I.D. WELDED TO 8"x8" STEEL PLATE
GROUT JOINTS - STRIKE HARD AND FLUSH WITH TOP OF BRICK
GALVANIZED CORRUGATED METAL MASONRY TIES EVERY OTHER BRICK COURSE
TOP OF CONCRETE
CONTINUOUS GALVANIZED METAL LATH
BRICK SOLDIER COURSE
VERTICAL CONTROL JOINTS AT FACE OF BUILDING TO CONTINUE OVER TOP OF WALL AND DOWN INSIDE FACE
ADJUSTABLE WALL TIES FASTENED TO CONCRETE AND SPACED AS SHOWN VERTICALLY
BRICK VENEER
3-OZ. METAL REINFORCED FABRIC FLASHING ATTACHED TO CONCRETE WITH CONTINUOUS 24 GAUGE GALVANIZED METAL BAND
FLOOR ELEVATION
PEA STONE FILL
3/4" STANDAND PEARLESS © WEDGE INSERT AT 2'-0" O.C.
CONTINUOUS 5"x5"x3/8" GALVANIZED RELIEVING ANGLE
WEEPHOLES @ 16" O.C. (TYP.)
BOTTOM OF RELIEVING ANGLE
CONTINUOUS COMPRESSIBLE FILLER
TYPICAL HIGH POINT OF SLOPED CONCRETE SLAB
1½" RIGID INSULATION APPLIED TO CONCRETE WITH ADHESIVE
2 SOLDIER COURSES @ ANGLE
GALVANIZED CORRUGATED METAL MASONRY TIES EVERY OTHER BRICK COURSE
BRICK SOLDIER COURSE CUT FOR SLOPE AT CAP
GROUT CAVITY SOLID
16" LONG DOVETAIL ANCHOR SLOT, 2'-0" O.C.
8"x8"x3/8" STEEL PLATE BOLTED TO CONCRETE WITH 4½" EXPANSION BOLTS - SHIM AS REQUIRED. COVER ENTIRE CONCEALED PORTION OF ASSEMBLY WITH BITUMINOUS COATING
CONTINUOUS SEALANT WITH FOAM ROD BACKUP
CUT BRICK TO CLEAR BOLTS
CORRUGATED DOVETAIL MASORY ANCHORS SPACED AS SHOWN VERTICALLY
CENTER LINE OF 1½" STEEL PIPE
4" HIGH CONTINUOUS FIBER-GLASS FILLER
WEEPHOLES @ 16" O.C.
2-PIECE LEAD COATED COPPER CAP FLASHING INTO PVC REG-LET IN CONCRETE
SARNAFIL© BASE FLASHING AD-HERED TO CONC. W/ ADHESIVE
1"x4" REDWOOD DECKING ON 2"x6" R.W. FRAME 16" O.C. SHIM AS RE-QUIRED TO MEET SLOPE OF GRAVEL. CROSS BRACE 2"x6" AS REQUIRED TO PROVIDE RIGID FRAME.
MOISTURE PERVIOUS POLYESTER FABRIC
3" RIDGID INSULATION
SARNAFIL© FIBERGLASS REINFORCED POLYVINYL SHEET MEMBRANE
WASHED ROUND STONE 3/4"Ø MIN. DIAMETER
8"
6"
6"
8"
8" RAD.
4"
1'-0"
4"
8"
1½"
7½"
3½"
½"R.
1'-9 3/8"
1'-0"
5"
3½"
3/8"
3½"

SECTION THROUGH PARAPET WALL AND RAILING SCALE 1½" = 1'-0"

6–1 SECTION THROUGH PARAPET WALL AND RAILING

This detail from the Rowland Institute for Science, Cambridge, Massachusetts, by Hugh Stubbins and Associates, Inc., shows brick veneer on a concrete structure where strong subtle horizontal stripes are made with one- and two-soldier courses. The top of the parapet wall terminates in a single brick soldier course surmounted by a single 1½″ pipe rail. Note how any possible moisture in the parapet wall cavity is drained through weepholes kept open with pea stone fill. The brick veneer on the parapet wall on the inside face is anchored using dovetail anchor slots, and adjustable wall ties are used on the exterior face. The whole reinforced concrete structure is thoroughly insulated with 3″ rigid insulation on the roof and 1½″ rigid insulation in the cavity.

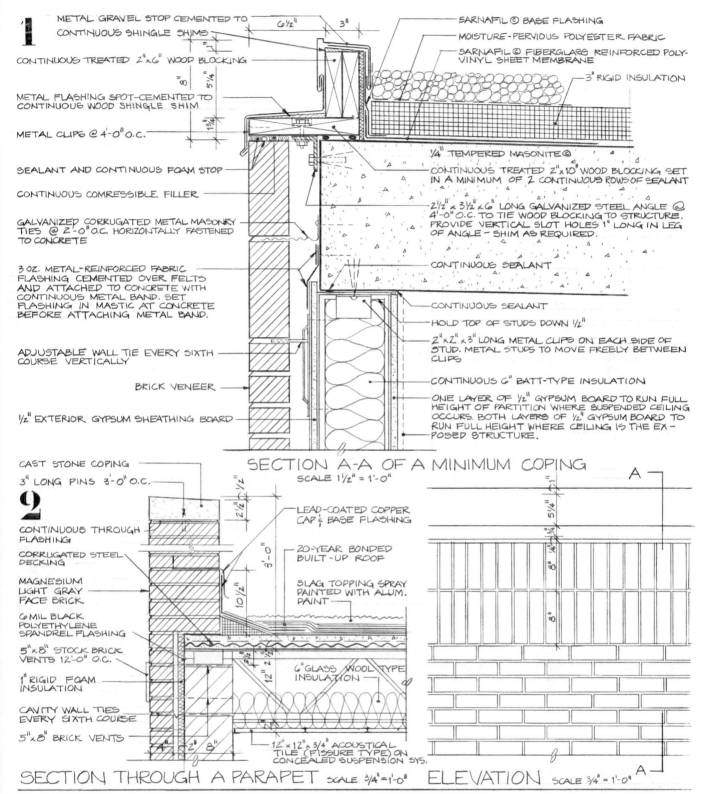

1 METAL GRAVEL STOP CEMENTED TO CONTINUOUS SHINGLE SHIMS

CONTINUOUS TREATED 2"×6" WOOD BLOCKING

METAL FLASHING SPOT-CEMENTED TO CONTINUOUS WOOD SHINGLE SHIM

METAL CLIPS @ 4'-0" O.C.

SEALANT AND CONTINUOUS FOAM STOP

CONTINUOUS COMPRESSIBLE FILLER

GALVANIZED CORRUGATED METAL MASONRY TIES @ 2'-0" O.C. HORIZONTALLY FASTENED TO CONCRETE

3 OZ. METAL-REINFORCED FABRIC FLASHING CEMENTED OVER FELTS AND ATTACHED TO CONCRETE WITH CONTINUOUS METAL BAND. SET FLASHING IN MASTIC AT CONCRETE BEFORE ATTACHING METAL BAND.

ADJUSTABLE WALL TIE EVERY SIXTH COURSE VERTICALLY

BRICK VENEER

½" EXTERIOR GYPSUM SHEATHING BOARD

SARNAFIL© BASE FLASHING

MOISTURE-PERVIOUS POLYESTER FABRIC

SARNAFIL© FIBERGLASS REINFORCED POLY-VINYL SHEET MEMBRANE

3" RIGID INSULATION

¼" TEMPERED MASONITE©

CONTINUOUS TREATED 2"×10" WOOD BLOCKING SET IN A MINIMUM OF 2 CONTINUOUS ROWS OF SEALANT

2½" × 3½" × 6" LONG GALVANIZED STEEL ANGLE @ 4'-0" O.C. TO TIE WOOD BLOCKING TO STRUCTURE. PROVIDE VERTICAL SLOT HOLES 1" LONG IN LEG OF ANGLE - SHIM AS REQUIRED.

CONTINUOUS SEALANT

CONTINUOUS SEALANT

HOLD TOP OF STUDS DOWN ½"

2"×2"×3" LONG METAL CLIPS ON EACH SIDE OF STUD. METAL STUDS TO MOVE FREELY BETWEEN CLIPS

CONTINUOUS 6" BATT-TYPE INSULATION

ONE LAYER OF ½" GYPSUM BOARD TO RUN FULL HEIGHT OF PARTITION WHERE SUSPENDED CEILING OCCURS. BOTH LAYERS OF ½" GYPSUM BOARD TO RUN FULL HEIGHT WHERE CEILING IS THE EX-POSED STRUCTURE.

SECTION A-A OF A MINIMUM COPING SCALE 1½" = 1'-0"

2 CAST STONE COPING

3" LONG PINS 3'-0" O.C.

CONTINUOUS THROUGH FLASHING

CORRUGATED STEEL DECKING

MAGNESIUM LIGHT GRAY FACE BRICK

6 MIL BLACK POLYETHYLENE SPANDREL FLASHING

5"×8" STOCK BRICK VENTS 12'-0" O.C.

1" RIGID FOAM INSULATION

CAVITY WALL TIES EVERY SIXTH COURSE

5"×8" BRICK VENTS

LEAD-COATED COPPER CAP & BASE FLASHING

20-YEAR BONDED BUILT-UP ROOF

SLAG TOPPING SPRAY PAINTED WITH ALUM. PAINT

6" GLASS WOOL TYPE INSULATION

12"×12"×¾" ACOUSTICAL TILE (FISSURE TYPE) ON CONCEALED SUSPENSION SYS.

SECTION THROUGH A PARAPET SCALE ¾" = 1'-0"   **ELEVATION** SCALE ¾" = 1'-0"

PARAPET AND COPING   **6–2**

DETAIL 1: This detail of the top of the brick veneer facing of the Rowland Institute for Science in Cambridge, Massachusetts, designed by Hugh Stubbins and Associates, Inc., shows the careful design treatment of the top of a brick veneer wall crowned with two soldier courses of brick, where a minimum of coping is visible. Viewed from the river, only the small 2" metal drip is visible because the actual coping is 6½" back from the brick face. Careful study of all parts of this detail section will show how thoroughly the whole coping design was studied and detailed.

DETAIL 2: This is a section of a solid brick parapet wall with cast stone coping. Here the insulation of the top floor is located directly above the suspended acoustical ceiling. To eliminate any problems of condensation in this dead air space, brick vents are installed on 12'-0" spacing.

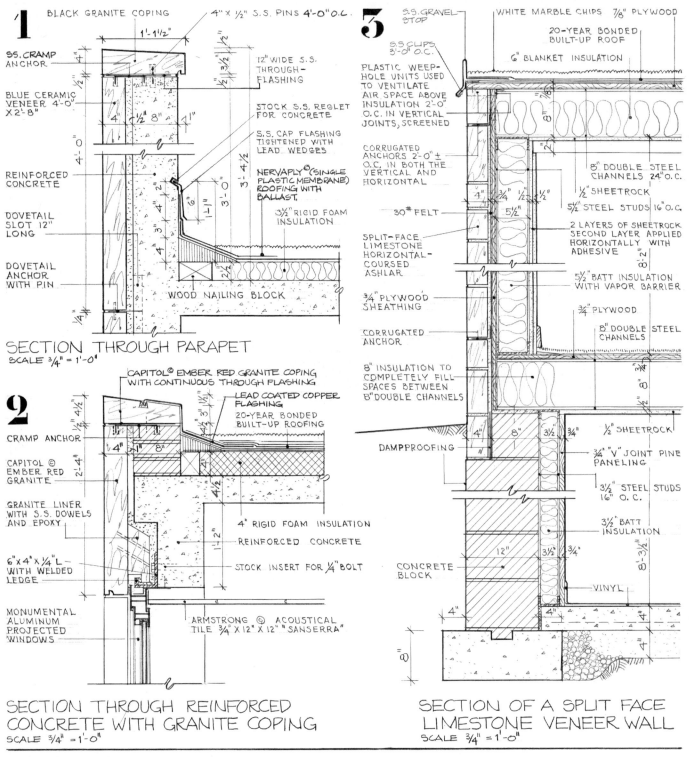

1 SECTION THROUGH PARAPET
SCALE 3/4" = 1'-0"

Labels (Detail 1): BLACK GRANITE COPING · 4" × 1/2" S.S. PINS 4'-0" O.C. · S.S. CRAMP ANCHOR · 12" WIDE S.S. THROUGH-FLASHING · BLUE CERAMIC VENEER 4'-0" × 2'-8" · STOCK S.S. REGLET FOR CONCRETE · S.S. CAP FLASHING TIGHTENED WITH LEAD WEDGES · NERVAPLY® (SINGLE PLASTIC MEMBRANE) ROOFING WITH BALLAST · REINFORCED CONCRETE · 3½" RIGID FOAM INSULATION · DOVETAIL SLOT 12" LONG · DOVETAIL ANCHOR WITH PIN · WOOD NAILING BLOCK

2 SECTION THROUGH REINFORCED CONCRETE WITH GRANITE COPING
SCALE 3/4" = 1'-0"

Labels (Detail 2): CAPITOL® EMBER RED GRANITE COPING WITH CONTINUOUS THROUGH FLASHING · LEAD COATED COPPER FLASHING · 20-YEAR BONDED BUILT-UP ROOFING · CRAMP ANCHOR · CAPITOL® EMBER RED GRANITE · GRANITE LINER WITH S.S. DOWELS AND EPOXY · 4" RIGID FOAM INSULATION · REINFORCED CONCRETE · STOCK INSERT FOR ¼" BOLT · 6"×4"×¼" L WITH WELDED LEDGE · MONUMENTAL ALUMINUM PROJECTED WINDOWS · ARMSTRONG® ACOUSTICAL TILE ¾" × 12" × 12" "SANSERRA"

3 SECTION OF A SPLIT FACE LIMESTONE VENEER WALL
SCALE 3/4" = 1'-0"

Labels (Detail 3): S.S. GRAVEL STOP · WHITE MARBLE CHIPS · 7/8" PLYWOOD · 20-YEAR BONDED BUILT-UP ROOF · 6" BLANKET INSULATION · S.S. CLIPS 3'-0" O.C. · PLASTIC WEEP-HOLE UNITS USED TO VENTILATE AIR SPACE ABOVE INSULATION 2'-0" O.C. IN VERTICAL JOINTS, SCREENED · 8" DOUBLE STEEL CHANNELS 24" O.C. · ½" SHEETROCK · 5½" STEEL STUDS 16" O.C. · CORRUGATED ANCHORS 2'-0" ± O.C. IN BOTH THE VERTICAL AND HORIZONTAL · 2 LAYERS OF SHEETROCK SECOND LAYER APPLIED HORIZONTALLY WITH ADHESIVE · 30# FELT · SPLIT-FACE LIMESTONE HORIZONTAL-COURSED ASHLAR · 5½" BATT INSULATION WITH VAPOR BARRIER · ¾" PLYWOOD · 8" DOUBLE STEEL CHANNELS · ¾" PLYWOOD SHEATHING · CORRUGATED ANCHOR · ½" SHEETROCK · ¾" "V" JOINT PINE PANELING · 3½" STEEL STUDS 16" O.C. · 8" INSULATION TO COMPLETELY FILL SPACES BETWEEN 8" DOUBLE CHANNELS · 3½" BATT INSULATION · DAMPPROOFING · CONCRETE BLOCK · VINYL

6–3 **WALLS AND SKINS**

DETAIL 1: This building is a reinforced concrete structure with a blue ceramic veneer facing. The parapet terminates in a black granite coping to accent the building against the sky. The stainless steel cap flashing wedges into a stainless steel reglet, and the roofing is of the ballast type with the base flashing an integral part of the roofing membrane.

DETAIL 2: This reinforced concrete building has a red granite facing and a red granite coping. The granite facing over the windows has granite liners using epoxy and stainless steel dowels to meet the continuous angle anchored to the structure. The coping has a reglet to receive the base flashing.

DETAIL 3: Shown is a simple one-story administration building of light steel construction with a split-face limestone facing. The top concrete blocks of the foundation wall are filled with mortar; a leveling mortar coat is then applied to which double steel channels are secured.

CROSS-REFERENCES TO *PARAPETS*
IN OTHER CHAPTERS

Chapter Number	Drawing Number	Drawing Title	Described on Page	Drawing on Page
2	2-2	Curtain wall	7	10
	2-3	Residential wall sections	7	11
	2-5	Exterior skin curtain wall	7	12
3	3-2	Four common flashing conditions	17	19
7	7-2	Intermediate platform stairs	51	54, 55
11	11-3	Light construction roof details	99	103

7

Stairs and Stair Railings

INTRODUCTION

Stairs can be divided into three types: straight run, platform, and circular. A fourth, less common type is the scissor stairs, which consists of two straight-run stairs going in opposite directions.

The height of the riser in relation to the width of the tread can be found in almost any architectural or construction handbook. A simple rule to follow is that the product of the riser height multiplied by the width of the tread should equal between 70 and 80 to create a good stair. For example, a stair with a $7\frac{1}{2}''$ riser and a $10\frac{1}{2}''$ tread would give us a product $7.5 \times 10.5 = 78.75$, which is between 70 and 80. For circular stairs, calculate the tread and riser on a circular line $12''$ from the most used handrail.

Stair treads and risers are supported by what are called stringers, located at the sides of the stairs. These stringers can be set in from the sides of the stairs, or be decreased to a single center stringer, or even eliminated completely if the staircase is made of reinforced concrete or if the stair construction is self-supporting.

When the treads and risers are exposed, the resulting design is referred to as an open stringer stairs. When the treads and risers butt into the stringers and only the face of the stringer is exposed, this type is known as a closed stringer stairs. The intersection of a stairs, with or without stringers, at a platform or landing represents one of the most difficult problems in detailing, which can enhance or spoil the entire appearance of a stairs. The various stairs illustrated show answers to these problems.

The surface of the treads should be easily maintained and made of highly durable materials, which, at the same time, are not slippery, particularly at the nosings. The tread should project beyond the riser so that the face of the riser will not be marred by the toes of the shoes as people walk up the stairs.

Stair and wall railings are a basic part of a staircase. There are several major design problems with all stair rails: the joining of the handrail to the vertical supports and the joining of the supports to the stair proper; and in like manner, how the wall railing is supported at the wall. What is particularly difficult is how to take care of a handrail as it follows up the stair slope and meets the handrail which follows the down stairs slope. Difficulty may also be encountered where the stair railing meets the railing of a balcony. In both cases the final design must produce a smooth flow and interesting design from the beginning to the end of the railing.

This integration of the handrail and its vertical supports with the stairs proper without any easements if possible, or else with easements that seem a natural part of the stair design, should not be underestimated. In easements of the handrail, the difficult problem is to eliminate sharp and awkward joints which may be formed by the intersection of the angle of the stairs and the platform or landing. The problem can be simplified by off-setting one tread at the platform and at the landing; this makes it possible for the up and the down railings to meet at the same level. A careful study of the details in this chapter will explain how this is accomplished.

The wall railings raise another difficulty: how to support the railings at the wall. These supports must place the railing away from the wall, leaving space for a comfortable hand and finger grip and be of such a shape that the fingers will not hit the supports when a person is going up or down the stairs. One solution to wall railing supports is to find a method of inserting something rigid in the basic structure of the wall to which the wall railing supports can be secured.

CHAPTER DETAIL TEXT

7-1 Tread-Riser Table for Stairs

This table shows combinations of treads and risers that create good comfortable stairs. In general, building codes for buildings used by the public limit the height of the riser to $7\frac{1}{2}''$, and the minimum width of the tread to $10''$. For residential work the $8''$ riser and $9''$ to $9\frac{3}{4}''$ tread are used for basement stairs and secondary stairs. For secondary schools, nursing homes, and housing for the elderly a $6''$ riser is used. Exterior stairs vary from a $5''$ riser to a $7''$ riser, depending on the character and design of the stairs.

7-2 Intermediate Platform Stairs

This stair detail shows a method of taking care of a fire escape stairs where first-to-second floor height is over $12'\text{-}0''$. Its value lies in showing how to use an intermediate platform to allow the stairs to exit at ground level.

Also note how the usual stair structure above the roof has been integrated with the building's parapet wall so as not to be visible from the street by simply making the roof slope the same as the stair slope and installing a built-in gutter which spills at both sides of the stair roof structure onto the roof of the building.

The use of terne stainless steel metal roofing answers the difficult problem of a built-in gutter and a $3'\text{-}0''$ high parapet wall. The gutter spills at each side onto splashblocks on the built-up roof. Note the flashing at the sill of the roof exit door.

7-3 Straight-Run Stairs in a Club

This detail, designed by Alley Friends Architects of Philadelphia, shows how, by using simple stock materials, an interesting original decorative staircase was created from stock store fixture rack rings, acorn nuts, $\frac{3}{4}''$ pipe washers, and $1\frac{1}{2}''$ balls. Note how at the stair treads the carpet is wrapped around the $\frac{3}{4}''$ nosing and at the sides the carpet edge binding is back $3''$ from the sides of the treads. At the balcony the fascia has a $\frac{3}{4}''$ round moulding and the carpet is wrapped around in the same manner as at the treads. Also note that the round rack rings at balcony are kept away from the fascia with $1''$ pipe washers so that the wrapped-around carpet makes a continuous horizontal line.

7-4 Straight-Run Stairs in a Residence

This detail from the Perlman residence in Riverdale, New York, shows a simple straight-run wood stairs with $2'' \times 12''$ Douglas fir wood stringers. It illustrates uncomplicated yet design-noteworthy solutions to typical stair problems. Here the stair design uses the formula of offsetting one riser at both landing and balcony, to make the handrail coming up the platform and the handrail coming down to the platform meet exactly at the $2'\text{-}8''$ height. As a result no easement is required and, in this case, by tipping the handrail, a simple $45°$ cut is made for the intersection. At the balcony where a railing higher than $2'\text{-}8''$ is needed, the offset allows the handrail to continue on up so that it intersects the balcony railing at a $3'\text{-}0''$ height. Once again, by tipping the balcony handrail, a simple $90°$ intersection is created and only a simple $45°$ cut is necessary.

7-5 Platform Stairs

The stairs shown on this illustration is an example of a carefully designed stairs that looks very straightforward, but on close scrutiny has answered simply and easily many of the difficult detail problems encountered in designing a stairs. By using a bent plate for a stringer, a $10''$ depth was obtained and a certain delicacy in design resulted. By widening the entire well to $10'\text{-}0''$, a more open feeling and a certain gracefulness were achieved. Just widening the run of the stairs to the exit door completely cleans up the termination of the wide well between stairs. Offsetting a riser at the platform eliminates any easements in the handrails and by keeping the handrails $3\frac{1}{2}''$ away from the balusters takes care of the $2'\text{-}8''$ height at stairs and the $3'\text{-}0''$ height required at the second floor. Note that the balusters are placed $\frac{1}{2}''$ away from the stringers. The entire visible underside of the stairs is covered with wire lath and plaster.

7-6 Fire Stairs in an Elementary School

This detail was developed for an elementary (K-6) school in Commack, New York, by the author's office. The simple platform stairs also served as the fire stairs at the end of a two-story classroom wing with kindergartens and first and second grades on grade (ground level), and grades 3 through 6 on the second floor. The use of deeper center stringers allows for a very simple answer to the platform closure plate and stringer intersection at second floor landing.

Elementary school stairs should have smaller risers, in this case $6\frac{3}{4}''$ ones, and two handrails, one for children and one at the normal $2'\text{-}8''$ height.

In this school the glazed masonry units were deep Kingston blue, and the handrails, stringers, closure plate, and balusters were painted a deep Swedish red flat enamel.

7-7 Horseshoe Stairs

This staircase should be studied closely as there are so many creative details which are simple because they had been carefully worked out to answer specific design criteria. Hugh Stubbins and Associates, Inc., are responsible for this truly distinctive horseshoe stairs in the Rowland Institute for Science in Cambridge, Massachusetts. It is worth noting that the stair manufacturer, Atlantic Stairways, Inc., Newburyport, Massachusetts, helped to work out the details of the stair during construction.

Note that the handrails are laminated vertically. Thus easements and curved areas can be easily made without the normal large number of joints and difficult grain matching.

TREADS \ RISERS	5"	5¼"	5½"	5¾"	6"	6¼"	6½"	6¾"	7"	7¼"	7½"	7¾"	8"
9"													72.00
9¼"												71.69	74.00
9½"											71.25	73.63	76.00
9¾"										70.69	73.13	75.56	78.00
10"									70.00	72.50	75.00	77.50	80.00
10¼"									71.75	74.31	76.88	79.44	
10½"								70.88	73.50	76.13	78.75		
10¾"								72.76	75.25	77.94			
11"							71.50	74.25	77.00	79.75			
11¼"						70.31	73.13	75.94	78.75				
11½"						71.88	74.75	77.63					
11¾"					70.50	73.44	76.38	79.31					
12"					72.00	75.00	78.00						
12¼"				70.44	73.50	76.56	79.63						
12½"				71.88	75.00	78.13							
12¾"			70.13	73.31	76.50	79.69							
13"			71.50	74.75	78.00								
13¼"			72.98	76.19	79.50								
13½"			74.25	77.53									
13¾"		72.19	75.63	79.06									
14"	70.00	73.50	77.00										

THIS TABLE SHOWS COMBINATIONS OF TREAD WIDTHS AND RISER HEIGHTS THAT CREATE A COMFORTABLE STAIR. FORMULA: RISER HEIGHT × TREAD WIDTH = 70 TO 80

7–1 TREAD-RISER TABLE FOR STAIRS

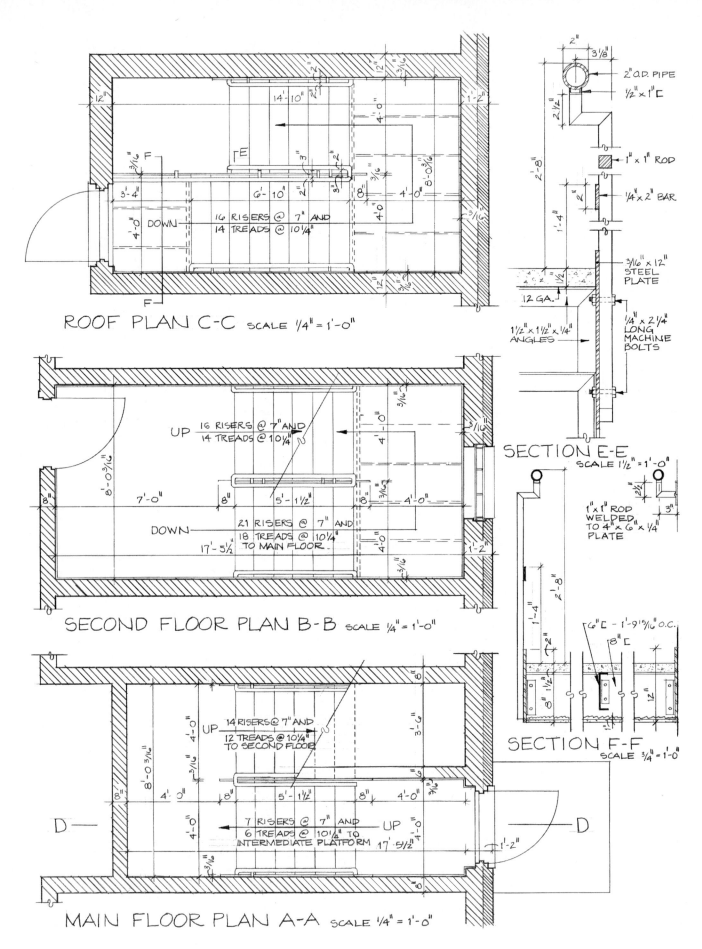

ROOF PLAN C-C SCALE ¼" = 1'-0"

16 RISERS @ 7" AND
14 TREADS @ 10¼"

SECOND FLOOR PLAN B-B SCALE ¼" = 1'-0"

UP 16 RISERS @ 7" AND
14 TREADS @ 10¼"

DOWN 21 RISERS @ 7" AND
18 TREADS @ 10¼"
TO MAIN FLOOR

MAIN FLOOR PLAN A-A SCALE ¼" = 1'-0"

UP 14 RISERS @ 7" AND
12 TREADS @ 10¼"
TO SECOND FLOOR

7 RISERS @ 7" AND
6 TREADS @ 10¼" TO
INTERMEDIATE PLATFORM

SECTION E-E
SCALE 1½" = 1'-0"

2" O.D. PIPE
½" x 1" L
1" x 1" ROD
¼" x 2" BAR
3/16" x 12" STEEL PLATE
¼" x 2¼" LONG MACHINE BOLTS
1½" x 1½" x ¼" ANGLES
12 GA.

SECTION F-F
SCALE ¾" = 1'-0"

1" x 1" ROD WELDED TO 4" x 6" x ¼" PLATE
6" L - 1'-9 15/16" O.C.
8" L

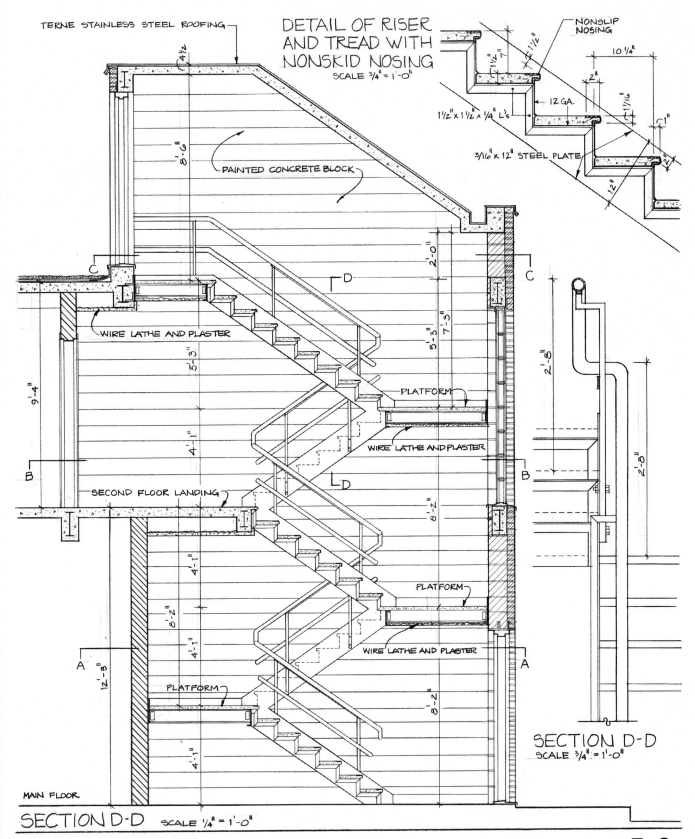

TERNE STAINLESS STEEL ROOFING

DETAIL OF RISER
AND TREAD WITH
NONSKID NOSING
SCALE 3/4" = 1'-0"

NONSLIP
NOSING

1 1/2"

7"

10 1/4"

1 1/2"

12 GA.

2"

1 11/16"

1 1/2" x 1 1/2" x 1/4" L's

3/16" x 12" STEEL PLATE

1"

12"

2"

2"

8'-6"

PAINTED CONCRETE BLOCK

C

D

C

2'-0"

7'-3"

5'-3"

2'-8"

WIRE LATHE AND PLASTER

5'-3"

9'-4"

4'-1"

PLATFORM

WIRE LATHE AND PLASTER

B

B

2'-0"

SECOND FLOOR LANDING

D

8'-2"

PLATFORM

4'-1"

8'-2"

WIRE LATHE AND PLASTER

A

A

12'-3"

PLATFORM

4'-1"

SECTION D-D
SCALE 3/4" = 1'-0"

MAIN FLOOR

SECTION D-D   SCALE 1/4" = 1'-0"

INTERMEDIATE PLATFORM STAIRS

This stairs, part of an addition to an existing school, had a first-to-second floor height of 12'-3" and had to serve as a fire escape also. This detail shows the use of an intermediate platform to allow the stairs to exit directly at grade. Note that three runs of stairs with seven risers each allows for clearance at both platforms. The stringer at the center of the stairs is a 3/16" welded steel plate; the wall stringers are also plates. The 2" continuous pipe railing is supported by 1" X 1" bars, and at landings and platforms, the railing just bends down 7", crosses, and continues on down. Note that the usual stair structure above the roof is not visible from the street.

7–2

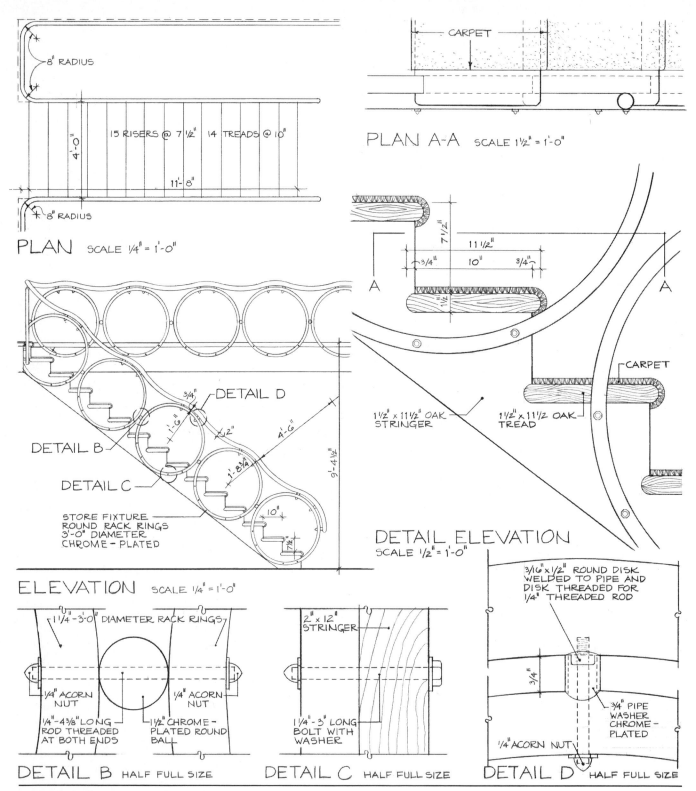

CARPET

PLAN A-A SCALE 1½" = 1'-0"

8" RADIUS

4'-0"

15 RISERS @ 7½" 14 TREADS @ 10"

11'-8"

8" RADIUS

PLAN SCALE ¼" = 1'-0"

7½"

11½"

¾" 10" ¾"

1½"

A   A

CARPET

DETAIL D

¾"

1'-6"

½"

4'-6"

DETAIL B

DETAIL C

1'-8¾"

9'-4½"

STORE FIXTURE
ROUND RACK RINGS
3'-0" DIAMETER
CHROME-PLATED

10"

7½"

1½" x 11½" OAK
STRINGER

1½" x 11½ OAK
TREAD

DETAIL ELEVATION
SCALE ½" = 1'-0"

ELEVATION SCALE ¼" = 1'-0"

3/16" x ½" ROUND DISK
WELDED TO PIPE AND
DISK THREADED FOR
¼" THREADED ROD

1¼"-3'-0" DIAMETER RACK RINGS

2" x 12"
STRINGER

¾"

¼" ACORN
NUT

¼" ACORN
NUT

¼"-4⅜" LONG
ROD THREADED
AT BOTH ENDS

1½" CHROME-
PLATED ROUND
BALL

1¼"-3" LONG
BOLT WITH
WASHER

¾" PIPE
WASHER
CHROME-
PLATED

¼"ACORN NUT

DETAIL B HALF FULL SIZE

DETAIL C HALF FULL SIZE

DETAIL D HALF FULL SIZE

7–3 **STRAIGHT-RUN STAIRS IN A CLUB**

This detail, designed by Alley Friends Architects, is from the Black Banana, a private club in Philadelphia. The dramatic effect evolves from the use of stock chrome-plated store fixtures—round rack rings, 3'-0" in diameter, connected by 1½" chrome-plated balls at midpoint and secured to the stringers at four points with ¼" bolts with chrome-plated acorn nuts. A 2" chrome-plated round nandrail, which is made to undulate by the use of two radii, one 1'-8¾" and the other 4'-6", is connected at two points to the round racks using ¾" chrome-plated washers. The oak treads are rounded and extend beyond stringers by 1".

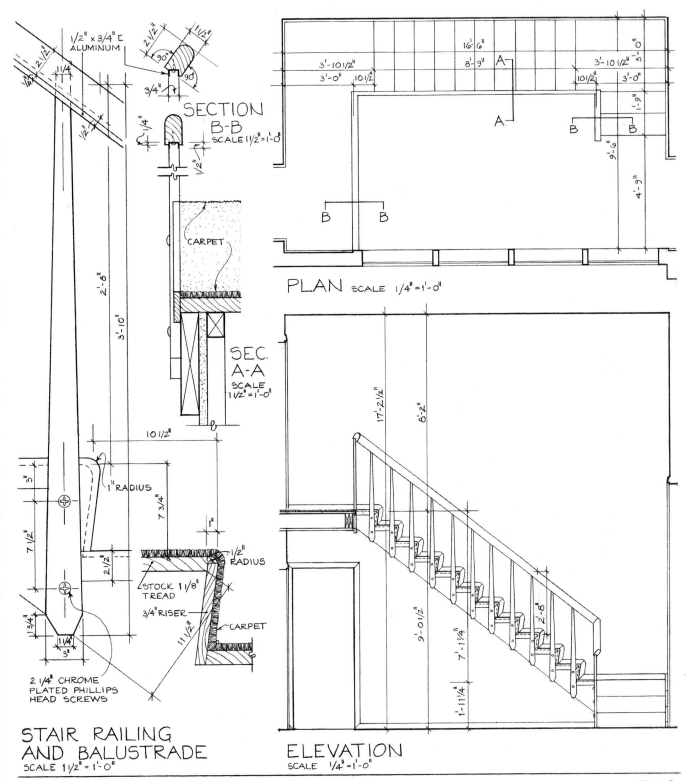

SECTION
B-B
SCALE 1½"=1'-0"

½" x ¾" ⊏
ALUMINUM

PLAN SCALE ¼"=1'-0"

CARPET

SEC.
A-A
SCALE
1½"=1'-0"

1" RADIUS

7 ¾"

STOCK 1⅛"
TREAD

¾" RISER

CARPET

½"
RADIUS

2 ¼" CHROME
PLATED PHILLIPS
HEAD SCREWS

STAIR RAILING
AND BALUSTRADE
SCALE 1½"=1'-0"

ELEVATION
SCALE ¼"=1'-0"

STRAIGHT-RUN STAIRS IN A RESIDENCE   **7–4**

In this straight-run wood stairs the use of a ¼" X ¾" aluminum channel allows each baluster to be secured with wood screws and accurately spaced both horizontally and vertically. The wood railing is also secured to the channel with wood screws. The shape of the balusters and the use of carefully spaced chrome-plated Phillips head screws to secure them to the 2" X 12" stringers give the stairs a pleasing design touch. In these stairs there are three interesting solutions to typical stair problems: (1) the use of stock wood treads cut so that the stair risers are slanted; (2) the use of two small trim pieces between balusters, thus allowing stair carpeting to extend the full width of the stairs; and (3) tipping the stock wood handrail at the landing at the small balcony as well as at the lower platform, to meet the sloping stair handrail at 90°, thus eliminating any handrail easements.

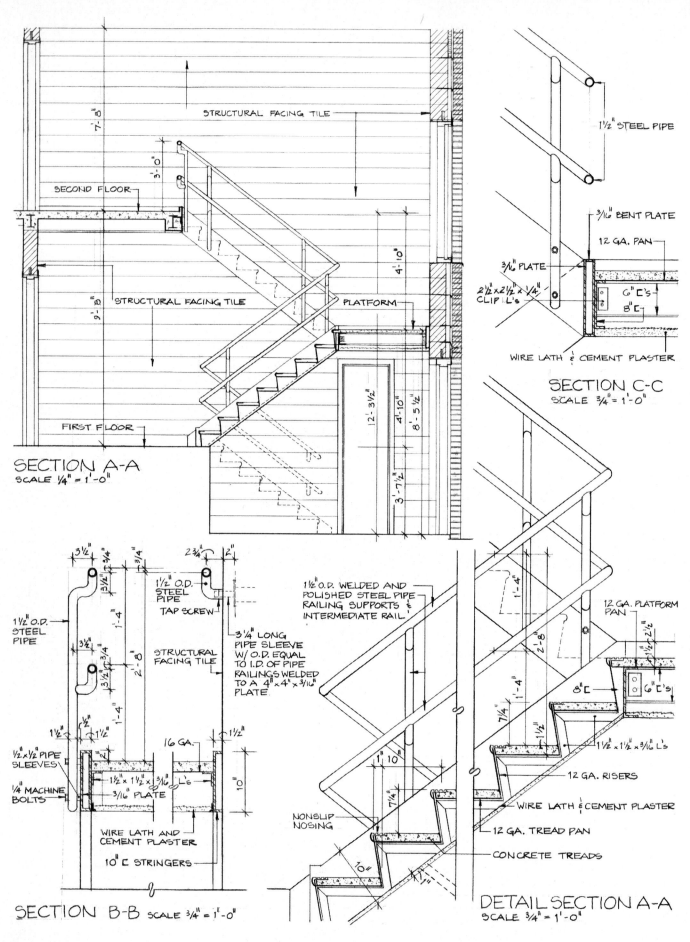

STRUCTURAL FACING TILE

7'-8"

3'-0"

SECOND FLOOR

9'-10"

STRUCTURAL FACING TILE

4'-10"

PLATFORM

FIRST FLOOR

12'-3½"

4'-10"

8'-5½"

3'-7½"

SECTION A-A
SCALE ¼" = 1'-0"

1½" STEEL PIPE

3/16" BENT PLATE

12 GA. PAN

3/16" PLATE

2½"x2½"x¼"
CLIP L's

6" C's

8" C

WIRE LATH & CEMENT PLASTER

SECTION C-C
SCALE ¾" = 1'-0"

3½" ¾" ¾" 2¾" 2"

1½" O.D.
STEEL
PIPE

TAP SCREW

3/16" 3/16"

1½" O.D.
STEEL
PIPE

1'-4"

2'-8"

3½" ¾"

3/16" 3/16"

1'-4"

STRUCTURAL
FACING TILE

3¾" LONG
PIPE SLEEVE
W/ O.D. EQUAL
TO I.D. OF PIPE
RAILINGS WELDED
TO A 4"x4"x3/16"
PLATE

1½" ½" 1½"

1½"

16 GA.

1½"

½"x½" PIPE
SLEEVES

¼" MACHINE
BOLTS

1½"x1½"x3/16" L's

3/16" PLATE

10"

WIRE LATH AND
CEMENT PLASTER

10" C STRINGERS

SECTION B-B SCALE ¾" = 1'-0"

1½" O.D. WELDED AND
POLISHED STEEL PIPE
RAILING SUPPORTS &
INTERMEDIATE RAIL

1'-4"

2'-8"

1'-4"

7¼"

1' 10"

7¼"

NONSLIP
NOSING

10"

12 GA. PLATFORM
PAN

1½" 2½"

8" C

6" C's

1½"x1½"x3/16" L's

12 GA. RISERS

WIRE LATH & CEMENT PLASTER

12 GA. TREAD PAN

CONCRETE TREADS

DETAIL SECTION A-A
SCALE ¾" = 1'-0"

58

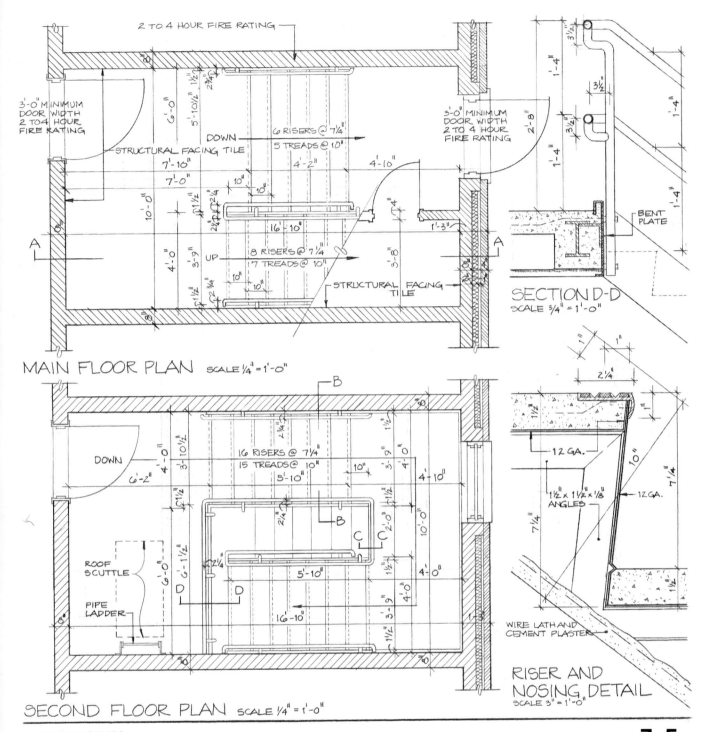

MAIN FLOOR PLAN SCALE ¼" = 1'-0"

SECTION D-D SCALE ¾" = 1'-0"

SECOND FLOOR PLAN SCALE ¼" = 1'-0"

RISER AND NOSING DETAIL SCALE 3" = 1'-0"

PLATFORM STAIRS

This is a very straightforward stairs where the first floor is 3'-7½" above exterior grade. This stairs takes advantage of this change in level by increasing the opening between the stairs and, at the first floor, widens the stair leading to the exterior. One of the difficult problems with stairs occurs when the exterior grade is at the same level as the first floor. Here twelve 7¾" risers or thirteen 7½" risers must be installed for the first straight run to the platform to provide the +7'-0" headroom needed to exit directly to the exterior. This stairs offsets one riser at the platform by the width of one tread; thus the pipe handrails are at the exact same level at the platform and simply take two 90° turns and connect horizontally. At the second floor, by not offsetting a riser, railing can continue and arrive at a 3'-0" height. The wall railing is secured by a pipe sleeve with a plate that is securely anchored within the wall, and the wall railing is shoved right onto the sleeve and secured by a tap screw.

7–5

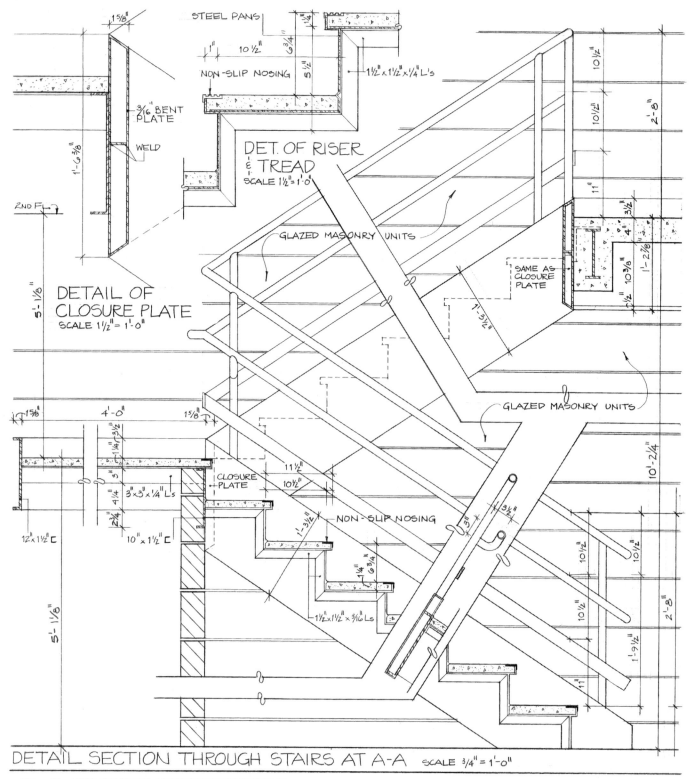

STEEL PANS

NON-SLIP NOSING

DET. OF RISER & TREAD
SCALE 1½" = 1'-0"

1½" x 1½" x ¼" L's

3/16" BENT PLATE

WELD

2ND FL.

DETAIL OF CLOSURE PLATE
SCALE 1½" = 1'-0"

GLAZED MASONRY UNITS

SAME AS CLOSURE PLATE

GLAZED MASONRY UNITS

CLOSURE PLATE

NON-SLIP NOSING

3 x 3 x ¼" Ls

12" x 1½" C

10" x 1½" C

1½" x 1½" x 3/16 Ls

DETAIL SECTION THROUGH STAIRS AT A-A   SCALE ¾" = 1'-0"

7–6 **FIRE STAIRS IN AN ELEMENTARY SCHOOL**

This very simple fire stairs answers several difficult detail problems that are common to any stairs: (1) by offsetting one riser at the platform, the pipe railings meet at the same elevation (see Plan at Platform), and so do the children's pipe railings; (2) by increasing the depth of both center stringers, the closure plate at platform and at second floor landing has its top and bottom angles equal to the up-and-down stringer angles. By this method a very simple joint is obtained, as shown both on the large detail of the closure plate and at the landing in the large section of the stairs.

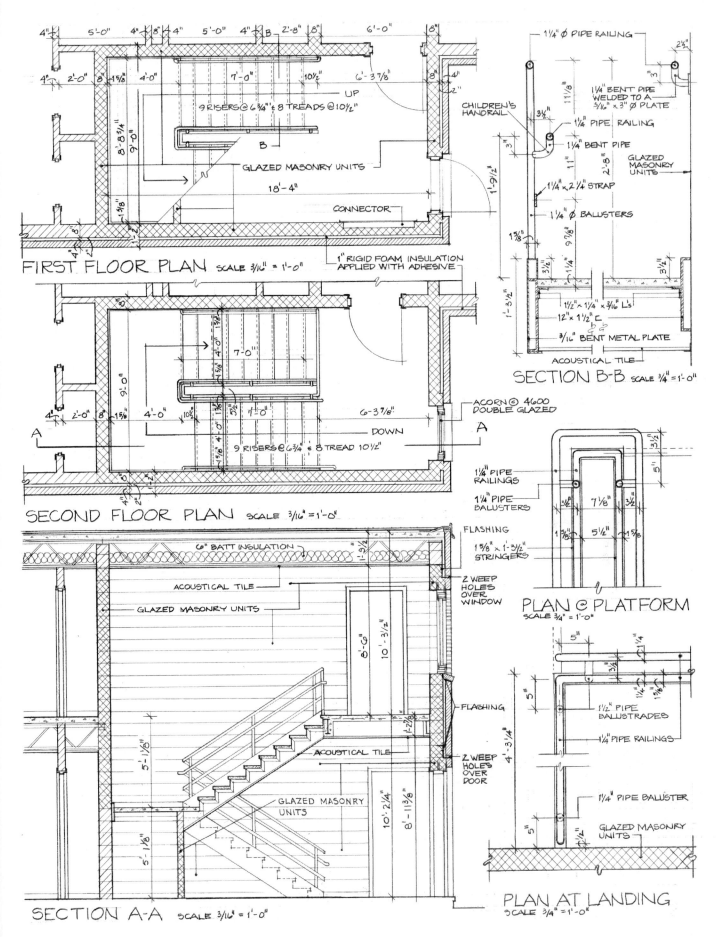

FIRST FLOOR PLAN SCALE 3/16" = 1'-0"

UP
9 RISERS @ 6¾" & 8 TREADS @ 10½"
B
GLAZED MASONRY UNITS
18'-4"
CHILDREN'S HANDRAIL
CONNECTOR
1" RIGID FOAM INSULATION APPLIED WITH ADHESIVE

SECOND FLOOR PLAN SCALE 3/16" = 1'-0"

A
7'-0"
9'-0"
4'-0"
7'-0"
DOWN
9 RISERS @ 6¾" & 8 TREAD 10½"
A
ACORN © 4600 DOUBLE GLAZED

SECTION B-B SCALE 3/4" = 1'-0"

1¼" Ø PIPE RAILING
1¼" BENT PIPE WELDED TO A 3/16" x 3" Ø PLATE
1¼" PIPE RAILING
1¼" BENT PIPE
GLAZED MASONRY UNITS
1¼" x 2¼" STRAP
1¼" Ø BALUSTERS
1½" x ¼" x 3/16" L's
12" x 1½" C
3/16" BENT METAL PLATE
ACOUSTICAL TILE

PLAN @ PLATFORM SCALE 3/4" = 1'-0"

1¼" PIPE RAILINGS
1¼" PIPE BALUSTERS
FLASHING
1 5/8" x 1-3½" STRINGERS
2 WEEP HOLES OVER WINDOW
7 1/8"
5½"

SECTION A-A SCALE 3/16" = 1'-0"

6" BATT INSULATION
ACOUSTICAL TILE
GLAZED MASONRY UNITS
8'-0"
10'-3½"
FLASHING
2 WEEP HOLES OVER DOOR
ACOUSTICAL TILE
GLAZED MASONRY UNITS
10'-2¼"
8'-11 3/8"
5'-1 1/8"
5'-1 1/8"

PLAN AT LANDING SCALE 3/4" = 1'-0"

1½" PIPE BALUSTRADES
1¼" PIPE RAILINGS
1¼" PIPE BALUSTER
GLAZED MASONRY UNITS
4'-3¼"
5"
5"
5"
5"

61

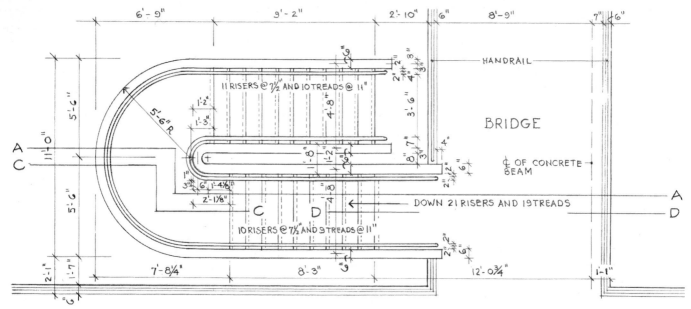

PLAN OF HORSESHOE STAIRS SCALE 3/16" = 1'-0"

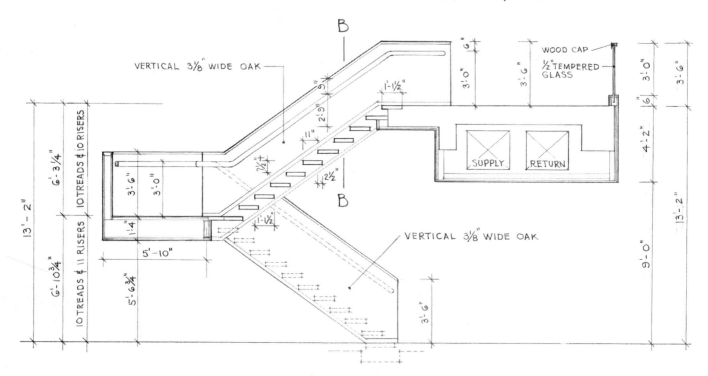

SECTION A-A THROUGH HORSESHOE STAIRS SCALE 3/16" = 1'-0"

7–7 HORSESHOE STAIRS

Hugh Stubbins and Associates, Inc., designed this handsome horseshoe stairs for the Rowland Institute for Science, Cambridge, Massachusetts. The detailing has to be looked at very closely to appreciate the care, design, and creativity that went into this stairs. For example, the small 3/16" reveal at top and bottom of the solid railing gives a slight, subtle accent between cap, base, and the 3 1/8" wide vertical T & G hardwood. The 3 1/8" width also takes care of the 3 1/8" X 1'-2" high glass lens with light fixture within the solid railing. These are installed at every other tread. Note the solid wood tread with 2 1/2" deep carpet cutout and small thin trim piece at the back with half-round top to terminate the wraparound carpet. This stairs starts from a bridge with glass handrails in a two-story atrium and descends to a planted reception area. The cap of the solid railing is laminated vertically; thus all curved areas do not require quantities of joints and difficult grain matching.

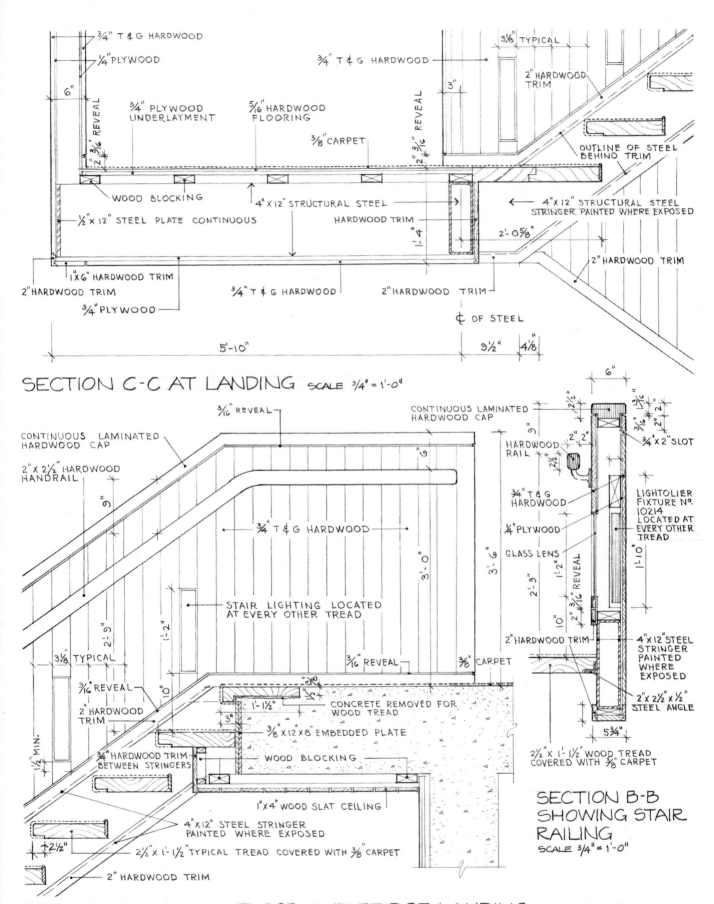

SECTION C-C AT LANDING SCALE 3/4" = 1'-0"

3/4" T & G HARDWOOD
1/4" PLYWOOD
6"
2" REVEAL
3/16
2"
3/4" PLYWOOD UNDERLAYMENT
5/16" HARDWOOD FLOORING
3/8" CARPET
2" REVEAL
2" 3/16
3/4" T & G HARDWOOD
3"
3/8" TYPICAL
2" HARDWOOD TRIM
3"
OUTLINE OF STEEL BEHIND TRIM
WOOD BLOCKING
4" X 12" STRUCTURAL STEEL
HARDWOOD TRIM
4" X 12" STRUCTURAL STEEL STRINGER PAINTED WHERE EXPOSED
1/2" X 12" STEEL PLATE CONTINUOUS
1'-4"
2'-0 5/8"
2" HARDWOOD TRIM
1"X 6" HARDWOOD TRIM
2" HARDWOOD TRIM
3/4" PLYWOOD
3/4" T & G HARDWOOD
2" HARDWOOD TRIM
Ȼ OF STEEL
5'-10"
9 1/2"
4 1/8"

CONTINUOUS LAMINATED HARDWOOD CAP
3/16" REVEAL
CONTINUOUS LAMINATED HARDWOOD CAP
CONTINUOUS LAMINATED HARDWOOD CAP
2" X 2 1/2" HARDWOOD HANDRAIL
3/4" T & G HARDWOOD
9"
6"
6"
3'-0"
3'-6"
9"
HARDWOOD RAIL
2 1/2"
2 1/2"
2"
2"
3/16" 3/8" 2" 2"
3/4" X 2" SLOT
3/4" T & G HARDWOOD
1/4" PLYWOOD
GLASS LENS
LIGHTOLIER FIXTURE Nᵒ. 10214 LOCATED AT EVERY OTHER TREAD
1'-10"
STAIR LIGHTING LOCATED AT EVERY OTHER TREAD
2'-9"
1'-2"
10"
2'-9"
1'-2"
2" 3/16" REVEAL
3/16" REVEAL
3/8" CARPET
2" HARDWOOD TRIM
4" X 12" STEEL STRINGER PAINTED WHERE EXPOSED
3 1/8" TYPICAL
3/16" REVEAL
2" HARDWOOD TRIM
10"
3 1/2
1'-1 1/2"
3"
CONCRETE REMOVED FOR WOOD TREAD
3/8" X 12 X 8" EMBEDDED PLATE
WOOD BLOCKING
1 1/2" MIN.
1/2 MIN.
3/4" HARDWOOD TRIM BETWEEN STRINGERS
1" X 4" WOOD SLAT CEILING
2" X 2 1/2" X 1/2" STEEL ANGLE
5 3/4"
2 1/2" X 1-1 1/2" WOOD TREAD COVERED WITH 3/8" CARPET
4" X 12" STEEL STRINGER PAINTED WHERE EXPOSED
2 1/2"
2 1/2" X 1-1 1/2" TYPICAL TREAD COVERED WITH 3/8" CARPET
2" HARDWOOD TRIM

SECTION B-B SHOWING STAIR RAILING SCALE 3/4" = 1'-0"

SECTION D-D AT 3RD FLOOR AND BRIDGE LANDING SCALE 3/4" = 1'-0"

CROSS-REFERENCES TO *STAIRS AND STAIR RAILINGS*
IN OTHER CHAPTERS

Chapter Number	Drawing Number	Drawing Title	Described on Page	Drawing on Page
3	3-2	Four common flashing conditions	17	19
	3-3	Four special flashing conditions	17	20
6	6-1	Section through parapet wall and railing	42	44
8	8-1	Residential railings	67	70
	8-2	Railings	67	71
	8-4	Metal railings	68	73
	8-5	Terrace railings	68	74

8

Railings

INTRODUCTION

Stair railings are discussed and detailed in Chapter 7. Here mezzanine, balcony, retaining wall, bridge, and roof railings are examined. All of these have a common problem and that is how to support the railings and how to treat the space between railing and floor or roof.

The supports (balusters) can be let into the floor, structure, or coping with sleeves or set onto preset dowels of a size to meet the inside diameter of the balusters. The support can also be attached to floor, structure, or coping with flanges. It is possible to attach the supports with a space separating them from the face of the wall of the mezzanine, balcony, or retaining wall, or the face of the roof edge.

Another problem is how to secure the railings to the supports (balusters). If pipe is used for both the railing and the supports, it can easily be welded or joined with wedge-type connectors and concealed screws. The supports can also be of any metal form, such as channel, angle, rod, bar, or square or rectangular tube. In these cases, the method of attaching the railing depends on the type of railing.

Some examples are (1) a small continuous channel of the same size as the supports (balusters) to which the supports are secured and the railing is then secured to the channel, and (2) special flanges secured to the supports and the railing secured to the flanges. When the railing is some wood form, the same systems as described above are used. In all exterior metal railings and support systems, all metal parts should be of the same metal or of a compatible metal so as not to have galvanic action occur. Wood supports (balusters) are generally secured to the mezzanine, balcony, retaining wall, or roof edge. Sometimes they are let into the floor and secured there, or they may extend through the floor and be secured to the structure below the floor.

The space between the railing and the floor structure or coping must be treated with intermediate railings, solid or transparent panels, wire mesh, or stretched fabric. Some codes require three intermediate railings. The spacing of intermediate railings is very important because it can completely block the view of a person sitting in a balcony or mezzanine. Also, the space from floor or roof to first intermediate railing must not be such that somebody, particularly a child, could slip through the opening and fall to the ground level below.

CHAPTER DETAIL TEXT

8-1 Residential Railings   The three residential railings shown here are particularly interesting because they were designed for the specific decor requirements of clients with extensive knowledge and experience in the arts.

DETAIL 1. The railing here is designed to be very secure and safe yet not block the view. The hand railing, balusters, intermediate railing, and 2″ by 4″ decking are of redwood, and the structural joists and two 2″ × 12″ fascia are structural Douglas fir but painted flat black. The balusters are separated from the black fascia with pipe washers and are secured with bolts and 1½″ square washers.

DETAIL 2. This interior railing in the main entrance serves as the divider between a window wall with large planter and glass shelves for art objects and the main stairs descending to a lower level of the residence. The top of the cypress fascia is carefully raised above the subfloor to give a termination to the carpet. Balustrades are secured to structure with large Phillips Head® wood screws.

DETAIL 3. Shown is a simple wood railing for a balcony and terrace. The entire railing, balusters, decking, fascia, and supporting beams are all stained a silver gray. The use of silver gray stain allows the use of standard yard lumber for structure, decking, and railing.

8-2 Railings   This detail shows two balcony railings; one combines aluminum and redwood, and the other is a combination of aluminum supports and railing with filler panels of patterned glass, in this case, with a pebble finish.

DETAIL 1. The decking, fascia, structural members, handrail, and intermediate railings are all redwood and are contrasted against the slender aluminum balusters which are separated from redwood fascia with pipe washers.

DETAIL 2. The tempered patterned glass panels are secured to the aluminum balusters with square felt washers, square aluminum washers, and round-head Phillips Head® machine screws. When using any tempered glass, any holes have to be made by the glass manufacturer because tempered glass cannot be drilled, sandblasted, etc., once it has been tempered.

8-3 Ladders   Four types of ladders used extensively in buildings are shown. These are strictly functional, i.e., utilitarian. Their purpose is to give access to areas that require only periodic inspection or are very rarely used.

Another type of ladder, known as a ship ladder, is easily obtained, as it is used extensively on ships and boats. It consists of light channels for the stringers and special wide channels with a nonslip top surface for the rungs.

8-4   Metal Railings   The three details in this illustration are all simple metal railings. However, the railing in the first detail (see DETAIL 1 below) presents more complexity, as it had to be designed to correlate with the driveway and guest parking area of a residence. Both the retaining wall (top $2\frac{1}{2}''$ above grade) and the slate walk start at the edge of the sidewalk and, as they approach the house, the slate walk slowly pitches to $3'\text{-}4''$ below the parking area. The driveway here is designed an extra two-car width and the parking area is $30'\text{-}0''$ wide, plus $20'\text{-}0''$ for additional parking, so the chances of cars bumping the railing are negligible, as the area is wide enough for a car to turn around easily.

DETAIL 1. This shows a $2''$ diameter aluminum pipe supported by $1''$ by $1\frac{1}{4}''$ aluminum balusters $2'\text{-}8''$ o.c. and two $\frac{1}{2}'' \times 1\frac{1}{2}''$ aluminum intermediate bars. The $1'' \times 1\frac{1}{4}''$ balusters are kept away from the face of the retaining wall with $\frac{1}{2}'' \times 1''$ diameter pipe washers. Note that a $\frac{1}{2}'' \times 1''$ aluminum channel is used to secure the $2''$ pipe railing with aluminum machine screws at two points between balusters, and the channel is secured to the balusters the tops of which have been drilled and threaded to receive machine screws.

There are $\frac{1}{4}''$ vertical reinforcing rods $2'\text{-}0''$ o.c. which project $2''$ above the concrete foundation wall; then, when the first course of concrete blocks is laid and the voids filled, $\frac{1}{4}''$ reinforcing rods $2'\text{-}0''$ long are installed in the filled voids adjacent to the foundation wall rods.

DETAIL 2. This shows a complete $1''$ aluminum pipe railing with balusters and intermediate railings of the same $1''$ diameter. Large $2'' \times 4''$ deep sleeves are placed in the concrete of the balcony when it is poured. These sleeves are spaced $2'\text{-}10''$ apart and $3''$ from the balcony's edge. Then $7''$ sleeves with their O.D. equal to the I.D. of the $1''$ pipe balusters are very accurately placed in the installed sleeve with nonshrink grout, with their top $4''$ above balcony slab. Now the entire railing can be installed by being shoved down tight until the $3''$ diameter collar meets the slab.

DETAIL 3. This shows simple bent steel pipe balusters that place the handrailing flush with the edge of the balcony. Balusters are secured to balcony structure with four $\frac{1}{4}''$ bolts, washers, and nuts. Note that the intermediate railing is only $8''$ up from the redwood decking. This allows noninterrupted vision for one sitting on the deck. The location of the intermediate railings allow for a clear vision from seats and the bottom $6''$ space stops anybody from slipping through.

8-5   Terrace Railings   DETAIL 1. This railing on the terrace of an addition to a townhouse in Philadelphia by Alley Friends Architects shows the simple use of wood, aluminum pipe, and canvas to create a very decorative yet sturdy railing.

DETAIL 2. One of the difficult problems of installing a railing on a concrete terrace is answered in this case by the use of $6''$ high sleeves whose outside diameter is equal to the inside diameter of the pipe railing to be installed. These 6″ high sleeves are welded to a circular steel plate and the combined units are bolted to the concrete slab comprising the terrace. In this way, when the railing is finally installed, the pipe sleeves, circular plates, and bolts are concealed by the inverted washer cups welded to the bottom of the outside pipe supports of the entire railing.

Note that the two intermediate railings are projected out from the balusters, thus adding a three-dimensional feeling to the railing.

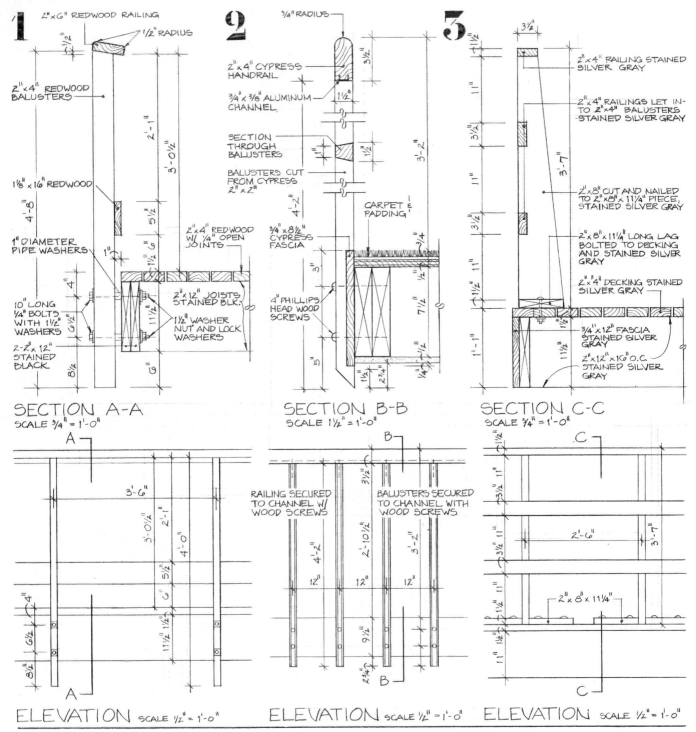

1 2"×6" REDWOOD RAILING
½" RADIUS
2"×4" REDWOOD BALUSTERS
2'-1"
3'-0½"
1⅛"×16" REDWOOD
4'-0"
5½"
1" DIAMETER PIPE WASHERS
1"
2"×4" REDWOOD W/ ¼" OPEN JOINTS
2"×12" JOISTS STAINED BLK.
1½" WASHER NUT AND LOCK WASHERS
10" LONG ¼" BOLTS WITH 1½" WASHERS
2-2"×12" STAINED BLACK

SECTION A-A
SCALE ¾" = 1'-0"

2 ¾" RADIUS
3½"
2"×4" CYPRESS HANDRAIL
1½"
¾"×⅜" ALUMINUM CHANNEL
SECTION THROUGH BALUSTERS
BALUSTERS CUT FROM CYPRESS 2"×2"
1½"
3'-2"
4'-2"
CARPET & PADDING
¾"×8½" CYPRESS FASCIA
¾"
½"
4" PHILLIPS HEAD WOOD SCREWS
7½"
5"

SECTION B-B
SCALE 1½" = 1'-0"

3 3½"
½"
2"×4" RAILING STAINED SILVER GRAY
11"
2"×4" RAILINGS LET INTO 2"×4" BALUSTERS STAINED SILVER GRAY
3½"
3'-7"
3½"
2"×8" CUT AND NAILED TO 2"×8"×11¼" PIECE, STAINED SILVER GRAY
11"
2"×8"×11¼" LONG LAG BOLTED TO DECKING AND STAINED SILVER GRAY
1½"
2"×4" DECKING STAINED SILVER GRAY
1½"
3"
1'-1"
¾"×12" FASCIA STAINED SILVER GRAY
11½"
2"×12"×16' O.C. STAINED SILVER GRAY

SECTION C-C
SCALE ¾" = 1'-0"

A
3'-6"
3'-0½"
2'-1"
4'-0"
5½"
6"
4"
6½"
11½" 1½"
8½"
6"
A

ELEVATION SCALE ½" = 1'-0"

B
3½"
RAILING SECURED TO CHANNEL W/ WOOD SCREWS
BALUSTERS SECURED TO CHANNEL WITH WOOD SCREWS
4'-2"
2'-10½"
3'-2"
12"
12"
12"
9½"
2¾"
B

ELEVATION SCALE ½" = 1'-0"

C
½"
3½"
11"
3½"
11"
2'-6"
3'-7"
3½"
11"
2"×8"×11¼"
1½"
11"
C

ELEVATION SCALE ½" = 1'-0"

8–1 RESIDENTIAL RAILINGS

DETAIL 1: This railing was installed on the Button house in North Hero, Vermont, designed by the author's office as part of an extensive modern addition to the original farmhouse. This railing terminates the addition, which is cantilevered 35'-0" over Lake Champlain. Since the porch is 25'-0" above the lake, the railing had to be designed to be very strong and safe, but it was also planned not to cut off the view for any person seated on the porch. Redwood 2" × 4" balusters were installed 3'-6" o.c. and the one horizontal intermediate railing was installed only 11½" above the deck. DETAIL 2: This railing for the Politan residence in Riverdale, New York, was installed on the right side of the front entrance and overlooked the stairs going down to the lower level. The large handrail (1½" × 3½" deep) with delicate balusters created a fine balance between the glass and plants on the left side and the cypress wall of the stairs on the other side. The use of cypress with its warm yellow-browns gave the entire entrance a unity. DETAIL 3: This very simple railing, installed on a balcony terrace of the Ackermann residence, Southampton, New York, was also designed by the author's office. Here 2" × 8"s are cut on the splay and become balusters with a 2" × 4" railing at top, and two 2" × 4" intermediate railings are let into the balusters. At the bottom the balusters are secured to horizontal 2" × 8"s × 11¼" long, which in turn are secured to the decking and deck beams.

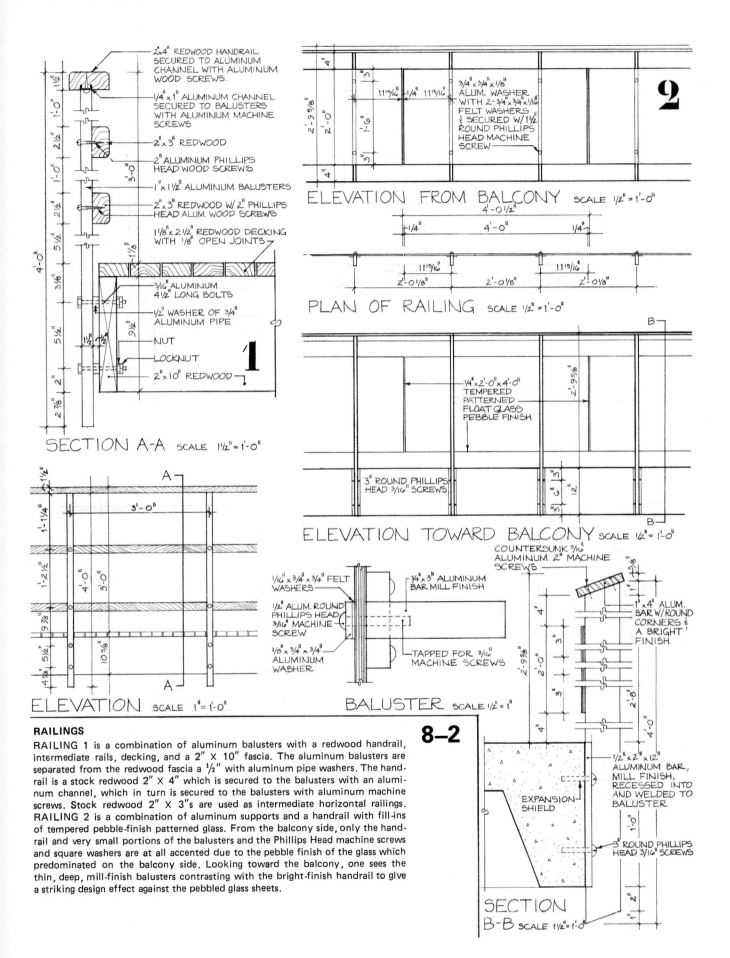

SECTION A-A SCALE 1½" = 1'-0"

ELEVATION FROM BALCONY SCALE ½" = 1'-0"

PLAN OF RAILING SCALE ½" = 1'-0"

ELEVATION TOWARD BALCONY SCALE ½" = 1'-0"

ELEVATION SCALE 1" = 1'-0"

BALUSTER SCALE ½" = 1"

SECTION B-B SCALE 1½" = 1'-0"

8–2

RAILINGS

RAILING 1 is a combination of aluminum balusters with a redwood handrail, intermediate rails, decking, and a 2" X 10" fascia. The aluminum balusters are separated from the redwood fascia a ½" with aluminum pipe washers. The handrail is a stock redwood 2" X 4" which is secured to the balusters with an aluminum channel, which in turn is secured to the balusters with aluminum machine screws. Stock redwood 2" X 3"s are used as intermediate horizontal railings. RAILING 2 is a combination of aluminum supports and a handrail with fill-ins of tempered pebble-finish patterned glass. From the balcony side, only the handrail and very small portions of the balusters and the Phillips Head machine screws and square washers are at all accented due to the pebble finish of the glass which predominated on the balcony side. Looking toward the balcony, one sees the thin, deep, mill-finish balusters contrasting with the bright-finish handrail to give a striking design effect against the pebbled glass sheets.

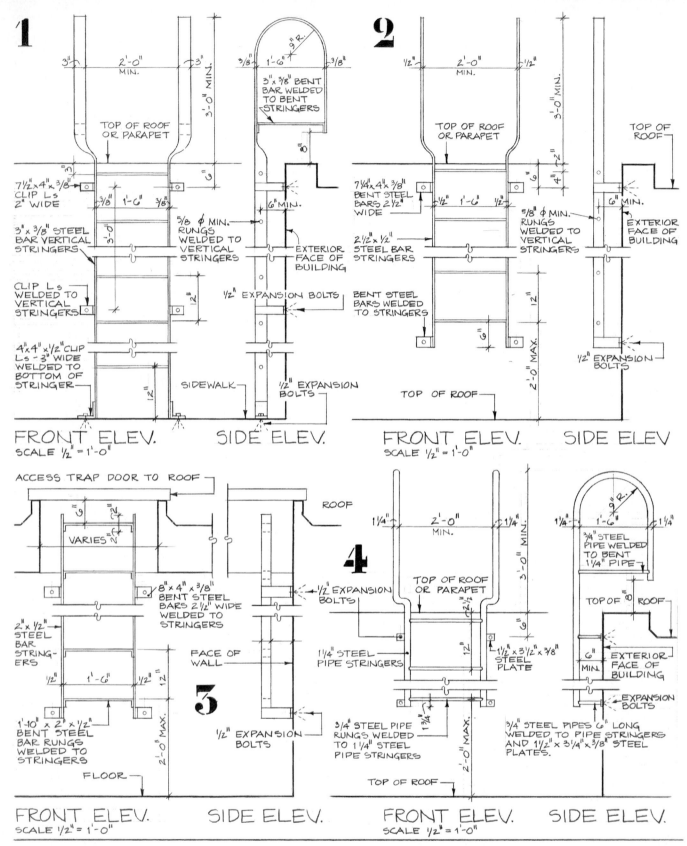

1

3"

2'-0" MIN.

3"

3'-0" MIN.

TOP OF ROOF OR PARAPET

3/8" 1'-6" 3/8"

9" R.

3" x 3/8" BENT BAR WELDED TO BENT STRINGERS

7½"x4"x3/8" CLIP Ls 2" WIDE

3/8" 1'-6" 3/8"

6" MIN.

3" x 3/8" STEEL BAR VERTICAL STRINGERS

5/8" ∅ MIN. RUNGS WELDED TO VERTICAL STRINGERS

EXTERIOR FACE OF BUILDING

CLIP Ls WELDED TO VERTICAL STRINGERS

½" EXPANSION BOLTS

4"x4"x½" CLIP Ls - 3" WIDE WELDED TO BOTTOM OF STRINGER

12"

SIDEWALK

½" EXPANSION BOLTS

FRONT ELEV.
SCALE ½" = 1'-0"

SIDE ELEV.

2

½"

2'-0" MIN.

½"

3'-0" MIN.

TOP OF ROOF OR PARAPET

TOP OF ROOF

7¼"x4"x3/8" BENT STEEL BARS 2½" WIDE

½" 1'-6" ½"

5/8" ∅ MIN. RUNGS WELDED TO VERTICAL STRINGERS

6" MIN.

2½"x½" STEEL BAR STRINGERS

EXTERIOR FACE OF BUILDING

BENT STEEL BARS WELDED TO STRINGERS

12"

½" EXPANSION BOLTS

2'-0" MAX.

TOP OF ROOF

FRONT ELEV.
SCALE ½" = 1'-0"

SIDE ELEV

3

ACCESS TRAP DOOR TO ROOF

ROOF

VARIES

8" x 4" x 3/8" BENT STEEL BARS 2½" WIDE WELDED TO STRINGERS

½" EXPANSION BOLTS

2" x ½" STEEL BAR STRINGERS

FACE OF WALL

½" 1'-6" ½"

12"

1'-0" x 2" x ½" BENT STEEL BAR RUNGS WELDED TO STRINGERS

2'-0" MAX.

½" EXPANSION BOLTS

FLOOR

FRONT ELEV.
SCALE ½" = 1'-0"

SIDE ELEV.

4

1¼"

2'-0" MIN.

1¼"

3'-0" MIN.

1¼" 1'-6" 1¼"

9" R.

TOP OF ROOF OR PARAPET

¾" STEEL PIPE WELDED TO BENT 1¼" PIPE

½" EXPANSION BOLTS

TOP OF ROOF

1¼" STEEL PIPE STRINGERS

1½" x 3½" x 3/8" STEEL PLATE

6" MIN.

EXTERIOR FACE OF BUILDING

12"

¾" STEEL PIPE RUNGS WELDED TO 1¼" STEEL PIPE STRINGERS

2'-0" MAX.

EXPANSION BOLTS

TOP OF ROOF

¾" STEEL PIPES 6" LONG WELDED TO PIPE STRINGERS AND 1½" x 3¼" x 3/8" STEEL PLATES.

FRONT ELEV.
SCALE ½" = 1'-0"

SIDE ELEV.

8-3   LADDERS

Four types of ladders are shown in this detail. LADDER 1 is made with flat steel bars as vertical stringers and round steel rods as ladder rungs. At the top, the flat steel bars are twisted to form a type of semicircular railing used to help climb onto a roof or a residential terrace. LADDER 2 is a similar type of ladder used to climb from one roof to another, higher roof. Here, a heavier steel bar is used for the vertical stringers, and it extends just 3'-0" up beyond the top of the roof or parapet. LADDER 3 is similar to No. 2 but uses lighter steel bar stringers and bent steel bar rungs. LADDER 4 uses pipe for both stringers and rungs.

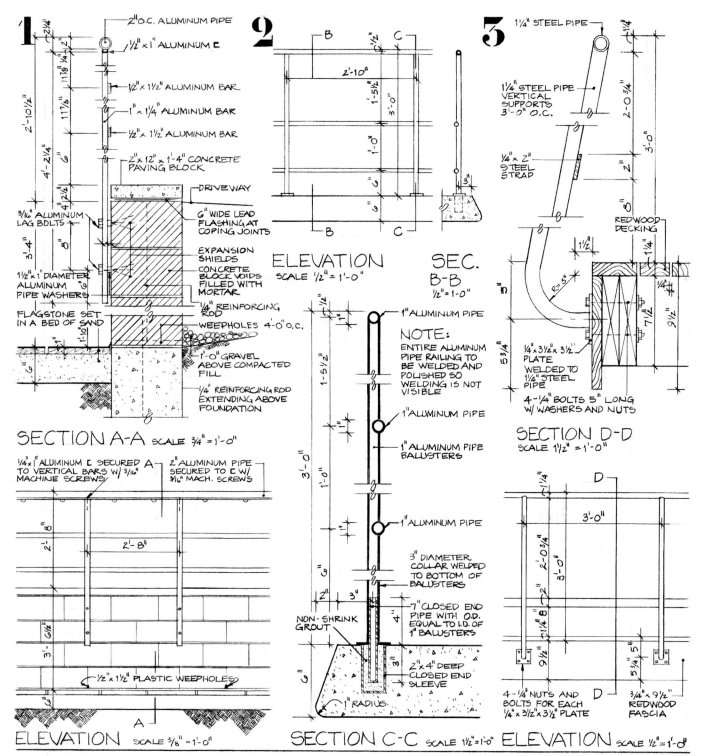

1

2" O.C. ALUMINUM PIPE
1/2" x 1" ALUMINUM ⊏
1/2" x 1 1/2" ALUMINUM BAR
1" x 1/4" ALUMINUM BAR
1/2" x 1 1/2" ALUMINUM BAR
2" x 12" x 1'-4" CONCRETE PAVING BLOCK
DRIVEWAY
6" WIDE LEAD FLASHING AT COPING JOINTS
EXPANSION SHIELDS
CONCRETE BLOCK VOIDS FILLED WITH MORTAR
1/4" REINFORCING ROD
WEEPHOLES 4'-0" O.C.
1'-0" GRAVEL ABOVE COMPACTED FILL
1/4" REINFORCING ROD EXTENDING ABOVE FOUNDATION
3/16" ALUMINUM LAG BOLTS
1 1/2" x 1" DIAMETER ALUMINUM PIPE WASHERS
FLAGSTONE SET IN A BED OF SAND

2'-10 1/2"   4'-2 1/4"   3'-4"

SECTION A-A SCALE 3/4" = 1'-0"

1/4" x 1" ALUMINUM ⊏ SECURED TO VERTICAL BARS W/ 3/16" MACHINE SCREWS
2" ALUMINUM PIPE SECURED TO ⊏ W/ 3/16" MACH. SCREWS

2'-8"
3'-
1/2" x 1 1/2" PLASTIC WEEPHOLES

ELEVATION SCALE 3/8" = 1'-0"

2

B   C
2'-10"
1'-5 1/2"
3'-0"
1'-0"

ELEVATION
SCALE 1/2" = 1'-0"

SEC. B-B
1/2" = 1'-0"

1" ALUMINUM PIPE

NOTE:
ENTIRE ALUMINUM PIPE RAILING TO BE WELDED AND POLISHED SO WELDING IS NOT VISIBLE

1" ALUMINUM PIPE
1" ALUMINUM PIPE BALUSTERS
1" ALUMINUM PIPE
3" DIAMETER COLLAR WELDED TO BOTTOM OF BALUSTERS
7" CLOSED END PIPE WITH O.D. EQUAL TO I.D. OF 1" BALUSTERS
NON-SHRINK GROUT
2" x 4" DEEP CLOSED END SLEEVE
1" RADIUS

1'-5 1/2"   1'-0"   3'-0"

SECTION C-C SCALE 1 1/2" = 1'-0"

3

1 1/4" STEEL PIPE
1 1/4" STEEL PIPE VERTICAL SUPPORTS 3'-0" O.C.
1/4" x 2" STEEL STRAP
2'-0 3/4"   3'-0"
R=3"
REDWOOD DECKING
1/4" x 3 1/2" x 3 1/2" PLATE WELDED TO 1 1/4" STEEL PIPE
4-1/4" BOLTS 5" LONG W/ WASHERS AND NUTS

SECTION D-D
SCALE 1 1/2" = 1'-0"

D
3'-0"
2'-0 3/4"
4-1/4" NUTS AND BOLTS FOR EACH 1/4" x 3 1/2" x 3 1/2" PLATE
3/4" x 9 1/2" REDWOOD FASCIA

ELEVATION SCALE 1/2" = 1'-0"

8-4

METAL RAILINGS

This page shows three types of metal railings in detail. DETAIL 1: Here is a railing that took care of a change in grade for a residence in Darien, Connecticut, in which the driveway and guest parking area are both slightly higher than the slate walk to the house. The retaining wall starts at the parking grade and the slate walk slowly pitches to 3'-4" below the parking area. The entire railing here is composed of stock aluminum units of sufficient strength to take a jolt from a car. DETAIL 2: This is a simple 1" round aluminum pipe railing with all parts shop-welded together. The support of the balusters is very simple. Sleeves 2" in diameter and 4" deep were installed in the apartment's concrete balcony every 2'-10" when the slab was poured. Then 7" long sleeves with O.D. equal to I.D. of the 1" pipe railing were placed in the installed 2" sleeves and adjusted to the exact 2'-10" spacing dimension, extending 4" above the slab. The prefabricated pipe railing could now be installed and the connection covered by the third round collar at the bottom. DETAIL 3: Here a 1 1/4" pipe railing of steel is bent on a 3" radius at the bottom and then the bottom extends another 1 1/2", at which point a 3 1/2" square is welded to the pipe. Each baluster slopes in, so the handrail is in line with the edge of the wood porch. In order not to block the view, the 1/4" X 2" intermediate railing is only 8" above the porch floor.

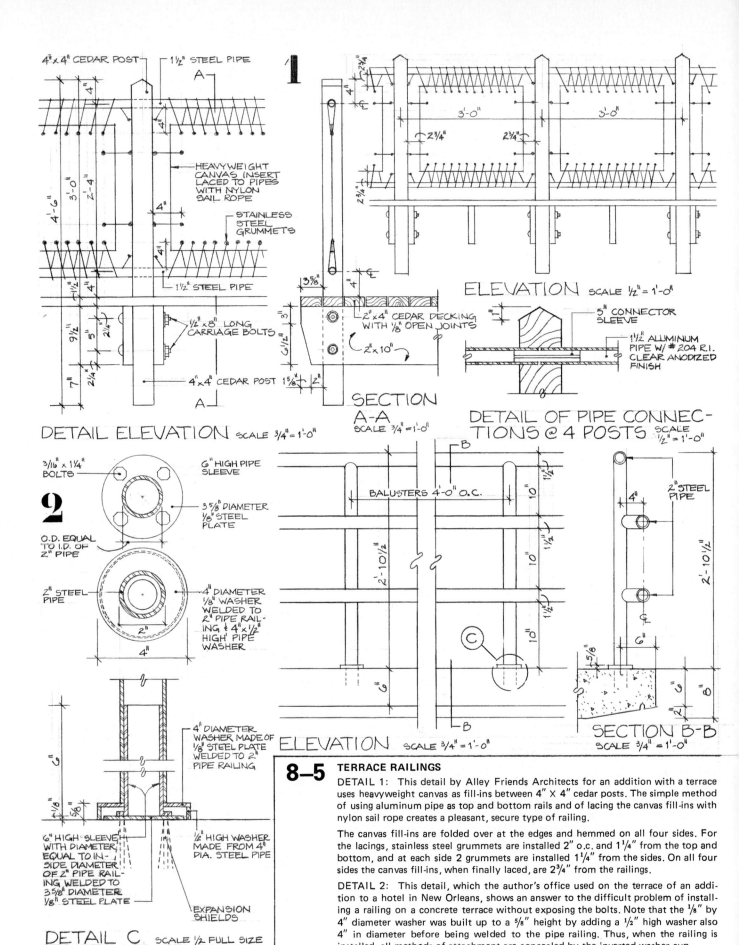

4"x4" CEDAR POST

1½" STEEL PIPE

A

HEAVYWEIGHT
CANVAS INSERT
LACED TO PIPES
WITH NYLON
SAIL ROPE

STAINLESS
STEEL
GRUMMETS

1½" STEEL PIPE

½"x8" LONG
CARRIAGE BOLTS

4"x4" CEDAR POST

DETAIL ELEVATION SCALE ¾" = 1'-0"

3-0"
2'-4"
4'-6"
3'-0"
2'-4"
9½"
5"
7"

ELEVATION SCALE ½" = 1'-0"

2"x4" CEDAR DECKING
WITH ⅛" OPEN JOINTS

2"x10"

SECTION A-A SCALE ¾" = 1'-0"

5" CONNECTOR
SLEEVE

1½" ALUMINUM
PIPE W/ #204 R.I.
CLEAR ANODIZED
FINISH

DETAIL OF PIPE CONNECTIONS @ 4 POSTS SCALE ½" = 1'-0"

3-0"   3-0"
2¾"   2¾"

3/16" x 1¼"
BOLTS

6" HIGH PIPE
SLEEVE

3⅝" DIAMETER
⅛" STEEL
PLATE

O.D. EQUAL
TO I.D. OF
2" PIPE

2" STEEL
PIPE

4" DIAMETER
⅛" WASHER
WELDED TO
2" PIPE RAIL-
ING & 4"x½"
HIGH PIPE
WASHER

2"
4"

4" DIAMETER
WASHER MADE OF
⅛" STEEL PLATE
WELDED TO 2"
PIPE RAILING

6" HIGH SLEEVE
WITH DIAMETER
EQUAL TO IN-
SIDE DIAMETER
OF 2" PIPE RAIL-
ING WELDED TO
3⅝" DIAMETER
⅛" STEEL PLATE

½" HIGH WASHER
MADE FROM 4"
DIA. STEEL PIPE

EXPANSION
SHIELDS

DETAIL C SCALE ½ FULL SIZE

BALUSTERS 4'-0" O.C.

2'-10½"

C

ELEVATION SCALE ¾" = 1'-0"

B

2" STEEL
PIPE

4"

2'-10½"

6"

SECTION B-B SCALE ¾" = 1'-0"

8–5   TERRACE RAILINGS

DETAIL 1: This detail by Alley Friends Architects for an addition with a terrace uses heavyweight canvas as fill-ins between 4" X 4" cedar posts. The simple method of using aluminum pipe as top and bottom rails and of lacing the canvas fill-ins with nylon sail rope creates a pleasant, secure type of railing.

The canvas fill-ins are folded over at the edges and hemmed on all four sides. For the lacings, stainless steel grummets are installed 2" o.c. and 1¼" from the top and bottom, and at each side 2 grummets are installed 1¼" from the sides. On all four sides the canvas fill-ins, when finally laced, are 2¾" from the railings.

DETAIL 2: This detail, which the author's office used on the terrace of an addition to a hotel in New Orleans, shows an answer to the difficult problem of installing a railing on a concrete terrace without exposing the bolts. Note that the ⅛" by 4" diameter washer was built up to a ⅝" height by adding a ½" high washer also 4" in diameter before being welded to the pipe railing. Thus, when the railing is installed, all methods of attachment are concealed by the inverted washer cup.

CROSS-REFERENCES TO *RAILINGS AND LADDERS* IN OTHER CHAPTERS

Chapter Number	Drawing Number	Drawing Title	Described on Page	Drawing on Page
3	3–2	Four common flashing conditions	17	19
	3–3	Four special flashing conditions	17	20
6	6–1	Section through parapet wall and railing	42	44
7	7–2	Intermediate platform stairs	51	54, 55
	7–3	Straight-run stairs in a club	51	56
	7–4	Straight-run stairs in a residence	52	57
	7–5	Platform stairs	52	58, 59
	7–6	Fire stairs in an elementary school	52	60, 61
	7–7	Horseshoe stairs	52	62, 63

9

Doors and Windows

INTRODUCTION

Doors and windows need screening; they must close tightly to keep out wind, rain, and snow, in other words, be weatherstripped; yet they must open easily; and, most important, they must be carefully insulated. The hardware must permit the door or window to open, close, latch, and lock. The type of hardware to use depends on the type of door or window.

DOORS.   Doors fall into the following types: swinging, sliding, revolving, overhead, folding, by-passing, and side-rolling. Overhead, side-rolling, revolving, by-passing, and folding doors are not shown in this book because the architect or designer who wishes to use these will find that for each type of door the manufacturer must be contacted for specific information and specialized details.

The swinging door is the most common. It may swing in only one direction or in both directions. The single-swing door requires door stops at the head and the two jambs. With the double-swing door, no stops are required and the hardware not only must allow the door to swing both ways but also must stop and hold it at the desired closed position or hold the door in the fully open position. Push plates also must be provided on both sides. In public buildings, swinging exit doors require panic-bolt type of hardware and must meet the fire code requirements. With all swinging doors, care should be taken that one door does not interfere with the swing of another door and that the door swing does not swing against a light switch. All doors that swing against a wall should have door stops.

The sill of a door to the exterior presents an especially difficult design problem because the sill is subjected to hard use and wear, and therefore it is difficult to weatherstrip, particularly at the point at which the interior floor finish meets exterior weather conditions. This joint presents problems in flashing, covering (saddle), drainage, and weatherstripping.

Entrance doors with or without side glass panels for buildings and store fronts are so well standardized by manufacturers that detailing them is not a difficult problem for the simple reason that the manufacturers are only too glad to give assistance in both the designing and detailing.

WINDOWS. Window functions include ventilation, light, screening, and insulation. The basic detail problems are weatherstripping, ease of operation, control of heat and cold, and accessibility for cleaning. Today, except in residential construction, the window often has become a wall or skin and often functions primarily as such. In fact, windows, doors, and wall are, in many cases, one and the same. Therefore ventilation is now considered as a separate function that includes heating and air conditioning and ventilation, and it is no longer necessarily a function of the window proper.

The diversity of new and improved materials has caused a host of new detail problems, for which it is advisable to have a full-size mock-up tested for all climatic conditions before the window wall is accepted and installed.

Fixed window details become fairly simple in that no screening, weatherstripping, and ventilation are encountered. Only heat loss in winter, heat gain in summer, and accessibility for cleaning from both exterior and interior must be taken into consideration.

The movable window, on the other hand, requires careful detailing, as it must operate easily and be well insulated. Location of the screen is important because, if it is located on the outside, the window operating hardware presents no difficulties; on the other hand, if the screen is located on the inside, either a remote control mechanism passing through the screen must be used to operate the window, or the screen must be easily removable. The movable section of the window must be weatherstripped on all four sides to keep out rain, snow, and most of all, wind. The head, jamb, and sill of the window frame must be designed to eliminate air and water leakage. Finally, the window must lock on the inside, and all movable parts must be easily reached for cleaning from both the outside and inside.

In detailing any glass panel, be it in a door or window, fixed or movable, a simple means of replacing broken glass must be allowed for in its construction.

It can easily be seen from the number of problems enumerated here that the detailing of doors and windows can become complicated; and the type of climate—be it tropical, subtropical, desert, mountain, temperate, cold, subarctic, or arctic—will dictate the type of door and windows to be used.

CHAPTER DETAIL TEXT

9-1 Sliding Wood Doors These details show a very simple method of concealing sliding doors without resorting to wall pockets. This method has been used many times in quite a few of the residences designed by the author's office. Once it was used to open one room into another with a 16'-0" opening and two specially built 8'-2" doors.

Standard sliding door hardware is available for single, double, or multiple sliding doors. Note that in a pair of sliding doors, when they are closed, one of the doors must be held in a fixed position with recessed flush bolts in order for the locking hardware on the other door to operate.

9-2 Up-Sliding Doors The utilization of up-sliding doors to completely convert a two-story living room into a summer screened porch is shown here. The detail illustrated is a refinement of the original, designed and built in the Van Wesep residence, Brewster, New York. The French doors on the exterior can be locked, as one of the doors has recessed flush bolts and the other a standard cylinder knob-type lock. The inside up-sliding combination screen and storm doors have two mortise bolts located on each side of the bottom wood member of the door. Note that for easy lifting up, a door pull is located in the middle of the bottom wood member of the door.

9-3   Location of Door Hardware and Door Identification

Although taken for granted many times, the exact location of all the various types of hardware used on doors can become a complicated detailing and specification problem. In a large structure such as a high school or a university building, the complete selection of hardware, the various master, sub-master, and sub-submaster keys, and all the various pieces for all the various types of doors does become a time-consuming and tedious job. If one adds to the normal hardware problems, all the automatic electrical locking and unlocking devices, one can see that the location of hardware as shown on this illustration can quickly help decisions on hardware.

The other half of this illustration shows types of doors by their opening action. Not shown are the double-swing rubber-type doors that are used in manufacturing plants where electrified carts, dollies, and forklifts are constantly passing from one area to another.

9-4   Types of Windows and Swing Doors and Their Symbols for Working Drawings

This detail shows not only all the various types of windows and swing doors but also shows the various symbols which are used on architectural working drawings to indicate the window and door types.

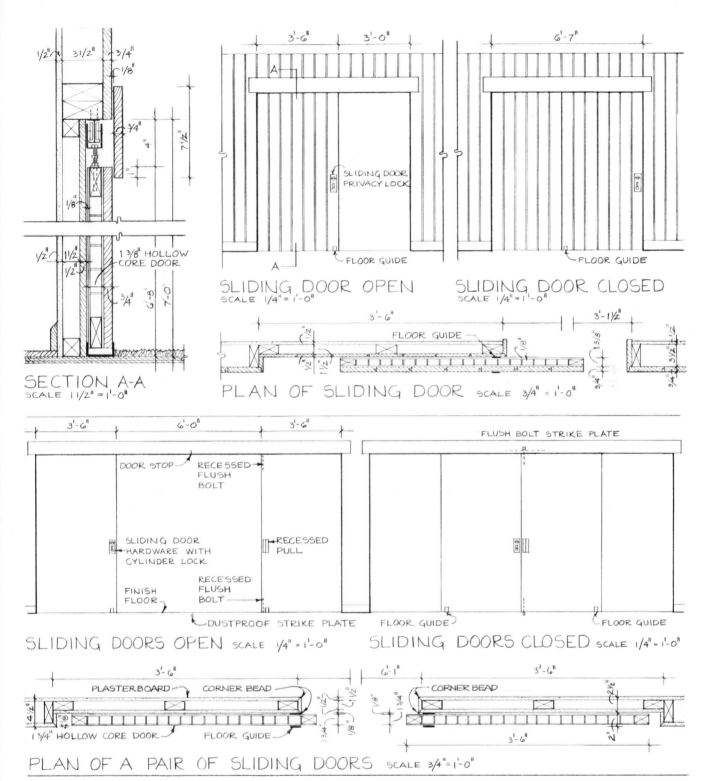

SECTION A-A
SCALE 1 1/2" = 1'-0"

1 3/8" HOLLOW CORE DOOR

SLIDING DOOR OPEN
SCALE 1/4" = 1'-0"

SLIDING DOOR PRIVACY LOCK

FLOOR GUIDE

SLIDING DOOR CLOSED
SCALE 1/4" = 1'-0"

FLOOR GUIDE

PLAN OF SLIDING DOOR SCALE 3/4" = 1'-0"

FLOOR GUIDE

SLIDING DOORS OPEN SCALE 1/4" = 1'-0"

DOOR STOP
RECESSED FLUSH BOLT
SLIDING DOOR HARDWARE WITH CYLINDER LOCK
RECESSED PULL
RECESSED FLUSH BOLT
FINISH FLOOR
DUSTPROOF STRIKE PLATE

SLIDING DOORS CLOSED SCALE 1/4" = 1'-0"

FLUSH BOLT STRIKE PLATE
FLOOR GUIDE
FLOOR GUIDE

PLAN OF A PAIR OF SLIDING DOORS SCALE 3/4" = 1'-0"

PLASTERBOARD
CORNER BEAD
1 3/4" HOLLOW CORE DOOR
FLOOR GUIDE
CORNER BEAD

SLIDING WOOD DOORS

9–1

Creating a recess as shown in the upper plan allows the door, when in the recess, to become part of the wall and, when slid closed, only a small change in the wall surface is apparent. Placing the wall studs horizontally and using a 1 3/8" stock hollow core wood door with 3/4" vertical paneling applied on one side and 1/2" vertical paneling applied on the recessed wall behind the door allows just enough space for the door to be flush with the paneled wall and still have 1/8" clearance at the back. The fascia board which hides the sliding door hardware is furred out from the paneled wall, so now there is 1/8" clearance at both back and front. This is shown in section A–A. This same system for a pair of doors is shown in the lower plan and elevation. In this detail, sheetrock is used and stock 1 3/4" flush hollow core wood doors are used. This allows 1/8" clearance at both back and front, and fascia board is applied directly to the wall.

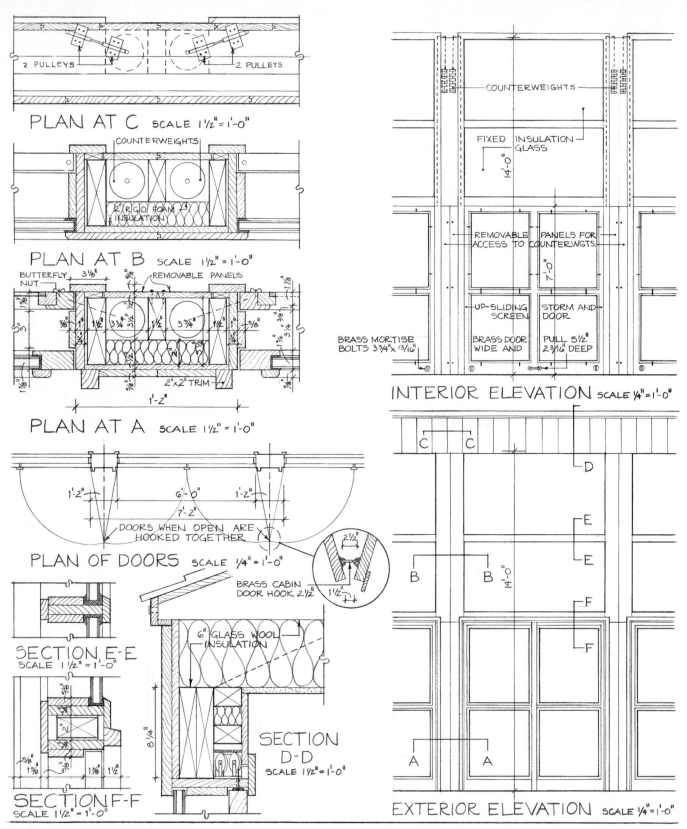

PLAN AT C SCALE 1½" = 1'-0"

2 PULLEYS   2 PULLEYS

COUNTERWEIGHTS

PLAN AT B SCALE 1½" = 1'-0"

2" RIGID FOAM INSULATION

BUTTERFLY NUT   REMOVABLE PANELS

2" x 2" TRIM

1'-2"

PLAN AT A SCALE 1½" = 1'-0"

1'-2"   6'-0"   1'-2"

7'-2"

DOORS WHEN OPEN ARE HOOKED TOGETHER

PLAN OF DOORS SCALE ¼" = 1'-0"

BRASS CABIN DOOR HOOK 2½"

SECTION E-E
SCALE 1½" = 1'-0"

6" GLASS WOOL INSULATION

8¼"

SECTION D-D
SCALE 1½" = 1'-0"

SECTION F-F
SCALE 1½" = 1'-0"

COUNTERWEIGHTS

FIXED INSULATION GLASS

14'-0"

REMOVABLE PANELS FOR ACCESS TO COUNTER-WGTS.

7'-0"

UP-SLIDING SCREEN   STORM AND DOOR

BRASS MORTISE BOLTS 3¾" x 13/16"

BRASS DOOR PULL 5½" WIDE AND 2 3/16" DEEP

INTERIOR ELEVATION SCALE ¼" = 1'-0"

C   C

D

E

E

B   B

14'-0"

F

F

A   A

EXTERIOR ELEVATION SCALE ¼" = 1'-0"

9–2   UP-SLIDING DOORS

In this detail counterweights are substituted for the spring balances used in the original. Combination screen and storm doors are used as the up-sliding doors and French doors on the exterior. The utilization of the double-hung window principle in a 14'-8" high two-story living room allows for the lower half of the two-floor window wall to become entirely open in summer, like a screened porch, when the up-sliding screen doors (combination screen and storm) doors are pulled down and the outside French glass doors are hooked together when open. In winter, when the French doors are closed and the inside up-sliding storm doors are pulled down, excellent insulation values are obtained. Stainless steel pulleys and wire rope and lead counterweights guarantee minimum maintenance. The removable panels allow for exact balancing of up-sliding doors.

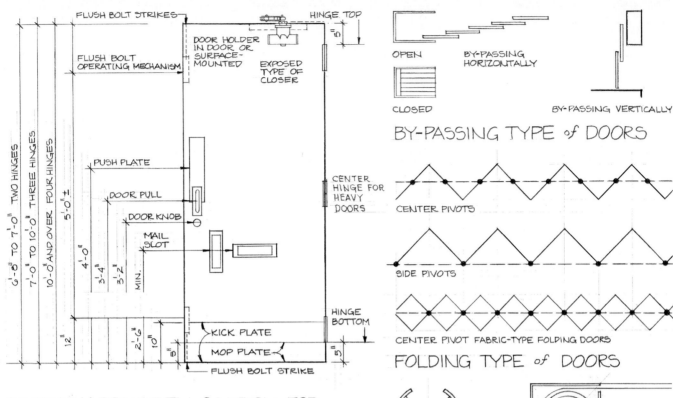

FINISH HARDWARE LOCATION FOR ALL TYPES of DOORS

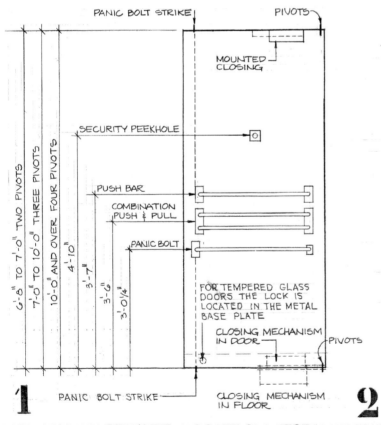

1

FINISH HARDWARE LOCATION FOR ALL TYPES of DOORS

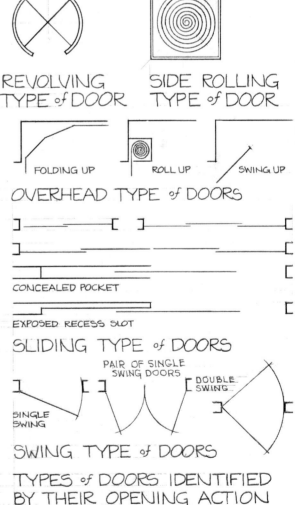

BY-PASSING TYPE of DOORS

FOLDING TYPE of DOORS

REVOLVING TYPE of DOOR   SIDE ROLLING TYPE of DOOR

OVERHEAD TYPE of DOORS

SLIDING TYPE of DOORS

SWING TYPE of DOORS

2

TYPES of DOORS IDENTIFIED BY THEIR OPENING ACTION

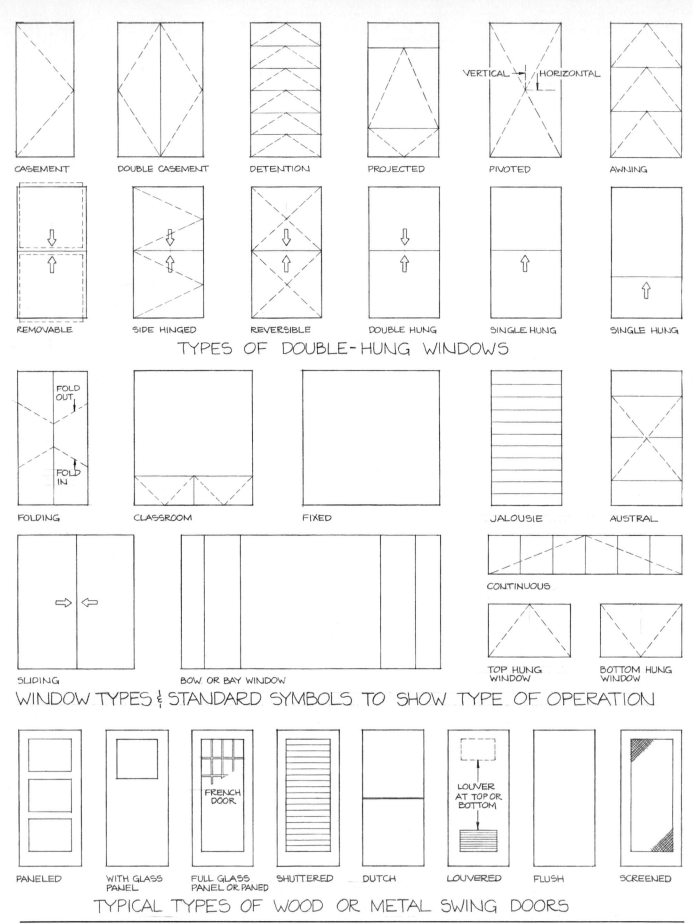

CASEMENT DOUBLE CASEMENT DETENTION PROJECTED PIVOTED AWNING

VERTICAL — HORIZONTAL

REMOVABLE SIDE HINGED REVERSIBLE DOUBLE HUNG SINGLE HUNG SINGLE HUNG

TYPES OF DOUBLE-HUNG WINDOWS

FOLD OUT FOLD IN

FOLDING CLASSROOM FIXED JALOUSIE AUSTRAL

SLIDING BOW OR BAY WINDOW CONTINUOUS

TOP HUNG WINDOW BOTTOM HUNG WINDOW

WINDOW TYPES & STANDARD SYMBOLS TO SHOW TYPE OF OPERATION

FRENCH DOOR

LOUVER AT TOP OR BOTTOM

PANELED WITH GLASS PANEL FULL GLASS PANEL OR PANED SHUTTERED DUTCH LOUVERED FLUSH SCREENED

TYPICAL TYPES OF WOOD OR METAL SWING DOORS

9—4 **TYPES OF WINDOWS AND SWING DOORS AND THEIR SYMBOLS FOR WORKING DRAWINGS**

CROSS-REFERENCES TO *DOORS AND WINDOWS*
IN OTHER CHAPTERS

Chapter Number	*Drawing Number*	*Drawing Title*	*Described on Page*	*Drawing on Page*
2	2-1	Reinforced concrete structure with cavity wall	6	9
	2-3	Residential wall sections	7	11
	2-4	Simple exterior and interior load-bearing walls	7	12
	2-5	Exterior skin curtain wall	8	13
5	5-4	Cabinet and millwork joints for plywood and solid wood	35	39
6	6-3	Walls and skins	43	46
7	7-2	Intermediate platform stairs	51	54, 55
	7-6	Fire stairs in an elementary school	52	60, 61
11	11-1	Sun control	99	101
	11-2	Sloping window with sill ventilation	99	102
	11-3	Light construction roof details	99	103
12	12-1	Solar residence	109	110, 111
	12-2	Underground house	109	112, 113
	12-3	Trombe wall	109	114
14	14-8	Built-in sofa and bookshelves	128	139
15	15-1	Interior planters for residences	147	149
	15-2	Interior planters for buildings	147	150
16	16-4	Bathroom window	156	162

10

Fireplaces

INTRODUCTION

All the early principles for designing fireplaces have not changed, but control of the heat going up the chimney and taking along the warm air already in the room has become of prime importance in designing a fireplace. The use of glass doors with dampers can accomplish the following: (1) cutting down on waste of room air going up the chimney, (2) control by dampers of the speed of burning of the fire to make the wood or coal last longer, and (3) no loss of or decrease in the amount of radiant heat reflected from the back and side walls. The most efficient fireplace ever encountered by the author was in an old Dutch colonial house in northern New Jersey. Here, somebody in the past had cut a hole in the side of the heating-cooking fireplace, and on the outside they had constructed two low parallel walls perpendicular to the side wall with the hole in it. By placing lengths of pipe across these walls to function as rollers, a whole 50' tree trunk could be slowly pushed into the fireplace, thus providing wood for an almost permanent fire for the whole winter.

In fireplace design an adequate draft is a must. The draft is controlled by the height of the chimney and the size of the flue. Most textbooks will give tables showing size of flue to fireplace opening. For an exceptional case the following formula can be followed: the flue must be equal to 10 percent of the fireplace opening. The chimney top must be a minimum of 3'-0" above the highest point of the roof. Dampers are installed to control the amount of draft and to shut off the draft when the fireplace is not in use; their size depends on the size of the fireplace opening.

A smoke chamber is the space directly above the damper. It can be compared to a funnel which decreases the large size of the damper opening to the small size of the flue. Within the smoke chamber is located a shelf called the smoke shelf, against which any chimney down drafts will hit and then be reflected back up the chimney again. The smoke shelf also acts as a trap for any water which may come down the chimney.

The fireplace proper, or firebox, is the area to which the actual fire is confined. The materials used here must withstand very high temperatures. The back hearth is the area directly beneath the fire. It, also, must be impervious to the effects of intense heat.

The fireplace should also be considered from a heating viewpoint. The back of a fireplace will reflect a tremendous amount of heat. Therefore, any form, shape, or material which adds direction to this heat and retains heat is advantageous to the design. In like manner, the side walls, if there are any, when tilted at an angle, will also reflect heat into the room. Utilization of any of the heat going up the chimney will further increase the efficiency of the fireplace, as shown in one of the details.

From a heating viewpoint, the use of glass doors which stop any smoke from coming into the room remove the usual limitations on the height of the fireplace. Therefore, taller back and side walls are possible and more reflected heat can be obtained. The hood, the built-in Heatilator®, and the set-in fireplace stove are other methods to obtain maximum heat from a fireplace. One should also remember that the fireplace is a better total heating unit if it is located within the building and not placed on the exterior wall, where a large quantity of heat is lost from the back wall to the exterior.

With the cost of fuel oil and gas, the Franklin stove has been reintroduced along with numerous types of wood-burning stoves and furnaces. There are models that fit into a fireplace opening and those which stand free. They all are highly efficient for maximum heat from minimum wood or coal. Eventually they all will contain the new catalytic converter, which will make them even more efficient and will almost eliminate chimney fires. All types mentioned so far require chimneys, either built of masonry or prefabricated. Draft and chimney height requirements, however, are the same as before.

CHAPTER DETAIL TEXT

10-1 Raised Fireplace with Hood This detail shows how a fireplace hood can effectively become a very efficient heating element. Copper is a very fast conductor of heat. Therefore, by forcing the normally wasted heat that goes up the chimney to follow the zigzag path formed by the internal baffles, the copper hood is quickly heated and gives off large quantities of radiant heat. This design uses the rivets that fix the interior baffles in place as an added hood design feature.

The triangular access hole not only gives access to the pulley, bead chain, and damper for repairs or replacement, but it also allows access for cleaning the hood and baffles. The triangular A-shaped removable panel here provided a desirable design feature—the owners' last name began with an A—a family monogram!

10-2 Double Fireplaces This detail of two fireplaces in the Button residence, North Hero, Vermont, shows how the chimney acts as bearing support for a large built-up beam and allows the chimney to incorporate two flues and at the same time allows 2″ clearance between chimney and the large built-up beam. The fireplace in the master bedroom is raised 1′-8″ above the floor so that the fire can be enjoyed when in bed. The master bedroom fireplace face and front hearth are finished with ceramic tile and ceramic mosaic tile. Note the use of cantilever slabs to support front hearths for both fireplaces.

The use of glass doors with draft controls on both fireplaces allows control of the quantity of air needed for the fire to burn. Without this control the wood burns very rapidly and large quantities of heated air in the room are pulled up the chimney. A stock damper can act only on an all-or-none basis, i.e., close off all draft or allow maximum draft.

10-3 Chimney Flashing at Pitched Roof

This detail shows a chimney penetrating a pitched roof somewhere below the ridge. It shows all the necessary flashing that must be installed to make this penetration completely watertight. It is an absolute *must* that the chimney pan be a complete single watertight unit. Therefore, if a metal is used, it must be of a type that is easily soldered; if a synthetic material is used, the synthetic and its appropriate adhesive must form a solid watertight unit.

To eliminate the possibility of the chimney getting sufficiently hot to ignite any wood in direct contact with it or built into it, all chimneys must have a space of 2″ between the chimney and any combustible materials. Usually this space is filled with fire-resistant material.

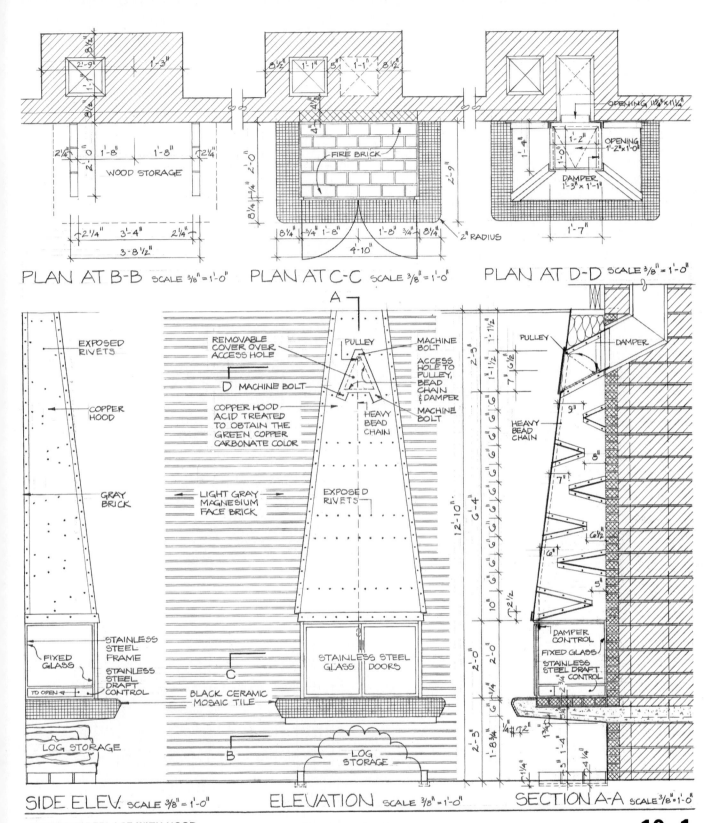

PLAN AT B-B SCALE 3/8" = 1'-0"   PLAN AT C-C SCALE 3/8" = 1'-0"   PLAN AT D-D SCALE 3/8" = 1'-0"

SIDE ELEV. SCALE 3/8" = 1'-0"   ELEVATION SCALE 3/8" = 1'-0"   SECTION A-A SCALE 3/8" = 1'-0"

RAISED FIREPLACE WITH HOOD

10–1

This fireplace was installed in a summer residence in Bridgton, Maine. Because the family likes to use the residence from early May until the middle of October, the copper hood with the internal baffles serves as the main heating unit in the large living-dining-kitchen area. The use of glass doors plus the forcing of the heat up through the baffles in the large copper hood to give off radiant heat worked very successfully. Two years later the family removed the fixed side glass panels and installed new glass panels with draft controls at the bottom in order to get maximum heat from minimum wood.

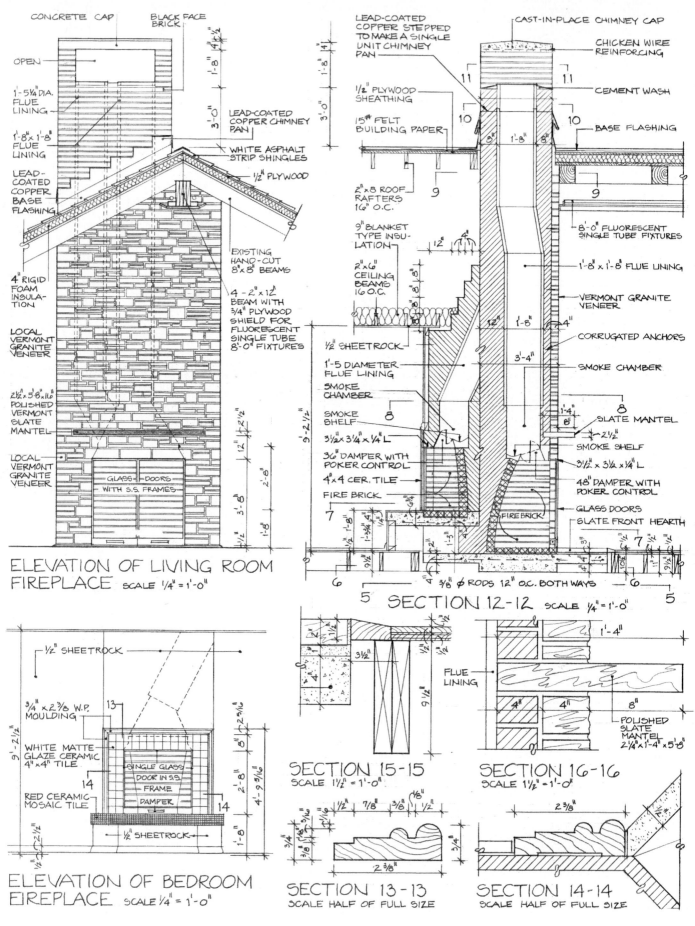

ELEVATION OF LIVING ROOM
FIREPLACE SCALE 1/4" = 1'-0"

CONCRETE CAP
BLACK FACE BRICK
OPEN
1-5 1/4" DIA. FLUE LINING
1'-8" x 1'-8" FLUE LINING
LEAD-COATED COPPER BASE FLASHING
4" RIGID FOAM INSULATION
LOCAL VERMONT GRANITE VENEER
2 1/2"x5'-8"x16" POLISHED VERMONT SLATE MANTEL
LOCAL VERMONT GRANITE VENEER
GLASS DOORS WITH S.S. FRAMES
LEAD-COATED COPPER CHIMNEY PAN
WHITE ASPHALT STRIP SHINGLES
1/2" PLYWOOD
EXISTING HAND-CUT 8"x8" BEAMS
4 - 2"x12" BEAM WITH 3/4" PLYWOOD SHIELD FOR FLUORESCENT SINGLE TUBE 8'-0" FIXTURES

ELEVATION OF BEDROOM
FIREPLACE SCALE 1/4" = 1'-0"

1/2" SHEETROCK
3/4" x 2 3/8" W.P. MOULDING
WHITE MATTE GLAZE CERAMIC 4"x4" TILE
RED CERAMIC MOSAIC TILE
SINGLE GLASS DOOR IN S.S. FRAME
DAMPER
1/2" SHEETROCK

LEAD-COATED COPPER STEPPED TO MAKE A SINGLE UNIT CHIMNEY PAN
1/2" PLYWOOD SHEATHING
15# FELT BUILDING PAPER
2"x8 ROOF RAFTERS 16" O.C.
9" BLANKET TYPE INSULATION
2"x6" CEILING BEAMS 16" O.C.
1/2" SHEETROCK
1'-5 DIAMETER FLUE LINING
SMOKE CHAMBER
SMOKE SHELF
3 1/2 x 3 1/4 x 1/4 L
36" DAMPER WITH POKER CONTROL
4"x4" CER. TILE
FIRE BRICK

CAST-IN-PLACE CHIMNEY CAP
CHICKEN WIRE REINFORCING
CEMENT WASH
BASE FLASHING
8'-0" FLUORESCENT SINGLE TUBE FIXTURES
1'-8" x 1'-8" FLUE LINING
VERMONT GRANITE VENEER
CORRUGATED ANCHORS
SMOKE CHAMBER
SLATE MANTEL
SMOKE SHELF
3 1/2 x 3 1/2 x 1/4 L
48" DAMPER WITH POKER CONTROL
GLASS DOORS
SLATE FRONT HEARTH
FIREBRICK

SECTION 12-12 SCALE 1/4" = 1'-0"
3/8" ⌀ RODS 12" O.C. BOTH WAYS

SECTION 15-15
SCALE 1 1/2" = 1'-0"

SECTION 16-16
SCALE 1 1/2" = 1'-0"

FLUE LINING
POLISHED SLATE MANTEL 2 1/4"x1'-4"x5'-8"

SECTION 13-13
SCALE HALF OF FULL SIZE

SECTION 14-14
SCALE HALF OF FULL SIZE

92

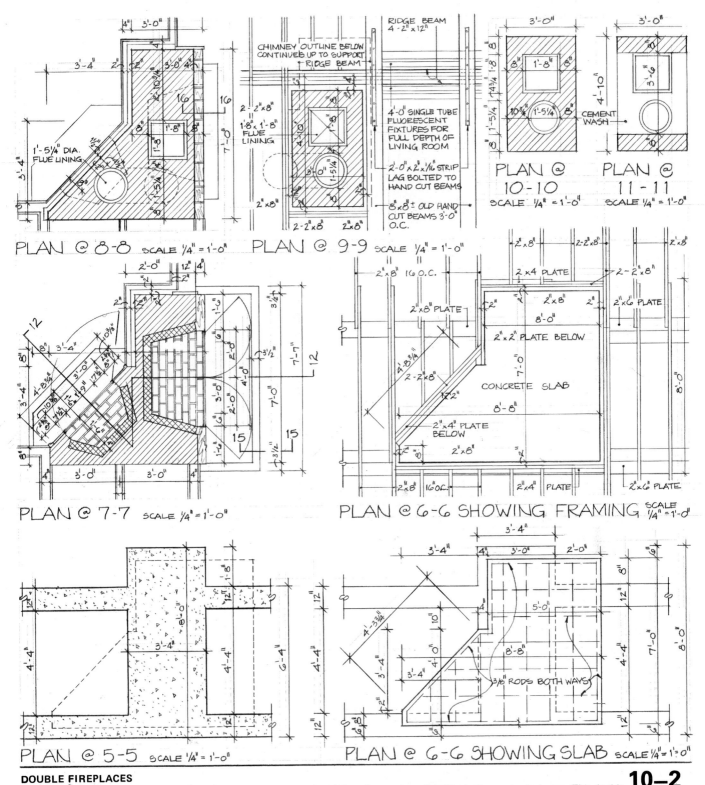

PLAN @ 8-8 SCALE ¼" = 1'-0"

PLAN @ 9-9 SCALE ¼" = 1'-0"

PLAN @ 10-10 SCALE ¼" = 1'-0"

PLAN @ 11-11 SCALE ¼" = 1'-0"

PLAN @ 7-7 SCALE ¼" = 1'-0"

PLAN @ 6-6 SHOWING FRAMING SCALE ¼" = 1'-0"

PLAN @ 5-5 SCALE ¼" = 1'-0"

PLAN @ 6-6 SHOWING SLAB SCALE ¼" = 1'-0"

DOUBLE FIREPLACES

10–2

This detail shows two fireplaces: one located in the living room, and the other a corner fireplace in the master bedroom. This double fireplace was the first of this type designed by the author in which glass doors were installed with damper controls, so that only a small amount of hot air was allowed to be wasted up the chimney. Located in North Hero, Vermont, where Vermont granite and slate are easily available, these materials were used for the living-room face of the fireplace. Note also the use of old handhewn 8″ × 8″ beams obtained from an old barn. These were exposed in the living-room ceiling. A center supporting beam of four 2″ × 12″s was used, with its bottom covered with plywood so that fluorescent cove lights could be installed.

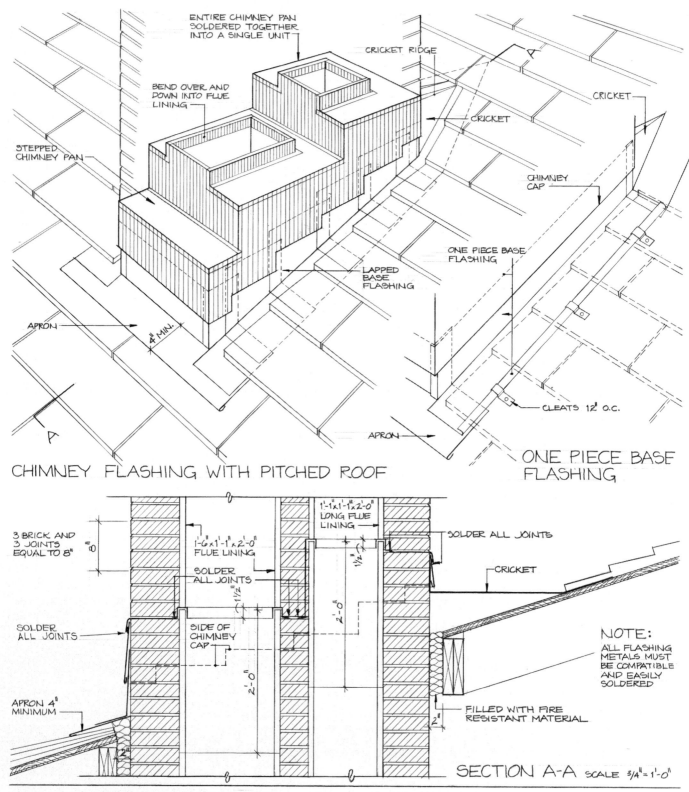

ENTIRE CHIMNEY PAN
SOLDERED TOGETHER
INTO A SINGLE UNIT

CRICKET RIDGE

BEND OVER AND
DOWN INTO FLUE
LINING

CRICKET

CRICKET

STEPPED
CHIMNEY PAN

CHIMNEY
CAP

ONE PIECE BASE
FLASHING

LAPPED
BASE
FLASHING

APRON

4" MIN.

CLEATS 12" O.C.

APRON

CHIMNEY FLASHING WITH PITCHED ROOF

ONE PIECE BASE
FLASHING

3 BRICK AND
3 JOINTS
EQUAL TO 8"

8"

1'-6"x1-1"x2'-0"
FLUE LINING

1'-1"x1-1"x2'-0"
LONG FLUE
LINING

SOLDER ALL JOINTS

SOLDER
ALL JOINTS

1½"

2'-0"

1½"

CRICKET

SOLDER
ALL JOINTS

SIDE OF
CHIMNEY
CAP

2'-0"

NOTE:
ALL FLASHING
METALS MUST
BE COMPATIBLE
AND EASILY
SOLDERED

APRON 4"
MINIMUM

2"

FILLED WITH FIRE
RESISTANT MATERIAL

SECTION A-A SCALE 3/4"=1'-0"

10–3 CHIMNEY FLASHING AT PITCHED ROOF

This detail shows the complete flashing of a chimney in a pitched roof. The chimney pan completely separates the masonry structure of the chimney above the roof from the chimney structure coming up through the roof. The chimney should be isolated from any combustible materials by a minimum of 2", and this void should be filled with fireproof material. To eliminate any possibility of water collecting and penetrating along the line where the chimney meets the down-sloping roof, a special flashing piece is installed. This piece, called a cricket, forces any water to be directed to the sides of the chimney. Two different methods of installing the base flashing are shown: the use of separate pieces that overlap, and the use of a one-piece base flashing.

CROSS-REFERENCES TO *FIREPLACES* IN OTHER CHAPTERS

Chapter Number	Drawing Number	Drawing Title	Described on Page	Drawing on Page
3	3-1	Chimney flashing at ridge and flat roofs	17	18
12	12-2	Underground house	109	112, 113

11 | Sun Control

INTRODUCTION

The effect of the sun upon buildings is one of the important design considerations that faces the architect in planning, orientation, and the selection of materials, colors, type and amount of glass, overhangs, awnings, and shades for any building. Since today's architects have commissions in all latitudes and climates, they must know exactly the yearly movements of the sun. These become important determinants in the design of a building for a particular climate and geographic location.

A simple example would be a building at the equator. For twelve months of the year the sun will rise directly in the east, perpendicular to the equator, make a complete arc, and set in the west. Consequently, any windows facing north and south would never get any direct sunlight.

North or south of the equator, while the sun rises in the east and sets in the west, it is no longer perpendicular to the ground but at an angle. The farther north or south, the greater the angle. This is an effect of latitude which enters into sun control.

The farther north or south of the equator one goes, the more the setting of the sun varies in winter and summer. For example, in the latitude through the New York City–Philadelphia area (40° latitude, roughly), on the longest day of the year the sun rises in the northeast and sets in the northwest. During the following twelve-month period the sun shifts each day until, on the shortest day of the year, it rises in the southeast and sets in the southwest. Thus a window facing due north would receive some sun during the longest day of the year and sunshine for only a very short period (about a couple of weeks) thereafter.

A window facing due south, during the longest day of the year, would have sunlight for the entire day; on the shortest day of the year it would get sunlight from about 8:30 a.m. until 3:30 p.m.

Any window facing the east would get direct morning sunlight during the whole year and, since the angle of the sun in the morning is low, direct sunlight could not be eliminated by overhangs.

The most dangerous and objectionable sun is the western sun, as its angle is low. Although western sun is not too objectionable in the winter and may even be desirable for solar heating purposes, in the summer it becomes highly undesirable and can become a very serious problem. The reason is that during the entire day, the air, ground, buildings, etc., are being heated and, as the sun slowly sets, the sun's rays pour in at either a slight angle or a horizontal one. The contemporary architect can utilize all this knowledge in the design of buildings not only for sun control but for the development of solar heat control systems.

CHAPTER DETAIL TEXT

11-1 Sun Control This detail shows the various possibilities for total control of the damaging sun rays on store merchandise or any other area where sun control is necessary. This is an updated detail of a Joseph Magnin store in California by Gruen & Krummeck, Architects. On close examination, one notes how the 5'-0″ recess from the face of the sun-control louver and the 7'-0″ clearance when the louver is lowered permit neither summer nor winter sun to penetrate to the display window, thus eliminating fading and sun damage to merchandise on display.

11-2 Sloping Window with Sill Ventilation These details, used by the author's office on the Cory House, Riverdale, New York, show a combination of sloping fixed glass, solar control, sill ventilation, a large window seat, and direct-indirect lighting.

The exterior walls were built of 2″ × 6″s, 16″ on center. This 6″ depth allows room for 5½″ batt-type insulation with vapor barrier. Then 2″ × 4″ horizontal members were installed. These permit all electrical wiring to be installed without touching either the vapor barrier or the 5½″ insulation. Finally, 1½″ insulation was installed in the 1½″ space.

The roof has cedar shingles on plywood sheathing. Note that the underside of the overhang has screened vents in order to ventilate the air space between the insulation and the underside of the roof sheathing. The sloping window is supported by using ¾″ plywood gussets at intermediate points, as shown at sections B-B and C-C.

Note the recess for both fluorescent lighting and the curtain track. When curtains are drawn at night, the fluorescent light not only gives outside lighting but also gives a pleasant soft light through the curtains.

11-3 Light Construction Roof Details This illustration includes three details, all for light construction, which deal with entirely different conditions and requirements for sun control.

DETAIL 1. In wall-bearing construction with steel studs and porcelain enamel on laminated steel exterior walls, by extending steel studs above the roof deck and installing a stainless steel cap, a simple solution for a roof flashing detail is obtained. Note that the steel studs are tied to the Flexicore® planks (prefabricated reinforced hollow planks) with small clip angles at each stud. The Flexicore® planks bear on masonry walls at the sides of the building, and at the middle on a steel I-beam, supported by columns.

DETAIL 2. Here a flat roof overhang is adjusted to control summer and winter sun. To increase the R factor a dead air space is used for the large fixed windows. Note that the supporting beam at the head of the large fixed glass windows consists of two $2'' \times 12''$s with spacers and $2\frac{1}{2}''$ of insulation, which is what the load calculations originally required.

DETAIL 3. A simple pitched roof overhang is achieved by increasing the size of the ceiling beams to take care of the cantilever overhang, and by using $\frac{1}{2}''$ plywood gussets to tie the roof rafters and ceiling beams rigidly together. In this manner the overhang can be adjusted to control summer and winter sun.

11–4   Exterior Adjustable Louvers

This detail shows how adjustable louvers can be used not only to control solar heat gain in summer, but also to block off northwest winter winds and, most important, to allow a fine northwest view to be seen.

The most difficult problem in designing these adjustable louvers was finding the exact positions in which to place the louvers to control summer sun, winter winds, and the view. Note that very heavy lumber was used and the control hardware had to be specially ordered to meet the architect's design and strength specifications.

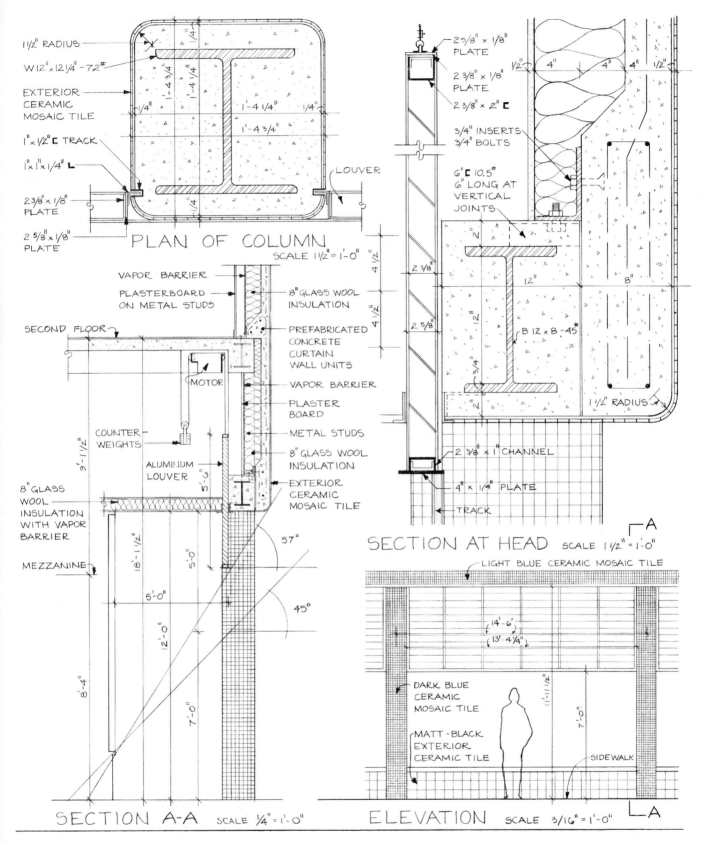

PLAN OF COLUMN SCALE 1 1/2" = 1'-0"

- 1 1/2" RADIUS
- W 12" x 12 1/4" - 72#
- EXTERIOR CERAMIC MOSAIC TILE
- 1" x 1/2" ⊏ TRACK
- 1" x 1" x 1/4" L
- 2 3/8" x 1/8" PLATE
- 2 5/8" x 1/8" PLATE
- LOUVER

- 2 5/8" x 1/8" PLATE
- 2 3/8" x 1/8" PLATE
- 2 3/8" x 2" ⊏
- 3/4" INSERTS 3/4" BOLTS
- 6" ⊏ 10.5# 6" LONG AT VERTICAL JOINTS
- B 12 x 8 - 45#
- 1 1/2" RADIUS
- 2 3/8" x 1" CHANNEL
- 4" x 1/4" PLATE
- TRACK

SECTION AT HEAD SCALE 1 1/2" = 1'-0"

- VAPOR BARRIER
- PLASTERBOARD ON METAL STUDS
- 8" GLASS WOOL INSULATION
- PREFABRICATED CONCRETE CURTAIN WALL UNITS
- VAPOR BARRIER
- PLASTER BOARD
- METAL STUDS
- 8" GLASS WOOL INSULATION
- EXTERIOR CERAMIC MOSAIC TILE
- SECOND FLOOR
- MOTOR
- COUNTER WEIGHTS
- ALUMINUM LOUVER
- 8" GLASS WOOL INSULATION WITH VAPOR BARRIER
- MEZZANINE
- 57°
- 45°

SECTION A-A SCALE 1/4" = 1'-0"

ELEVATION SCALE 3/16" = 1'-0"

- LIGHT BLUE CERAMIC MOSAIC TILE
- DARK BLUE CERAMIC MOSAIC TILE
- MATT-BLACK EXTERIOR CERAMIC TILE
- SIDEWALK

SUN CONTROL

This detail is updated from an earlier one for a Joseph Magnin store by Gruen & Krummeck, Architects. The store display windows are recessed in such a way that neither summer sun nor winter sun can fade merchandise. There are also motorized louvers controlled by a light-sensitive cell which raises and lowers the louvers, thereby eliminating direct sunlight upon merchandise. The depth of the recess and the extent of raising and lowering of the louvers are both controlled by the location of the store and its orientation. In this case the sun angles were 45° and 57°.

11–1

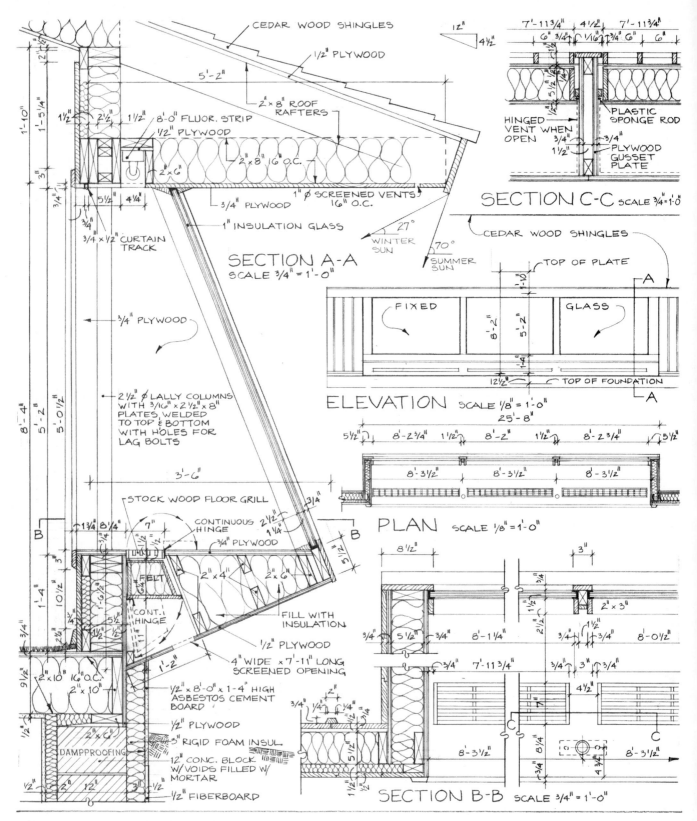

CEDAR WOOD SHINGLES

1/2" PLYWOOD

5'-2"

2" × 8" ROOF RAFTERS

1/2" PLYWOOD

8'-0" FLUOR. STRIP

1/2" PLYWOOD

2" × 6"

2" × 8" 16" O.C.

3/4" PLYWOOD

1" ∅ SCREENED VENTS, 16" O.C.

1" INSULATION GLASS

3/4" × 1/2" CURTAIN TRACK

SECTION A-A
SCALE 3/4" = 1'-0"

WINTER SUN 27°

SUMMER SUN 70°

3/4" PLYWOOD

2 1/2" ∅ LALLY COLUMNS WITH 3/16" × 2 1/2" × 8" PLATES, WELDED TO TOP & BOTTOM WITH HOLES FOR LAG BOLTS

3'-6"

STOCK WOOD FLOOR GRILL

CONTINUOUS HINGE

3/4" PLYWOOD

FELT

CONT. HINGE

2" × 4"

2" × 6"

FILL WITH INSULATION

1/2" PLYWOOD

4" WIDE × 7'-11" LONG SCREENED OPENING

1/2" × 8'-0" × 1'-4" HIGH ASBESTOS CEMENT BOARD

1/2" PLYWOOD

3" RIGID FOAM INSUL.

12" CONC. BLOCK W/ VOIDS FILLED W/ MORTAR

DAMPPROOFING

2" × 10" 16" O.C.

2" × 10"

2" × 6"

1/2" FIBERBOARD

7'-11 3/4"   4 1/2"   7'-11 3/4"

6"   6"   6"

HINGED VENT WHEN OPEN

PLASTIC SPONGE ROD

PLYWOOD GUSSET PLATE

SECTION C-C SCALE 3/4" = 1'-0"

CEDAR WOOD SHINGLES

TOP OF PLATE

FIXED

GLASS

8'-2"

5'-2"

TOP OF FOUNDATION

ELEVATION SCALE 1/8" = 1'-0"

25'-8"

5 1/2"   8'-2 3/4"   1 1/2"   8'-2"   1 1/2"   8'-2 3/4"   5 1/2"

8'-3 1/2"   8'-3 1/2"   8'-3 1/2"

PLAN SCALE 1/8" = 1'-0"

8 1/2"   3"

2" × 3"

3/4"   5 1/2"   3/4"   8'-1 1/4"   3/4"   3/4"   8'-0 1/2"

3/4"   7'-11 3/4"   3/4"   3"   3/4"

4 1/2"

8'-3 1/2"   8'-3 1/2"

SECTION B-B SCALE 3/4" = 1'-0"

11–2 SLOPING WINDOW WITH SILL VENTILATION

These details are a refinement of a sloping window on a residence in Riverdale, New York. A sloping window has four advantages over a vertical window: (1) privacy: on the exterior the glass picks up reflections in daytime, which means one cannot see into the house; (2) a large window seating area is obtained; (3) ventilation can be obtained through the windowsill; and (4) simple large fixed glass areas can be used. The overhang is built to allow winter sun to penetrate and thus gain solar heat, and to completely stop solar gain from summer sun.

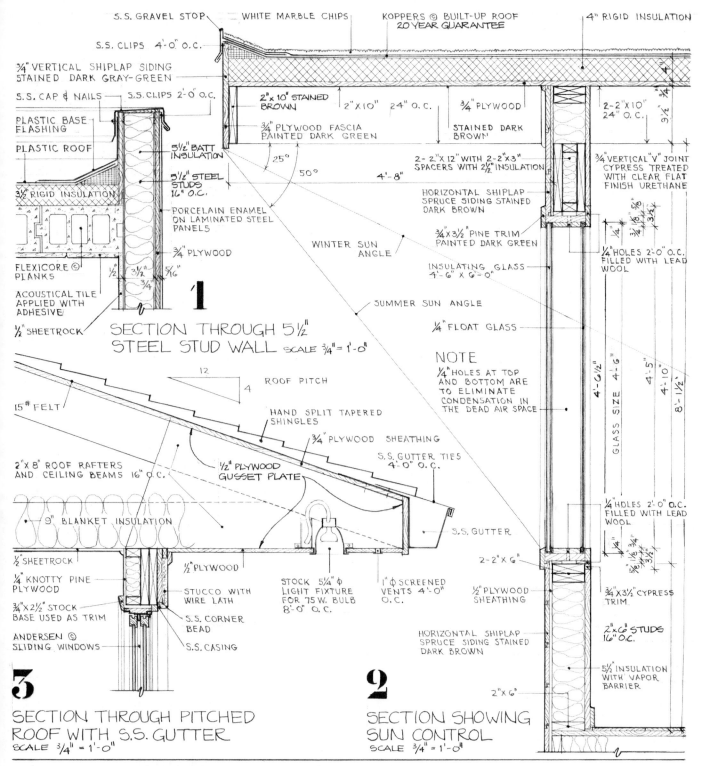

S.S. GRAVEL STOP — WHITE MARBLE CHIPS — KOPPERS © BUILT-UP ROOF 20 YEAR GUARANTEE — 4" RIGID INSULATION

S.S. CLIPS 4'-0" O.C.

¾" VERTICAL SHIPLAP SIDING STAINED DARK GRAY-GREEN

S.S. CAP & NAILS — S.S. CLIPS 2'-0" O.C.

PLASTIC BASE FLASHING

PLASTIC ROOF

3½" RIGID INSULATION

FLEXICORE © PLANKS

ACOUSTICAL TILE APPLIED WITH ADHESIVE

½" SHEETROCK

5½" BATT INSULATION

5½" STEEL STUDS 16" O.C.

PORCELAIN ENAMEL ON LAMINATED STEEL PANELS

¾" PLYWOOD

½" 3½" 5/16" ¾"

2"x 10" STAINED BROWN   2"X 10" 24" O.C.   ¾" PLYWOOD

¾" PLYWOOD FASCIA PAINTED DARK GREEN

STAINED DARK BROWN

25°   50°   4'-8"

2- 2"X 12" WITH 2-2"X 3" SPACERS WITH 2½" INSULATION

HORIZONTAL SHIPLAP SPRUCE SIDING STAINED DARK BROWN

¾"x 3½" PINE TRIM PAINTED DARK GREEN

WINTER SUN ANGLE

INSULATING GLASS 4'-6" X 6'-0"

SUMMER SUN ANGLE

¼" FLOAT GLASS

2- 2"X 10" 24" O.C.

¾" VERTICAL "V" JOINT CYPRESS TREATED WITH CLEAR FLAT FINISH URETHANE

¼" HOLES 2'-0" O.C. FILLED WITH LEAD WOOL

1
SECTION THROUGH 5½" STEEL STUD WALL SCALE ¾" = 1'-0"

NOTE
¼" HOLES AT TOP AND BOTTOM ARE TO ELIMINATE CONDENSATION IN THE DEAD AIR SPACE

12   4   ROOF PITCH

HAND SPLIT TAPERED SHINGLES

¾" PLYWOOD SHEATHING

S.S. GUTTER TIES 4'-0" O.C.

15# FELT

2"X 8" ROOF RAFTERS AND CEILING BEAMS 16" O.C.

½" PLYWOOD GUSSET PLATE

9" BLANKET INSULATION

½" SHEETROCK

¼" KNOTTY PINE PLYWOOD

¾"X 2½" STOCK BASE USED AS TRIM

ANDERSEN © SLIDING WINDOWS

½" PLYWOOD

STUCCO WITH WIRE LATH

S.S. CORNER BEAD

S.S. CASING

STOCK 5¼" Ø LIGHT FIXTURE FOR 75 W. BULB 8'-0" O.C.

1" Ø SCREENED VENTS 4'-0" O.C.

S.S. GUTTER

2- 2"X 6"

½" PLYWOOD SHEATHING

HORIZONTAL SHIPLAP SPRUCE SIDING STAINED DARK BROWN

2"X 6"

¼" HOLES 2'-0" O.C. FILLED WITH LEAD WOOL

¾"X 3½" CYPRESS TRIM

2"X 6" STUDS 16" O.C.

5½" INSULATION WITH VAPOR BARRIER

GLASS SIZE 4'-6"   4'-6½"   4'-5"   4'-10"   8'-1½"

3
SECTION THROUGH PITCHED ROOF WITH S.S. GUTTER
SCALE ¾" = 1'-0"

2
SECTION SHOWING SUN CONTROL
SCALE ¾" = 1'-0"

LIGHT CONSTRUCTION ROOF DETAILS

DETAIL 1 shows the flashing of a steel stud wall at roof of a wall-bearing multiple type of building. The metal studs have ¾" plywood sheathing, as does the other side of the parapet, for nailing. A simple stainless steel cap is secured with clips and then nailed over plastic base flashing. DETAIL 2 shows a flat roof overhang to eliminate summer sun solar heat gain and to let in winter sun to obtain maximum solar heat gain. Note that the fixed large glass windows have insulating glass on the outside and ¼" float glass on the inside, a combination that gives very fine *R* values. To eliminate condensation in the dead air space, small holes are drilled at both top and bottom. This allows a small amount of air movement. The lead wool both minimizes air movement and stops insects from entering the air space. DETAIL 3 shows a pitched roof overhang of sufficient size to check the summer sun and obtain the winter sun's solar heat. By installing stock exterior recessed light fixtures, a terrace or walk can be illuminated.

11–3

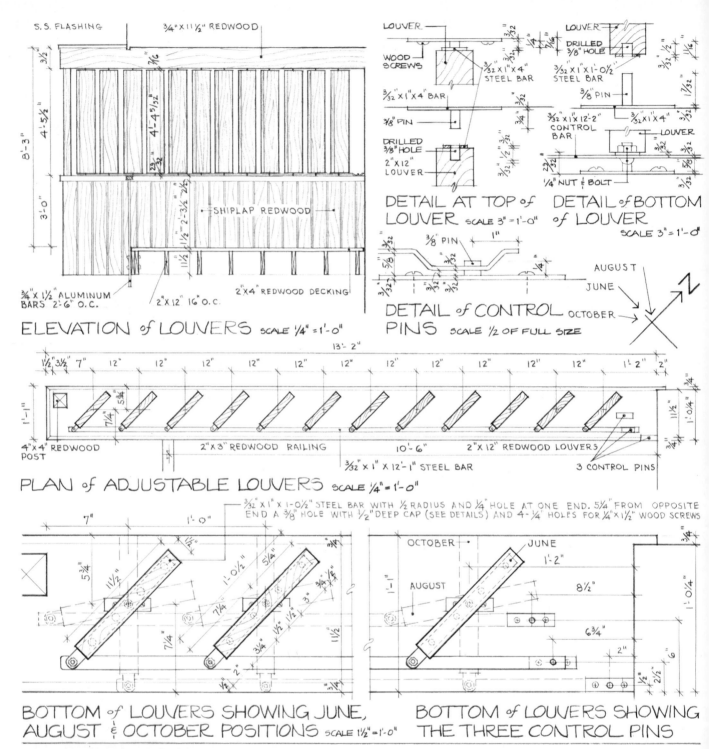

S.S. FLASHING ¾" X 11½" REDWOOD

8'-3" 3½" 4'-5½" 3'-0"

4'-4⁵⁄₃₂" ²⁹⁄₃₂"

1½" 2'-3½" 2½" 1½"

SHIPLAP REDWOOD

¾" X 1½" ALUMINUM BARS 2'-6" O.C. 2"X12" 16" O.C. 2"X4" REDWOOD DECKING

ELEVATION of LOUVERS SCALE ¼" = 1'-0"

LOUVER WOOD SCREWS ³⁄₃₂ X 1" X 4" STEEL BAR ³⁄₃₂ X 1" X 1'-0½" STEEL BAR LOUVER DRILLED ⅜" HOLE

³⁄₃₂ X 1" X 4" BAR ⅜" PIN DRILLED ⅜" HOLE 2" X 12" LOUVER ⅜" PIN ³⁄₃₂ X 1" X 12'-2" CONTROL BAR ³⁄₃₂ X 1" X 4" LOUVER ¼" NUT & BOLT

DETAIL AT TOP of LOUVER SCALE 3" = 1'-0"   **DETAIL of BOTTOM of LOUVER** SCALE 3" = 1'-0"

⅜" PIN 1"

DETAIL of CONTROL PINS SCALE ½ OF FULL SIZE

AUGUST JUNE OCTOBER

13'-2"
½" 3½" 7" 12" 12" 12" 12" 12" 12" 12" 12" 12" 12" 12" 1' 2" 2"

1'-1" 7¼" 5¾"

4"X4" REDWOOD POST 2"X3" REDWOOD RAILING 10'-6" 2"X12" REDWOOD LOUVERS ³⁄₃₂" X 1" X 12'-1" STEEL BAR 3 CONTROL PINS

PLAN of ADJUSTABLE LOUVERS SCALE ¼" = 1'-0"

³⁄₃₂" X 1" X 1'-0½" STEEL BAR WITH ½ RADIUS AND ¼" HOLE AT ONE END. 5¼" FROM OPPOSITE END A ⅜" HOLE WITH ½" DEEP CAP (SEE DETAILS) AND 4-¼" HOLES FOR ¼" X 1½" WOOD SCREWS

7" 1'-0" 5¾" 1½" 5¼" 1'-0½" 5¼" 7¼"

OCTOBER JUNE 1'-2" 8½" 6¾" AUGUST 2"

BOTTOM of LOUVERS SHOWING JUNE, AUGUST & OCTOBER POSITIONS SCALE 1½" = 1'-0"   **BOTTOM of LOUVERS SHOWING THE THREE CONTROL PINS**

11—4 EXTERIOR ADJUSTABLE LOUVERS

The author faced a very difficult sun-control problem for a residence in Greenwich, Connecticut, due to the fact that the better views were to the southwest and west, and the best view was to the northwest. It was relatively simple to answer the southwest sun, as this would give solar heat gain in winter. Therefore the major side of the house was angled to the southwest, and by extending a 10'-6" porch in front of the living and dining rooms, the sun was completely controlled from October through May to obtain solar heat gain. By extending a side wall of the porch to 13'-2" and installing adjustable louvers, the June-through-August sun could be completely cut out by control of the louvers. After August the louvers, when put in the October position and kept there until June, permitted one to enjoy the beautiful northwest view.

CROSS-REFERENCES TO *SUN CONTROL*
IN OTHER CHAPTERS

Chapter Number	Drawing Number	Drawing Title	Described on Page	Drawing on Page
12	12-1	Solar residence	109	110, 111
	12-2	Underground house	109	112, 113
	12-3	Trombe wall	109	114

12

Solar:
Active
and Passive

INTRODUCTION

The details in this chapter cover some of the methods of using the sun for heating in winter and eliminating solar gain in the summer. Only a few typical, efficient examples are shown, as this subject is beyond the scope of this book. The field is wide open to new ideas, materials, and methods. These come from a wide range of professionals and do-it-yourself organizations, as well as enterprising and sometimes surprisingly successful amateurs. The results of their efforts fill journals and library shelves with books, to which the author refers those with a serious interest in knowing more about active and passive methods of using the sun's energy. Only a brief outline about passive solar systems is included here.*

There are basically two distinct approaches to the solar heating of buildings: active and passive. In general, active systems enploy hardware and mechanical equipment to collect and transport heat. Passive systems, on the other hand, collect and transport heat by nonmechanical means. The most common definition of a passive solar heating and cooling system is that it is a system in which the thermal energy flows in the system are by natural means such as radiation, conduction, and natural convection. In essence, the building structure or some element of it is the system. The most striking difference between the systems is that the passive system operates on the energy available in its immediate environment and the active system imports energy, such as electricity, to power the fans and pumps which make the system work.

*Edward Mazria, *The Passive Solar Energy Book,* Rodale Press, Emmaus, Pa., 1979.

CHAPTER DETAIL TEXT

12-1 Solar Residence   The residence of Dr. William and Eleanor Inouye, in Elkins Park, Pennsylvania, designed by Alley Friends Architects, has been in use for three winters and three summers and has required minimum use of the wood stove in winter and has always been comfortable in the summer. The two large ceiling fans circulate the heated air in the winter, and in the summer they are used to circulate the air within the house and the cool air from the small fan connected to the underground cool-tube. The residence is very well insulated, so there is minimum heat loss or heat gain. The greenhouse is utilized as a heat collector for the house and even more as a source of pleasure, for both homeowners like gardening. The use of dark gray stucco on the wall in the greenhouse makes the solid concrete block wall a passive solar collector.

12-2 Underground House   Two pages of details show sections of the Lewis residence, Medfield, Massachusetts, by Don Metz, architect. The section through the south wall and front of the residence shows treatment of deep fascia due to earth on the roof, insulation, and the heavy wood structure needed to support the weight involved. The interior wall shows treatment of the space between $6'' \times 10''$ roof beams, and the section through the chimney shows detail of roofing, topsoil, insulation, and flashing where it penetrates the roof. The section through underground foundation wall shows all the answers to the problems of insulation, waterproofing, backfill, drainage, and the intersection of roof topsoil and backfill and finish grade.

Note that a very thick, permanent-type roofing membrane was selected because once installed, it would become very costly to repair or to install a new membrane.

STO® is one of the relatively new types of exterior plastic finish, which is available colored, textured or smooth; it is dampproof, waterproof, and most important, durable and long-lasting.

12-3 Trombe Wall   A two-car garage was converted into a work-study area and a single-car garage. By using a trombe wall the work-study area was heated in winter, had light the year round, and yet was spared overheating during the summer. By installing aluminum-faced plywood panels in summer, the trombe-wall heating was closed off. Naturally, the entire south wall had to be removed and the new wall adjusted to the angles of winter and summer sun. The entire work-study area was totally insulated and a small wood stove with standard prefabricated chimney was used for backup heat. After several years of use, a small fan was installed in the ceiling of the trombe wall space to allow any built-up summer heat to be exhausted into the attic space. In winter a small plywood sliding door closed the opening to the fan. This door was easily accessible from one Andersen® utility window.

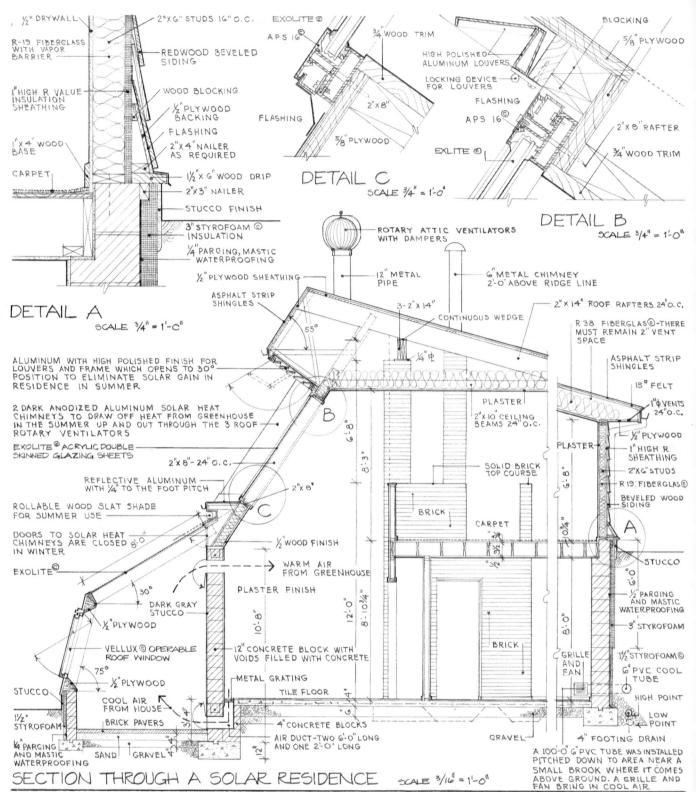

½" DRYWALL

R-19 FIBERGLASS WITH VAPOR BARRIER

1" HIGH R VALUE INSULATION SHEATHING

1"X 4" WOOD BASE

CARPET

2"X 6" STUDS 16" O.C.

REDWOOD BEVELED SIDING

WOOD BLOCKING

½" PLYWOOD BACKING

FLASHING

2"X 4" NAILER AS REQUIRED

1½ X 6" WOOD DRIP

2"X 3" NAILER

STUCCO FINISH

3" STYROFOAM © INSULATION

¼" PARGING, MASTIC WATERPROOFING

DETAIL A

SCALE ¾" = 1'-0"

EXOLITE ©

APS 16 ©

¾ WOOD TRIM

FLASHING

5/8" PLYWOOD

DETAIL C

SCALE ¾" = 1'-0"

BLOCKING

5/8" PLYWOOD

HIGH POLISHED ALUMINUM LOUVERS

LOCKING DEVICE FOR LOUVERS

FLASHING

APS 16 ©

EXLITE ©

2"X 8" RAFTER

¾ WOOD TRIM

DETAIL B

SCALE ¾" = 1'-0"

ROTARY ATTIC VENTILATORS WITH DAMPERS

12" METAL PIPE

6" METAL CHIMNEY 2'-0" ABOVE RIDGE LINE

3-2"X 14"

CONTINUOUS WEDGE

2"X 14" ROOF RAFTERS 24"O.C.

R 38 FIBERGLAS © -THERE MUST REMAIN 2" VENT SPACE

½" PLYWOOD SHEATHING

ASPHALT STRIP SHINGLES

55°

¼" ∅

PLASTER

2"X 10" CEILING BEAMS 24" O.C.

ASPHALT STRIP SHINGLES

15# FELT

1"∅ VENTS 24" O.C.

½" PLYWOOD

PLASTER

1" HIGH R SHEATHING

2"X 6" STUDS

R 19 FIBERGLAS ©

BEVELED WOOD SIDING

ALUMINUM WITH HIGH POLISHED FINISH FOR LOUVERS AND FRAME WHICH OPENS TO 30° POSITION TO ELIMINATE SOLAR GAIN IN RESIDENCE IN SUMMER

2 DARK ANODIZED ALUMINUM SOLAR HEAT CHIMNEYS TO DRAW OFF HEAT FROM GREENHOUSE IN THE SUMMER UP AND OUT THROUGH THE 3 ROOF ROTARY VENTILATORS

EXOLITE © ACRYLIC DOUBLE SKINNED GLAZING SHEETS

REFLECTIVE ALUMINUM WITH ¼" TO THE FOOT PITCH

ROLLABLE WOOD SLAT SHADE FOR SUMMER USE

DOORS TO SOLAR HEAT CHIMNEYS ARE CLOSED IN WINTER

EXOLITE ©

DARK GRAY STUCCO

½" PLYWOOD

VELLUX © OPERABLE ROOF WINDOW

STUCCO

½" PLYWOOD

½" STYROFOAM

¼" PARGING AND MASTIC WATERPROOFING

SAND

GRAVEL

COOL AIR FROM HOUSE

BRICK PAVERS

B

C

2"X 8"

2"X 8"- 24" O.C.

30°

75°

½ WOOD FINISH

WARM AIR FROM GREENHOUSE

PLASTER FINISH

12" CONCRETE BLOCK WITH VOIDS FILLED WITH CONCRETE

METAL GRATING

TILE FLOOR

4" CONCRETE BLOCKS

AIR DUCT-TWO 6'-0" LONG AND ONE 2'-0" LONG

SOLID BRICK TOP COURSE

BRICK

CARPET

BRICK

GRAVEL

A

STUCCO

½ PARGING AND MASTIC WATERPROOFING

3" STYROFOAM

1½ STYROFOAM ©

6" PVC COOL TUBE

HIGH POINT

LOW POINT

GRILLE AND FAN

4" FOOTING DRAIN

A 100'-0" 6" PVC TUBE WAS INSTALLED PITCHED DOWN TO AREA NEAR A SMALL BROOK WHERE IT COMES ABOVE GROUND. A GRILLE AND FAN BRING IN COOL AIR

SECTION THROUGH A SOLAR RESIDENCE   SCALE 3/16" = 1'-0"

12–1 SOLAR RESIDENCE

The two sections explain the workings of this solar residence designed by Alley Friends Architects for Dr. William and Eleanor Inouye in Elkins Park, Pennsylvania. In winter the heated air from the greenhouse is passed into the two-story living area and the cooler air at the floor of this area passes into the greenhouse, which is at a slightly lower level. Thus a continuous circulation by natural means occurs. The large fixed windows allow the winter sun to add solar heat to the two-story area. In the summer, doors close off the openings from the greenhouse to the two-story living space, and doors open to the solar heat chimneys which carry off the greenhouse heat through rotary attic ventilators. Recessed aluminum louvers are projected out and these keep summer sun from entering through the fixed glass areas. Also, a wood slat shade is lowered over the pitched glass area of the greenhouse. A 100'-0" cool-tube installed underground and connected to a fan brings cool air into the entire house during the summer.

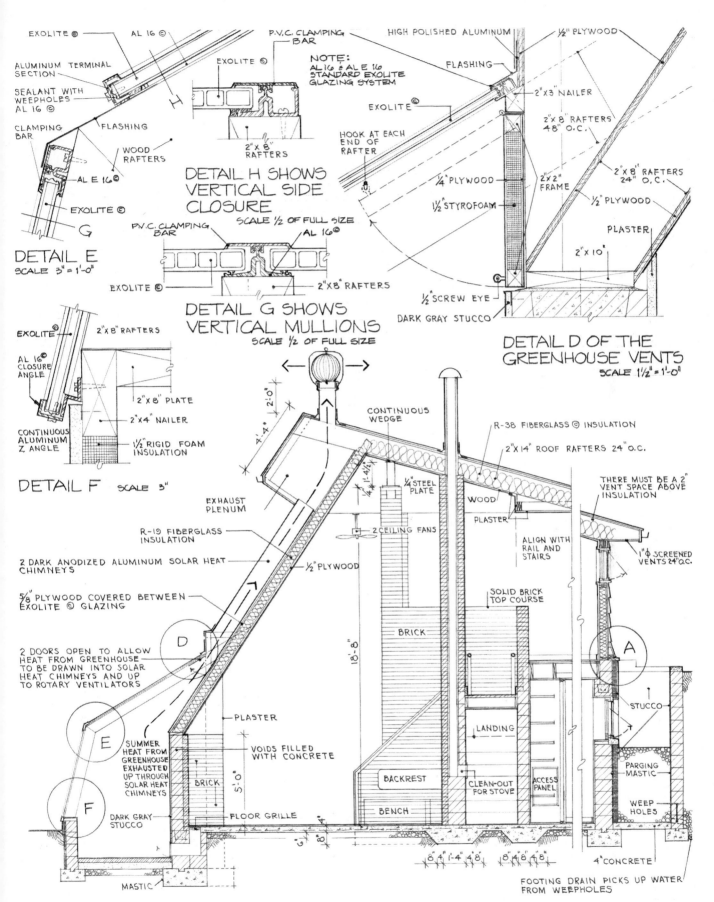

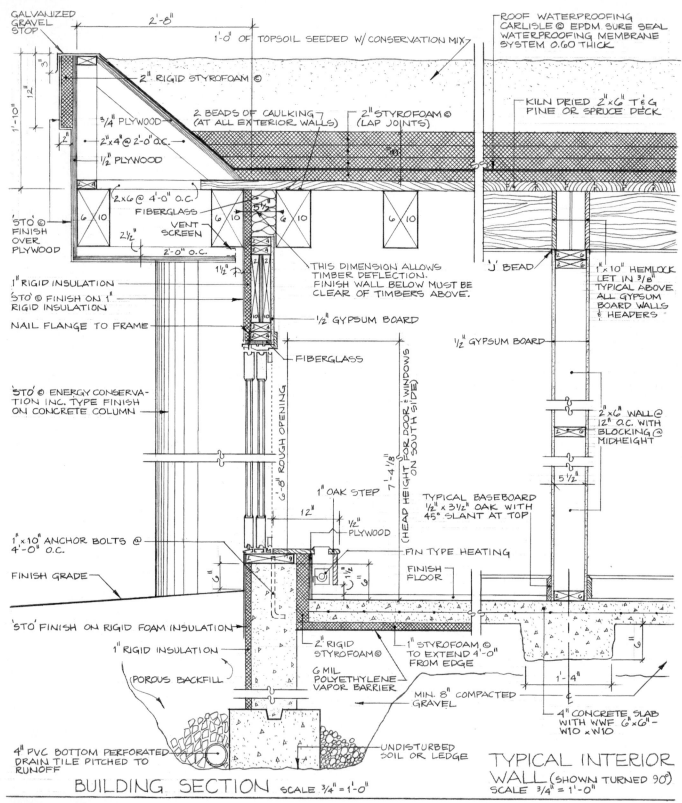

GALVANIZED GRAVEL STOP

2'-8"

1'-0" OF TOPSOIL SEEDED W/ CONSERVATION MIX

ROOF WATERPROOFING CARLISLE © EPDM SURE SEAL WATERPROOFING MEMBRANE SYSTEM 0.60 THICK

3"

12"

1'-10"

2"

2" RIGID STYROFOAM ©

3/4" PLYWOOD

2"x4 @ 2'-0" O.C.

1/2" PLYWOOD

2 BEADS OF CAULKING (AT ALL EXTERIOR WALLS)

2" STYROFOAM © (LAP JOINTS)

KILN DRIED 2"x6" T&G PINE OR SPRUCE DECK

6   10

6   10   5½"

10

6   10

'STO' © FINISH OVER PLYWOOD

(2x6 @ 4'-0" O.C.) FIBERGLASS

VENT SCREEN

2½"

2'-0" O.C.

1½"

THIS DIMENSION ALLOWS TIMBER DEFLECTION. FINISH WALL BELOW MUST BE CLEAR OF TIMBERS ABOVE.

'J' BEAD

1"x10" HEMLOCK LET IN 3/8" TYPICAL ABOVE ALL GYPSUM BOARD WALLS & HEADERS

1" RIGID INSULATION

'STO' © FINISH ON 1" RIGID INSULATION

NAIL FLANGE TO FRAME

½" GYPSUM BOARD

FIBERGLASS

½" GYPSUM BOARD

10   10

6'-8" ROUGH OPENING

(HEAD HEIGHT FOR DOOR & WINDOWS ON SOUTH SIDE)

7'-4⅛"

2"x6" WALL @ 12" O.C. WITH BLOCKING @ MIDHEIGHT

5½"

'STO' © ENERGY CONSERVATION INC. TYPE FINISH ON CONCRETE COLUMN

1" OAK STEP

½" PLYWOOD

12"

TYPICAL BASEBOARD ½" x 3½" OAK WITH 45° SLANT AT TOP

1"x10" ANCHOR BOLTS @ 4'-0" O.C.

FINISH GRADE

FIN TYPE HEATING

FINISH FLOOR

6"

'STO' FINISH ON RIGID FOAM INSULATION

1" RIGID INSULATION

(POROUS BACKFILL)

2" RIGID STYROFOAM ©

6 MIL POLYETHYLENE VAPOR BARRIER

1" STYROFOAM © TO EXTEND 4'-0" FROM EDGE

MIN. 8" COMPACTED GRAVEL

1'-4"

4" CONCRETE SLAB WITH WWF 6"x6"- W10 x W10

4" PVC BOTTOM PERFORATED DRAIN TILE PITCHED TO RUNOFF

UNDISTURBED SOIL OR LEDGE

BUILDING SECTION SCALE ¾" = 1'-0"

TYPICAL INTERIOR WALL (SHOWN TURNED 90°) SCALE ¾" = 1'-0"

12–2 UNDERGROUND HOUSE

This section through the south wall of the Lewis house in Medfield, Massachusetts, by architect Don Metz shows details of fascia treatment of the earth-covered insulated roof with sufficient overhang to eliminate summer sun from the sliding glass doors. Note treatment at the sliding door sill with a 1" thick oak step with narrow slots covered with metal grilles and incorporating a fin-type heating radiator below. The concrete foundation wall has 1" foam insulation on the outside treated with STO® finish, and 2" foam insulation on the inside extending down to meet the 1" foam insulation under the floor slab.

The interior wall detail is interesting because of the care taken in the treatment of the 1" X 10" hemlock so that it is flush with the ½" gypsum board, which terminates in a "J" bead.

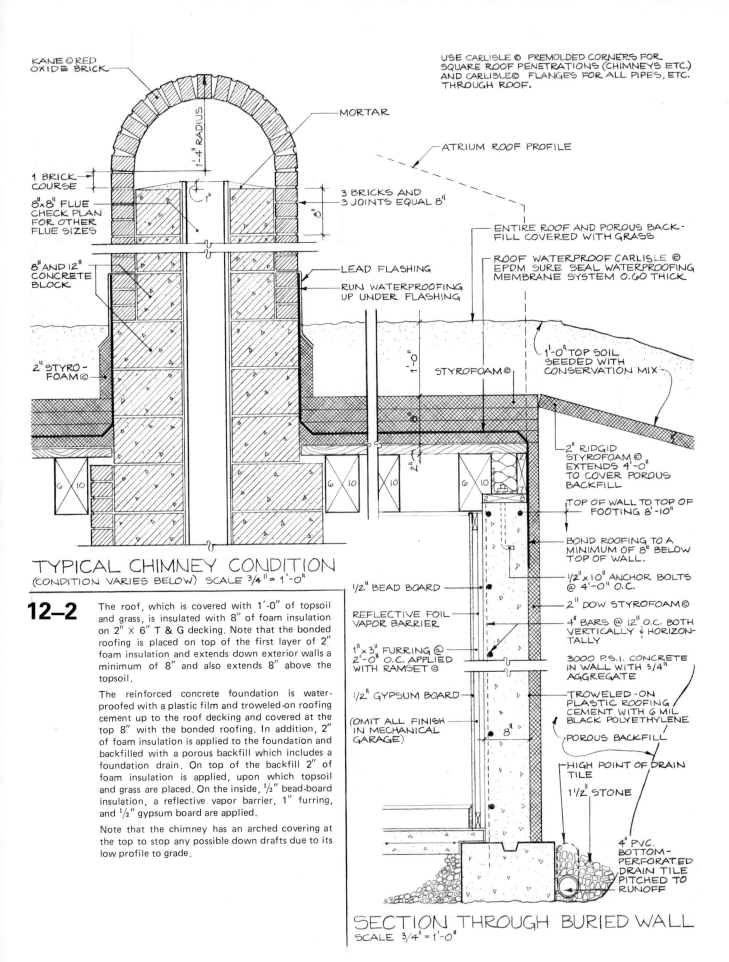

USE CARLISLE © PREMOLDED CORNERS FOR SQUARE ROOF PENETRATIONS (CHIMNEYS ETC.) AND CARLISLE© FLANGES FOR ALL PIPES, ETC. THROUGH ROOF.

KANE©RED OXIDE BRICK

MORTAR

1'-4 RADIUS

1 BRICK COURSE

8"x8" FLUE CHECK PLAN FOR OTHER FLUE SIZES

3 BRICKS AND 3 JOINTS EQUAL 8"

8"AND 12" CONCRETE BLOCK

ATRIUM ROOF PROFILE

LEAD FLASHING

RUN WATERPROOFING UP UNDER FLASHING

ENTIRE ROOF AND POROUS BACK-FILL COVERED WITH GRASS

ROOF WATERPROOF CARLISLE © EPDM SURE SEAL WATERPROOFING MEMBRANE SYSTEM 0.60 THICK

2" STYRO-FOAM©

1'-0"TOP SOIL SEEDED WITH CONSERVATION MIX

STYROFOAM©

2" RIDGID STYROFOAM© EXTENDS 4'-0" TO COVER POROUS BACKFILL

TOP OF WALL TO TOP OF FOOTING 8'-10"

BOND ROOFING TO A MINIMUM OF 8" BELOW TOP OF WALL.

1/2"x10" ANCHOR BOLTS @ 4'-0" O.C.

2" DOW STYROFOAM©

TYPICAL CHIMNEY CONDITION
(CONDITION VARIES BELOW) SCALE 3/4" = 1'-0"

12–2

The roof, which is covered with 1'-0" of topsoil and grass, is insulated with 8" of foam insulation on 2" X 6" T & G decking. Note that the bonded roofing is placed on top of the first layer of 2" foam insulation and extends down exterior walls a minimum of 8" and also extends 8" above the topsoil.

The reinforced concrete foundation is water-proofed with a plastic film and troweled-on roofing cement up to the roof decking and covered at the top 8" with the bonded roofing. In addition, 2" of foam insulation is applied to the foundation and backfilled with a porous backfill which includes a foundation drain. On top of the backfill 2" of foam insulation is applied, upon which topsoil and grass are placed. On the inside, 1/2" bead-board insulation, a reflective vapor barrier, 1" furring, and 1/2" gypsum board are applied.

Note that the chimney has an arched covering at the top to stop any possible down drafts due to its low profile to grade.

1/2" BEAD BOARD

REFLECTIVE FOIL VAPOR BARRIER

1"x 3" FURRING @ 2'-0" O.C. APPLIED WITH RAMSET ©

1/2" GYPSUM BOARD

(OMIT ALL FINISH IN MECHANICAL GARAGE)

4" BARS @ 12" O.C. BOTH VERTICALLY & HORIZON-TALLY

3000 P.S.I. CONCRETE IN WALL WITH 3/4" AGGREGATE

TROWELED-ON PLASTIC ROOFING CEMENT WITH 6 MIL BLACK POLYETHYLENE

POROUS BACKFILL

HIGH POINT OF DRAIN TILE

1 1/2" STONE

4" PVC. BOTTOM-PERFORATED DRAIN TILE PITCHED TO RUNOFF

SECTION THROUGH BURIED WALL
SCALE 3/4" = 1'-0"

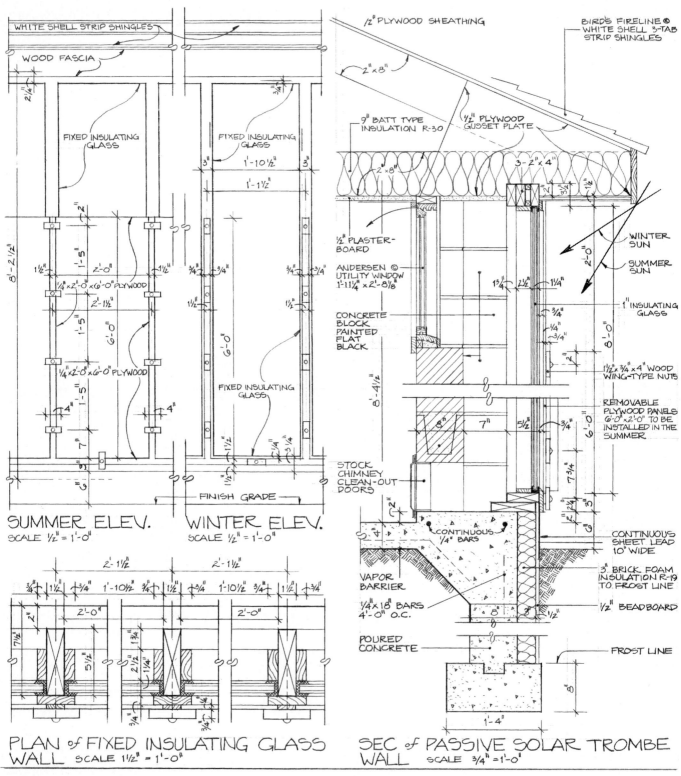

WHITE SHELL STRIP SHINGLES
WOOD FASCIA
FIXED INSULATING GLASS
FIXED INSULATING GLASS
FIXED INSULATING GLASS
¼"x2'-0"x6'-0" PLYWOOD
¼"x2'-0"x6'-0" PLYWOOD
FINISH GRADE

½" PLYWOOD SHEATHING
BIRD'S FIRELINE® WHITE SHELL 3-TAB STRIP SHINGLES
2"x8"
9" BATT TYPE INSULATION R-30
½" PLYWOOD GUSSET PLATE
2"x8"
3-2"x4"
½" PLASTER-BOARD
ANDERSEN © UTILITY WINDOW 1'-11¼" x 2'-8⅛"
CONCRETE BLOCK PAINTED FLAT BLACK
STOCK CHIMNEY CLEAN-OUT DOORS
VAPOR BARRIER
¼"x18 BARS 4'-0" O.C.
POURED CONCRETE
CONTINUOUS ¼" BARS
WINTER SUN
SUMMER SUN
1" INSULATING GLASS
1½"x ¾"x4" WOOD WING-TYPE NUTS
REMOVABLE PLYWOOD PANELS 6'-0"x2'-0" TO BE INSTALLED IN THE SUMMER
CONTINUOUS SHEET LEAD 10" WIDE
3" BRICK FOAM INSULATION R-19 TO FROST LINE
½" BEADBOARD
FROST LINE

SUMMER ELEV.
SCALE ½"=1'-0"

WINTER ELEV.
SCALE ½"=1'-0"

PLAN of FIXED INSULATING GLASS WALL SCALE 1½"=1'-0"

SEC of PASSIVE SOLAR TROMBE WALL SCALE ¾"=1'-0"

12–3 TROMBE WALL

An early client of the author asked if there was a simple way of turning his existing two-car garage into a work-study area and a single-car garage. He was also interested in solar energy. Fortunately, one of the side walls of the garage faced south. So the entire south wall was removed, and a wall was made up of large pieces of insulating glass. This wall was set back so that there was a considerable roof overhang. Then, 11¼" back of the glass on the inside, a concrete block wall was built. This concrete wall was painted black and simple utility-type Andersen® windows were installed at the top to give light both in winter and summer. The black concrete wall also had small clean-out doors installed which, in winter, could be opened so that the warm air in the trombe wall space could pass into and circulate throughout the work-study area. A small wood stove was installed for backup heating.

CROSS-REFERENCE TO *SOLAR: ACTIVE AND PASSIVE* IN ANOTHER CHAPTER

Chapter Number	Drawing Number	Drawing Title	Described on Page	Drawing on Page
11	11–4	Exterior adjustable louvers	100	104

13

Insulation

INTRODUCTION

Insulation has become a very important building material for architects for purely economic reasons. To obtain building loans, mortgages, and any other kind of investment money, all buildings now must meet R-factor requirements. This means that detailing the walls, foundations, roofs, windows, intersection of materials, etc., must be carefully considered. This book contains a large number of examples that show how to insulate under different conditions in a variety of buildings. Therefore the cross-indexing of this chapter was used as the means of making each of these details available; consequently the cross indexing is very large.

Today, with the advent of various types of synthetic foam materials, there has evolved a completely changed detailing for insulation of buildings. Standards have been set up for all types of insulation, based on the R factor, which is the rate by which a given material resists the flow of heat. Heat loss or gain occurs in three ways: radiation, conduction, and convection. In buildings, heat loss or gain occurs in all three of these ways.

Therefore the architect must be very careful in the selection and detailing of insulation. For example, $\frac{1}{2}''$ of one type of material can have a considerably lower R factor ($\frac{1}{2}''$ insulating board with R-1.39) than $\frac{1}{2}''$ of another material (foam sheathing with R-4.00). Also, time has shown that many of the synthetic foams cannot be used as perimeter insulation because they disintegrate when in contact with the earth.

It is always advisable to check both the flame-spread characteristics and the fire resistance of the material to be used. For example, glass wool as insulation is fireproof, whereas plastic foam materials are not fireproof but have various flame spread characteristics.

To summarize, it is not only the R factor that is important, but also flame spread, effect of contact with earth, and any latent chemical hazards, such as the giving off of dangerous, toxic, irritating, or allergy-producing fumes, which may occur soon after installation or only after some time has passed. Especially dangerous are synthetics that produce toxic fumes in case of fire, even a minor one.

CHAPTER DETAIL TEXT

13-1 Four Types of Insulated Walls

This group of details shows four different exterior walls with insulation that yields excellent R values.

DETAIL 1. The $5\frac{1}{2}''$ stud with an extra $1\frac{1}{2}''$ of insulation serves a double purpose: it allows space for all electrical wiring and also gives extra insulation. Offsetting the floor structure $4''$ beyond the face of the foundation wall allows for $4''$ of rigid foam insulation around the foundation walls, thus providing good R-factor perimeter insulation as well.

DETAIL 2. A brick veneer wall has $2''$ of rigid foam insulation between the sheathing and the brick. By extending the brick and the $2''$ of rigid foam insulation below grade, the usual gap between exterior and interior insulation is eliminated. The addition of the $9''$ of glass wool insulation between the floor joists stops the penetration of any cold through the concrete foundation wall.

DETAIL 3. This shows a simple concrete block wall with a $4''$ R-Wall®, an exterior insulation finish system which consists of a rigid foam insulation, reinforced with an adhesive-applied woven fiberglass fabric, and finished with a cement-sand-epoxy (or other special plastic) finish. To take care of the space between the $4''$ R-Wall® and grade, $\frac{1}{2}'' \times 9'' \times 9''$ quarry tile is adhesive-applied and the insulation is reduced by $1''$. This adhesive for the quarry tile continues down over the fiberboard to the footing.

DETAIL 4. This simple cavity wall has a $4''$ cavity to allow for an air space of $1''$ and $3''$ of rigid foam insulation. At grade a large steel angle is used to support the brick and at the same time allow $4''$ rigid foam perimeter insulation. Note that the protective dampproofing continues up and over the $8'' \times 8'' \times \frac{1}{2}''$ angle and then continues up behind the zinc flashing.

13-2 Residential Wall Sections

These four details show various conditions for obtaining good R factors.

DETAILS 1 AND 2. In DETAIL 1, we see that by projecting floor joists $4''$ beyond the face of the foundation wall, $4''$ of foam insulation can be applied to the exterior of the foundation wall. DETAIL 2 shows how conditions can be met when part of a residence is below grade by the use of high berm walls. Both DETAILS 1 and 2 take advantage of the masonry wall acting as a retainer of heat.

DETAILS 3 AND 4. Shown is a typical section through an exterior 4″ wood or metal stud wall. Here a 1½″ furred space is installed for a double purpose: first, to add more insulation, and second, to have space for electrical wiring so as not to break the vapor barrier or damage the insulation during installation of the electrical wiring. When wiring is completed, 1½″ more of insulation is installed. At grade, after dampproofing is applied, a continuous zinc termite shield and vertical strip are installed to have a finish surface from grade to siding.

Note that two different roof pitches are shown, and it is necessary to use not only roof shingles of a different type but also a different amount of shingle exposure for the two different roof pitches.

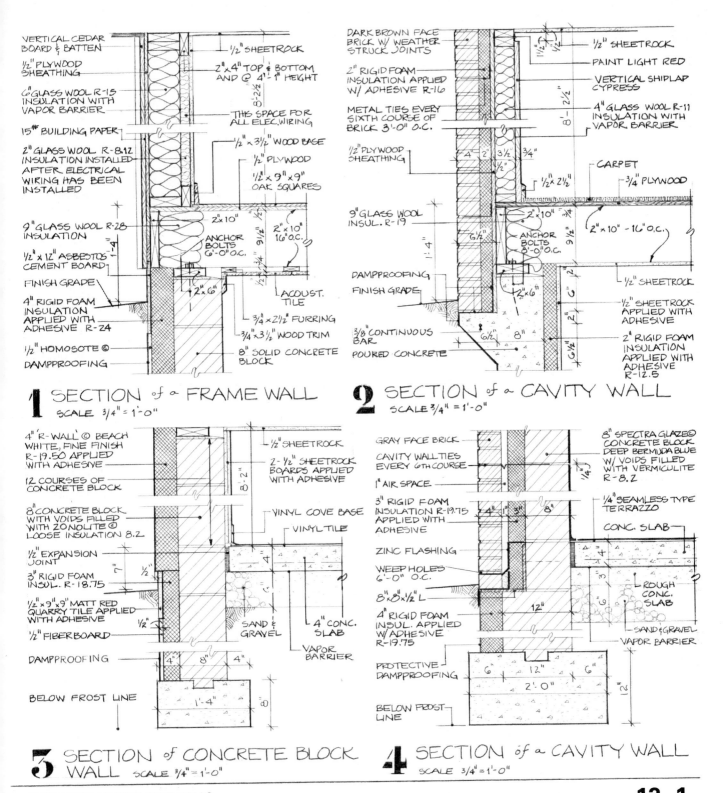

1 SECTION of a FRAME WALL
SCALE 3/4" = 1'-0"

VERTICAL CEDAR BOARD & BATTEN
1/2" PLYWOOD SHEATHING
6" GLASS WOOL R-15 INSULATION WITH VAPOR BARRIER
15# BUILDING PAPER
2" GLASS WOOL R-8.12 INSULATION INSTALLED AFTER ELECTRICAL WIRING HAS BEEN INSTALLED
9" GLASS WOOL R-28 INSULATION
1/2" x 12" ASBESTOS CEMENT BOARD
FINISH GRADE
4" RIGID FOAM INSULATION APPLIED WITH ADHESIVE R-24
1/2" HOMOSOTE ©
DAMPPROOFING

1/2" SHEETROCK
2" x 4" TOP & BOTTOM AND @ 4'-1" HEIGHT
THIS SPACE FOR ALL ELEC. WIRING
1/2" x 3 1/2" WOOD BASE
1/2" PLYWOOD
1/2" x 9" x 9" OAK SQUARES
ANCHOR BOLTS 6'-0" O.C.
2" x 10" 16" O.C.
2" x 6"
ACOUST. TILE
3/4" x 2 1/2" FURRING
3/4" x 3 1/2" WOOD TRIM
8" SOLID CONCRETE BLOCK

2 SECTION of a CAVITY WALL
SCALE 3/4" = 1'-0"

DARK BROWN FACE BRICK W/ WEATHER STRUCK JOINTS
2" RIGID FOAM INSULATION APPLIED W/ ADHESIVE R-16
METAL TIES EVERY SIXTH COURSE OF BRICK 3'-0" O.C.
1/2" PLYWOOD SHEATHING
9" GLASS WOOL INSUL. R-19
DAMPPROOFING
FINISH GRADE
3/8" CONTINUOUS BAR
POURED CONCRETE

1/2" SHEETROCK
PAINT LIGHT RED
VERTICAL SHIPLAP CYPRESS
4" GLASS WOOL R-11 INSULATION WITH VAPOR BARRIER
CARPET
3/4" PLYWOOD
2" x 10" - 16" O.C.
ANCHOR BOLTS 6'-0" O.C.
2" x 6"
1/2" SHEETROCK
1/2" SHEETROCK APPLIED WITH ADHESIVE
2" RIGID FOAM INSULATION APPLIED WITH ADHESIVE R-12.5

3 SECTION of CONCRETE BLOCK WALL
SCALE 3/4" = 1'-0"

4" 'R-WALL' © BEACH WHITE, FINE FINISH R-19.50 APPLIED WITH ADHESIVE
12 COURSES OF CONCRETE BLOCK
8" CONCRETE BLOCK WITH VOIDS FILLED WITH ZONOLITE © LOOSE INSULATION 8.2
1/2" EXPANSION JOINT
3" RIGID FOAM INSUL. R-18.75
1/2" x 9" x 9" MATT RED QUARRY TILE APPLIED WITH ADHESIVE
1/2" FIBERBOARD
DAMPPROOFING
BELOW FROST LINE

1/2" SHEETROCK
2 - 1/2" SHEETROCK BOARDS APPLIED WITH ADHESIVE
VINYL COVE BASE
VINYL TILE
SAND & GRAVEL
4" CONC. SLAB
VAPOR BARRIER

4 SECTION of a CAVITY WALL
SCALE 3/4" = 1'-0"

GRAY FACE BRICK
CAVITY WALL TIES EVERY 6TH COURSE
1" AIR SPACE
3" RIGID FOAM INSULATION R-19.75 APPLIED WITH ADHESIVE
ZINC FLASHING
WEEP HOLES 6'-0" O.C.
8" x 8" x 1/2" L
4" RIGID FOAM INSUL. APPLIED W/ ADHESIVE R-19.75
PROTECTIVE DAMPPROOFING
BELOW FROST LINE

8" SPECTRA GLAZE © CONCRETE BLOCK DEEP BERMUDA BLUE W/ VOIDS FILLED WITH VERMICULITE R-8.2
1/4" SEAMLESS TYPE TERRAZZO
CONC. SLAB
ROUGH CONC. SLAB
SAND & GRAVEL
VAPOR BARRIER

FOUR TYPES OF INSULATED WALLS   **13—1**

These details show four exterior walls with maximum insulation obtainable by using different types of insulating material. DETAIL 1 shows a 5 1/2" deep wood or metal stud wall with an extra depth of 1 1/2" to take care of the electrical wiring without damaging the vapor barrier. At grade the first floor extends 4" beyond the foundation wall to allow for 4" rigid foam insulation to be installed. DETAIL 2 shows a simple brick veneer wall with 2" of foam insulation between the sheathing and the back of the brick. The 3 1/2" stud wall is insulated with 4" glass wool and a vapor barrier. Note how the foundation wall has an extension at the top to allow for sheathing, insulation, and brick. DETAIL 3 is of a simple concrete block wall with a 4" *R*-Wall® with a beach-white exterior finish. The insulation is reduced to 3" of rigid foam, protected at grade with 1/2" quarry tile and 1/2" of fiberboard below grade. DETAIL 4 shows a simple cavity wall where the cavity is increased in depth to 4" and the voids in concrete block walls are filled with vermiculite. Note how a large 8 1/2" X 8 1/2" X 1/2" angle is used to support the brick and allow for 4" of rigid insulation below grade.

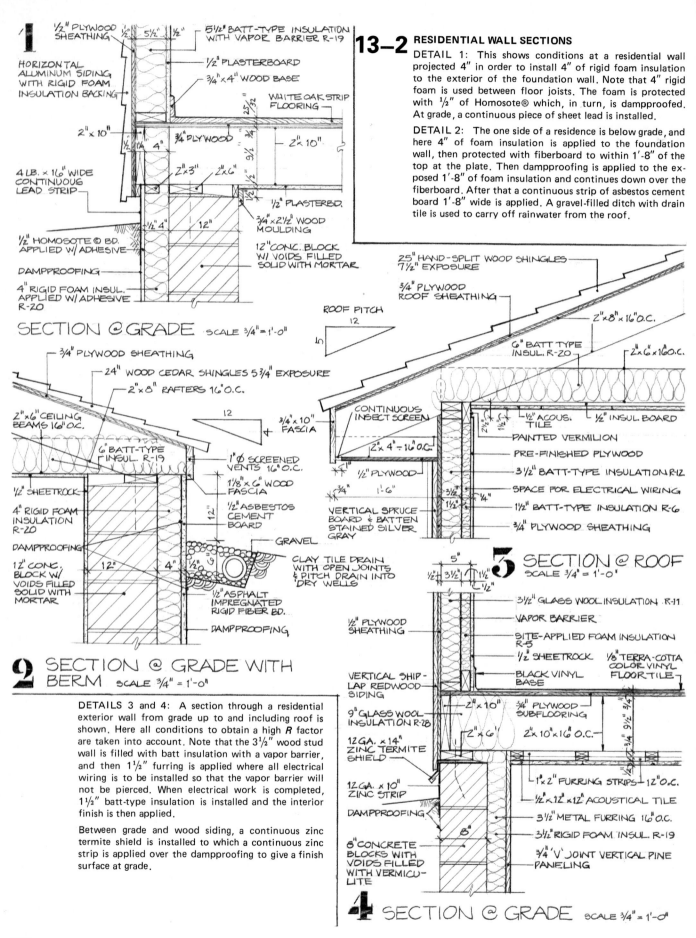

1 HORIZONTAL ALUMINUM SIDING WITH RIGID FOAM INSULATION BACKING

½" PLYWOOD SHEATHING

5½" BATT-TYPE INSULATION WITH VAPOR BARRIER R-19

½" PLASTERBOARD

¾" x 4" WOOD BASE

WHITE OAK STRIP FLOORING

2" x 10"

¾" PLYWOOD

2" x 10"

2" x 3"   2" x 6"

½" PLASTERBD.

¾" x 2½" WOOD MOULDING

4 LB. x 16" WIDE CONTINUOUS LEAD STRIP

12" CONC. BLOCK W/ VOIDS FILLED SOLID WITH MORTAR

½" HOMOSOTE © BD. APPLIED W/ ADHESIVE

DAMPPROOFING

4" RIGID FOAM INSUL. APPLIED W/ ADHESIVE R-20

SECTION @ GRADE SCALE ¾" = 1'-0"

13—2 RESIDENTIAL WALL SECTIONS

DETAIL 1: This shows conditions at a residential wall projected 4" in order to install 4" of rigid foam insulation to the exterior of the foundation wall. Note that 4" rigid foam is used between floor joists. The foam is protected with ½" of Homosote® which, in turn, is dampproofed. At grade, a continuous piece of sheet lead is installed.

DETAIL 2: The one side of a residence is below grade, and here 4" of foam insulation is applied to the foundation wall, then protected with fiberboard to within 1'-8" of the top at the plate. Then dampproofing is applied to the exposed 1'-8" of foam insulation and continues down over the fiberboard. After that a continuous strip of asbestos cement board 1'-8" wide is applied. A gravel-filled ditch with drain tile is used to carry off rainwater from the roof.

¾" PLYWOOD SHEATHING

24" WOOD CEDAR SHINGLES 5¾" EXPOSURE

2" x 8" RAFTERS 16" O.C.

2" x 6" CEILING BEAMS 16" O.C.

6" BATT-TYPE INSUL. R-19

½" SHEETROCK

4" RIGID FOAM INSULATION R-20

DAMPPROOFING

12" CONC. BLOCK W/ VOIDS FILLED SOLID WITH MORTAR

ROOF PITCH 12 / 5

3/4" x 10" FASCIA

1" Ø SCREENED VENTS 16" O.C.

1⅛" x 6" WOOD FASCIA

½" ASBESTOS CEMENT BOARD

GRAVEL

CLAY TILE DRAIN WITH OPEN JOINTS & PITCH DRAIN INTO DRY WELLS

½" ASPHALT IMPREGNATED RIGID FIBER BD.

DAMPPROOFING

2 SECTION @ GRADE WITH BERM SCALE ¾" = 1'-0"

25" HAND-SPLIT WOOD SHINGLES 7½" EXPOSURE

¾" PLYWOOD ROOF SHEATHING

2" x 8" x 16" O.C.

6" BATT TYPE INSUL. R-20

2" x 6" x 16" O.C.

CONTINUOUS INSECT SCREEN

2" x 4" x 16" O.C.

½" PLYWOOD

VERTICAL SPRUCE BOARD & BATTEN STAINED SILVER GRAY

½" ACOUS. TILE

½" INSUL. BOARD

PAINTED VERMILION

PRE-FINISHED PLYWOOD

3½" BATT-TYPE INSULATION R-12

SPACE FOR ELECTRICAL WIRING

1½" BATT-TYPE INSULATION R-6

¾" PLYWOOD SHEATHING

3 SECTION @ ROOF SCALE ¾" = 1'-0"

DETAILS 3 and 4: A section through a residential exterior wall from grade up to and including roof is shown. Here all conditions to obtain a high *R* factor are taken into account. Note that the 3½" wood stud wall is filled with batt insulation with a vapor barrier, and then 1½" furring is applied where all electrical wiring is to be installed so that the vapor barrier will not be pierced. When electrical work is completed, 1½" batt-type insulation is installed and the interior finish is then applied.

Between grade and wood siding, a continuous zinc termite shield is installed to which a continuous zinc strip is applied over the dampproofing to give a finish surface at grade.

½" PLYWOOD SHEATHING

VERTICAL SHIP-LAP REDWOOD SIDING

9" GLASS WOOL INSULATION R-28

12 GA. x 14" ZINC TERMITE SHIELD

12 GA. x 10" ZINC STRIP

DAMPPROOFING

8" CONCRETE BLOCKS WITH VOIDS FILLED WITH VERMICULITE

3½" GLASS WOOL INSULATION R-11

VAPOR BARRIER

SITE-APPLIED FOAM INSULATION R-5

½" SHEETROCK

BLACK VINYL BASE

⅛" TERRA-COTTA COLOR VINYL FLOOR TILE

2" x 10"   ¾" PLYWOOD SUBFLOORING

2" x 6"   2" x 10" x 16" O.C.

1" x 2" FURRING STRIPS 12" O.C.

½" x 12" x 12" ACOUSTICAL TILE

3½" METAL FURRING 16" O.C.

3½" RIGID FOAM INSUL. R-19

¾" 'V' JOINT VERTICAL PINE PANELING

4 SECTION @ GRADE SCALE ¾" = 1'-0"

CROSS-REFERENCES TO *INSULATION*
IN OTHER CHAPTERS

Chapter Number	Drawing Number	Drawing Title	Described on Page	Drawing on Page
2	2-1	Reinforced concrete structure with cavity wall	6	9
	2-2	Curtain wall	7	10
	2-3	Residential wall sections	7	11
	2-4	Simple exterior and interior load-bearing walls	7	12
	2-5	Exterior skin curtain wall	8	13
3	3-1	Chimney flashing at ridge and flat roofs	17	18
	3-2	Four common flashing conditions	17	19
	3-3	Four special flashing conditions	17	20
6	6-1	Section through parapet wall and railing	42	44
	6-3	Walls and skins	43	46
7	7-2	Intermediate platform stairs	51	54, 55
9	9-2	Up-sliding doors	79	82
10	10-2	Double fireplaces	89	92, 93
11	11-1	Sun control	99	101
	11-2	Sloping window with sill ventilation	99	102
	11-3	Light construction roof details	99	103
12	12-1	Solar residence	109	110, 111
	12-2	Underground house	109	112, 113
15	15-1	Interior planters for residences	147	149
	15-2	Interior planters for buildings	147	150

14

Built-Ins and Furniture

INTRODUCTION

One of the most difficult challenges in architecture is the creation of the design and detailing of various types of built-in furniture.

Almost all kinds of buildings require some built-in furniture, such as reception desks, showcases, cabinets, bookshelves, bars, beds, entrance lobbies, and store interiors, to mention a few.

Built-in furniture requires the designer not only to work within the building's architectural concept, but also and most important, to coordinate design, color, texture, light, and any other special design requirements of that particular piece of built-in furniture. Thus, such design comes very close to interior decoration, and in very many cases the division between architecture and interior decoration disappears. One such example is the main entrance lobby or atrium in a large commercial building. In residential work, the necessity for and the requirements of any built-in furniture become an accepted part of the job. In office space planning, built-in furniture is a "must" and is usually taken for granted as part of the job.

When designing built-in furniture that has to fit into a particular space, it is always advisable to take actual field measurements to be absolutely sure of the exact space dimensions. In many cases the walls may not meet at an exact 90° angle, and they may not be exactly vertical. Therefore, it is advisable to allow for what is known as *scribing* (tolerance). This means that the top flat surface of any built-in should extend a little beyond the unit below on which it is to rest so that it can be carefully fitted into the allotted space. In many instances a vertical trim piece is used to cover any leftover space between the flat vertical surfaces of the base units and the adjoining walls. In like manner the front of the base unit should allow on the side(s) which are to meet the wall or walls also to have extra length for scribing, to meet the vertical wall(s) without gaps.

CHAPTER DETAIL TEXT

14-1 Executive's Desk
This detail shows an executive-type desk originally designed for a major publishing company. All of the office furniture, as well as the layout, were designed by the author's firm for the original *TV Guide* major office in New York City. The addition of desk space for computer equipment has adapted the design for today's administrator. The entire office area was carefully color-coordinated. Carefully note that the wood base is painted to match the wall-to-wall carpet.

14-2 Built-In Bookshelves
A simple egg-crate system with one piece of trim is the method that Hugh Newell Jacobsen, FAIA, used to design built-in bookshelves, bar unit, etc., in a residence on the Eastern Shore of Maryland. Note that all plywood with exposed edges is banded and the entire unit is painted. The rough $1\frac{1}{2}''$ by $3\frac{3}{8}''$ supports for the bookcases act as base and the carpet is stretched up tight against the rough painted base.

14-3 Residential Bar
This residential bar, located in the basement playroom, not only has all the necessities of a bar, but also becomes an important decorative accent in the playroom. The burl-patterned plywood front, the stainless steel bar rail, the dark brown leatherette bar top, and the open shelves on the back bar with all the bar glassware and the liquor bottles sparkling in the indirect lighting—all these contribute to the decorative effect.

The playroom has light gray painted walls, a floor-to-ceiling southwest insulated glass wall, and a dark gray vinyl tile floor. The natural linen curtains at the window wall have an aluminized lining which reflects the sun in summer.

14-4 Emergency Nurse's Station
This detail for Sacred Heart General Hospital in Chester, Pennsylvania, by Robert D. Lynn Associates, architects and planners, is a basic design for nurse's stations of various types. The details show two types of emergency nurse's stations and examines other variations.

These details, when carefully examined, reveal many creative ideas. For example, the patients chart slots are carefully set at a $30°$ angle, which gives a slot depth of $12''$ and a front-to-back slot depth of only $6''$. This is accomplished by using a $60°$-$30°$ triangle in which the hypotenuse is equal to double the size of the short side of the triangle.

Both types of emergency stations have space for a mobile file unit, which is detailed and can become an integral part of the overall design concept. Note carefully how the removable panels in the base are shown in section D and the large-scale detail.

14-5 Two Display Cases
The two display cases shown in this detail were used frequently by the author's office on many jobs, with only the dimensions changed as required by the client for the kind of objects, or the particular manner or requirements of the display.

For both display cases, standard hardware was used: for display case No. 1 a standard stainless steel piano hinge with a key-operated cabinet-type lock; for display case No. 2, standard glass sliding-door hardware with a sliding-door key lock.

It is advisable always to check the exact length, width, and depth of the type of fluorescent fixture being installed in any display case.

14–6   Built-In Bed   This detail of a built-in bed shows all the design detail problems encountered by an architect when faced with the actual designing of a complete built-in bed unit. Here, simply detailed, are all the inherent requirements for normal double-size, queen-size, and king-size beds, where only the box spring and mattress must be purchased. Note how the backboard can be adjusted and can be covered to coordinate with the bed and pillow covers. The entire built-in bed unit is finished in white oak with walnut accents at the drawer pulls and the light fixture.

14–7   Removable Tackboards   These removable tackboards were used in several elementary schools designed by the author's office. The tackboards were made with standard frames and corkboard mounted on hardboard. Each classroom contained four of each shape, and by this means any class problem could be mounted on the tackboards, then removed from the classroom, to be displayed in the corridor either adjoining the classroom or along other corridor areas.

The specially designed hardware for attaching and removing the tackboards in the recesses was also used in the classrooms, with the exception of the spring clamps, which had to be redesigned for securing tackboards to the classroom wall.

14–8   Built-In Sofa and Bookshelves   The complete layout of office space for either a large corporation or a small business requires deft handling of the executive's offices. Company image, personalities, design preferences, psychology, and interior design all enter into the picture. This detail shows the minimum treatment necessary, using built-ins, for a vice-president's office in a large rayon and yarn manufacturing corporation. Note the simple use of dark walnut to match the dark oak desk, chairs, and computer units, all of which were selected and bought from a large commercial office furniture manufacturer.

The window treatment with double curtains and indirect lighting plus similar indirect lighting over the built-in sofa unit gave the office sufficient light for dark dull days, and for night work the desk and computer units had their own separate light sources.

The sofa was covered with a heavy fabric dyed to match the walnut, and the carpet for all the offices was a good grade of commercial carpet in a medium gray color.

14–9   Reception Desk   This detail show how two contrasting woods are used to dramatize the entrance reception desk of a publishing company. The use of a 7'-6" high curved floating partition covered with zebra wood not only allows for indirect lighting around the reception desk, but also accents the white-topped ebony desk.

The zebra wood, with its strong vertical grain pattern, allows for a simple butt joining of the plywood panels which almost completely eliminates any visible vertical joints.

Note that at the desk there is an access panel under the word processor and printer countertop to a space behind, which enables one to change the bulbs of the down lights and to adjust or change the indirect lighting flood bulbs. This space also gives access to the electrical connections for the word processor and printer and allows for any future electronic additions.

The wall-to-wall carpet is a top-quality commercial dark brown carpet. The color was chosen to accent the zebra wood, the ebony and matt white desk unit tops, and the white walls.

14-10 Library Charging Desk These illustrations show a simple, straightforward answer to a public library charging desk, designed for the Eastwick Branch Library in Philadelphia by B/JC Knowles, architects/planners. Here the charging desk has complete visual control, yet it carefully incorporates all the varied requirements of this special kind of desk. It is notable that the 6″ half-round cap serves not only as an important design material in contrast to the concrete masonry unit wall, but also as a stop for the cushions on the seating area and as a stop for the Plexiglas® front of the display area.

An interesting design requirement for the desk is that the grain of the oak on the entire desk top be in one direction only. By this simple requirement, all joints in the oak become practically invisible.

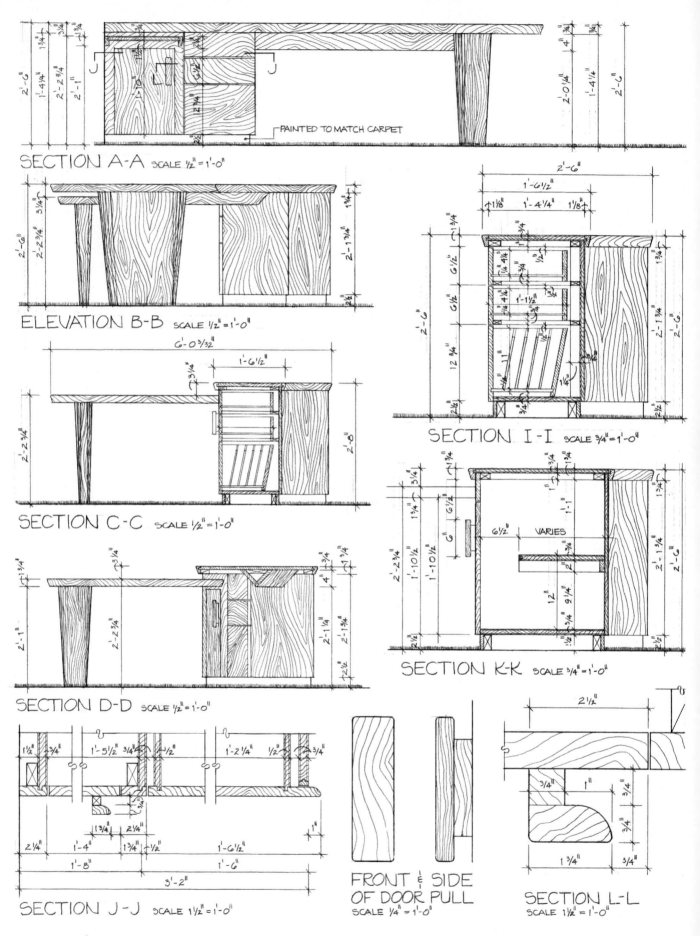

SECTION A-A SCALE ½"=1'-0"

PAINTED TO MATCH CARPET

ELEVATION B-B SCALE ½"=1'-0"

SECTION C-C SCALE ½"=1'-0"

SECTION D-D SCALE ½"=1'-0"

SECTION J-J SCALE 1½"=1'-0"

SECTION I-I SCALE ¾"=1'-0"

SECTION K-K SCALE ¾"=1'-0"

VARIES

FRONT & SIDE
OF DOOR PULL
SCALE ¼"=1'-0"

SECTION L-L
SCALE 1½"=1'-0"

130

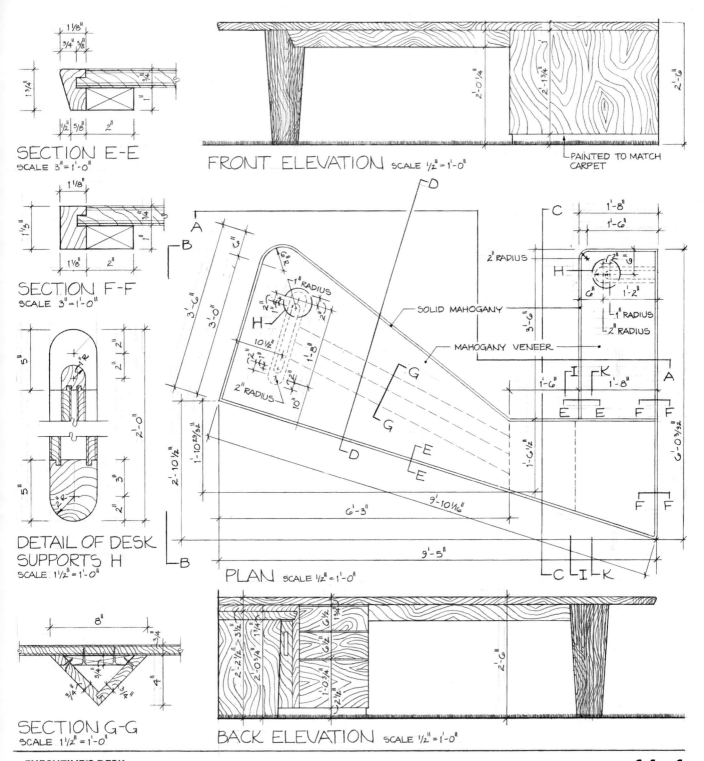

SECTION E-E
SCALE 3"=1'-0"

SECTION F-F
SCALE 3"=1'-0"

DETAIL OF DESK SUPPORTS H
SCALE 1 1/2"=1'-0"

SECTION G-G
SCALE 1 1/2"=1'-0"

FRONT ELEVATION SCALE 1/2"=1'-0"

PAINTED TO MATCH CARPET

SOLID MAHOGANY

MAHOGANY VENEER

2" RADIUS

1" RADIUS

2" RADIUS

PLAN SCALE 1/2"=1'-0"

BACK ELEVATION SCALE 1/2"=1'-0"

EXECUTIVE'S DESK

14—1

This detail shows an executive's desk. The entire desk top, including space for a computer setup, is cut from a 3/4" X 4'-0" X 10'-0" piece of mahogany veneer plywood, and the entire desk surface is stabilized by the drawer unit at one end, the 2'-0" tapered elongated post at the other end, and the triangular-shaped beam spanning between. This desk was made from Mexican mahogany with all pieces carefully matched for grain and color. The desktop veneer was from a fork in the tree to give exceptional curled grain. Note that the drawers overlap by 1" (see section J-J), which allows the overlaps to act as drawer pulls. It is interesting to note that the desk was delivered in four pieces and assembled at the job.

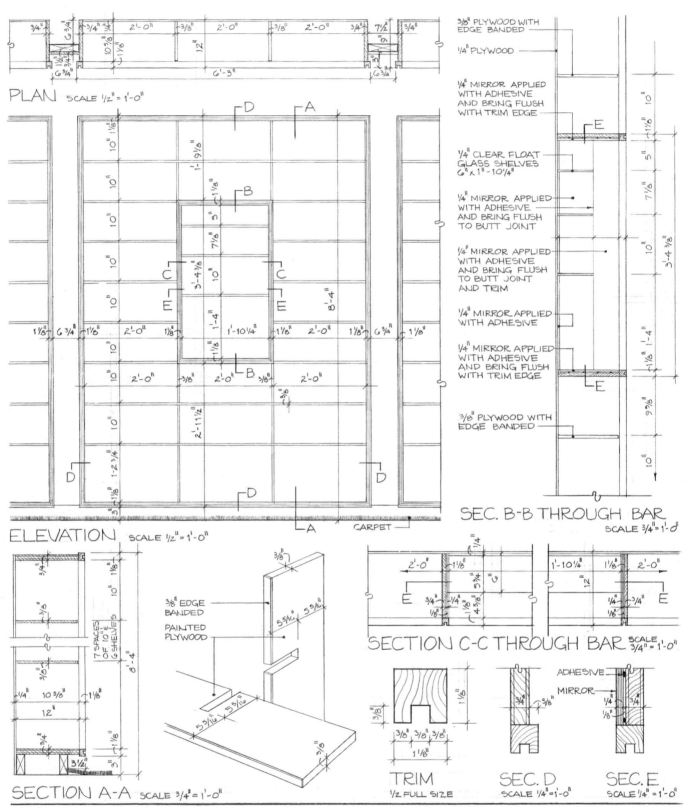

PLAN SCALE ½" = 1'-0"

ELEVATION SCALE ½" = 1'-0"

SECTION A-A SCALE ¾" = 1'-0"

SEC. B-B THROUGH BAR SCALE ¾" = 1'-0"

3/8" PLYWOOD WITH EDGE BANDED

1/4" PLYWOOD

1/4" MIRROR APPLIED WITH ADHESIVE AND BRING FLUSH WITH TRIM EDGE

1/4" CLEAR FLOAT GLASS SHELVES 6" X 1'-10¼"

1/4" MIRROR APPLIED WITH ADHESIVE AND BRING FLUSH TO BUTT JOINT

1/4" MIRROR APPLIED WITH ADHESIVE AND BRING FLUSH TO BUTT JOINT AND TRIM

1/4" MIRROR APPLIED WITH ADHESIVE

1/4" MIRROR APPLIED WITH ADHESIVE AND BRING FLUSH WITH TRIM EDGE

3/8" PLYWOOD WITH EDGE BANDED

3/8" EDGE BANDED

PAINTED PLYWOOD

SECTION C-C THROUGH BAR SCALE ¾" = 1'-0"

TRIM ½ FULL SIZE

SEC. D SCALE ¼" = 1'-0"

SEC. E SCALE ¼" = 1'-0"

ADHESIVE

MIRROR

CARPET

14—2 BUILT-IN BOOKSHELVES

Here is a simple method of building in bookshelves, bar units, etc., for residences and other types of buildings by using an egg-crate system. The front of the shelf is supported by the vertical members and the back of the shelf is nailed to the plywood back. These built-in bookshelves and bar unit were developed for a residence on the Eastern Shore of Maryland. In this design Hugh Newell Jacobsen, FAIA, divided the built-in bookcases into units of three shelf widths and introduced a recessed vertical divider 3" deep by 7½" wide between bookcase units. The major trim piece is solid wood 1⅛" X 1⅛" with a ⅜" wide by ⅜" deep groove at the middle. This simple trim piece acts as framing for sides, top, and bottom of the bookshelves and also for the bar unit with glass shelves and mirrored back, sides, top, and bottom.

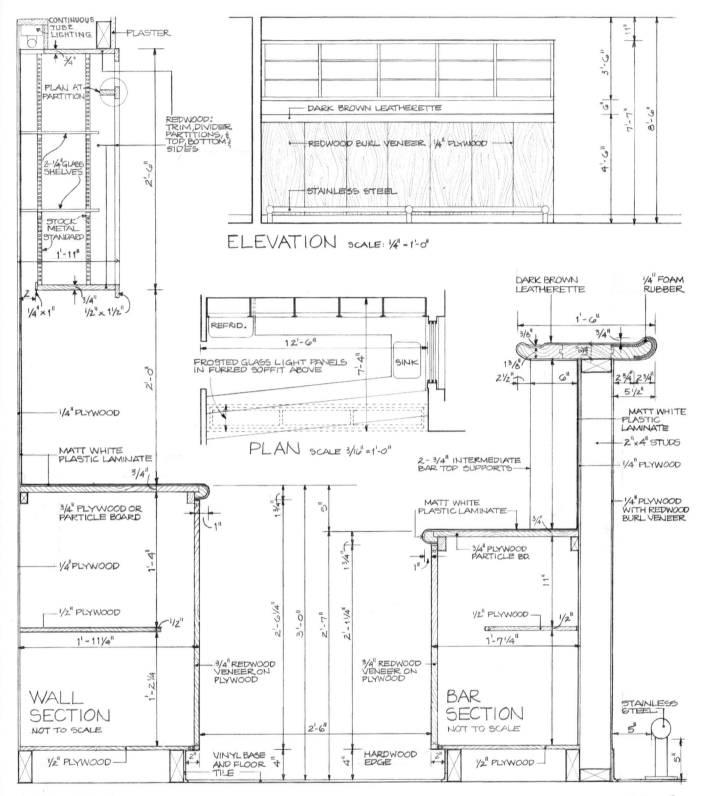

ELEVATION SCALE: 1/4" = 1'-0"

PLAN SCALE 3/16" = 1'-0"

WALL SECTION NOT TO SCALE

BAR SECTION NOT TO SCALE

RESIDENTIAL BAR

This small residential bar with double lighting was designed so that the back bar shelves would display all the types of bar glasses and the liquor bottles as a decorative element. Note how the recessed fluorescent tube fixtures indirectly light up all the glasses and the 2" open slot in the bottom shelf indirectly lights up the liquor bottles on the back bar shelf. The entire front bar has recessed light fixtures in the ceiling above; this allows for two different methods of lighting the bar area. Note also that the bar front is slightly padded with foam rubber and the entire bar top is finished with dark brown leatherette.

14—3

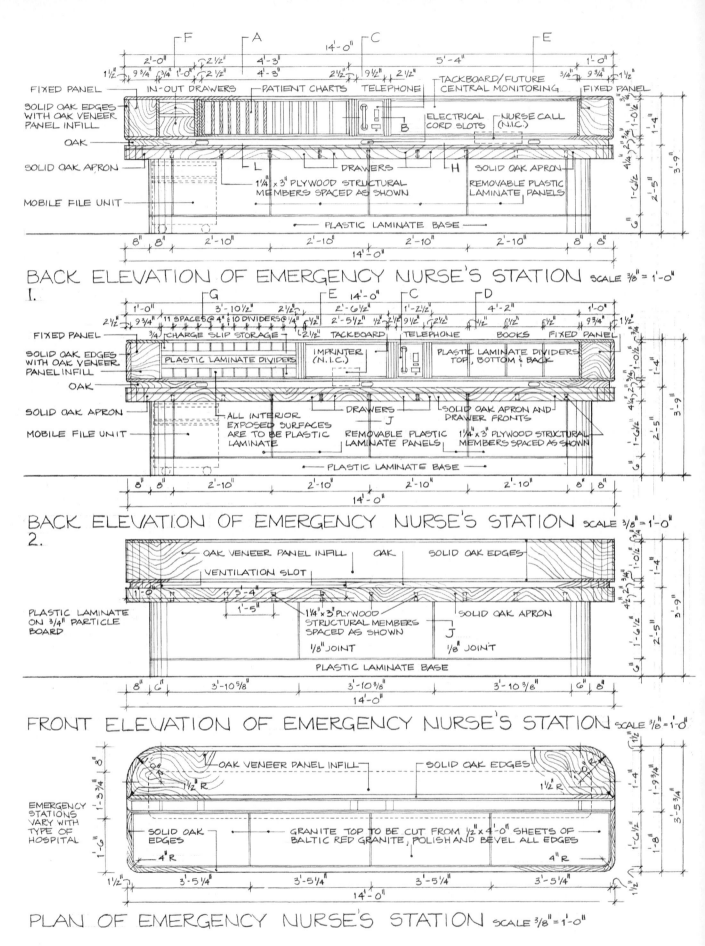

BACK ELEVATION OF EMERGENCY NURSE'S STATION SCALE 3/8" = 1'-0"
1.

BACK ELEVATION OF EMERGENCY NURSE'S STATION SCALE 3/8" = 1'-0"
2.

FRONT ELEVATION OF EMERGENCY NURSE'S STATION SCALE 3/8" = 1'-0"

PLAN OF EMERGENCY NURSE'S STATION SCALE 3/8" = 1'-0"

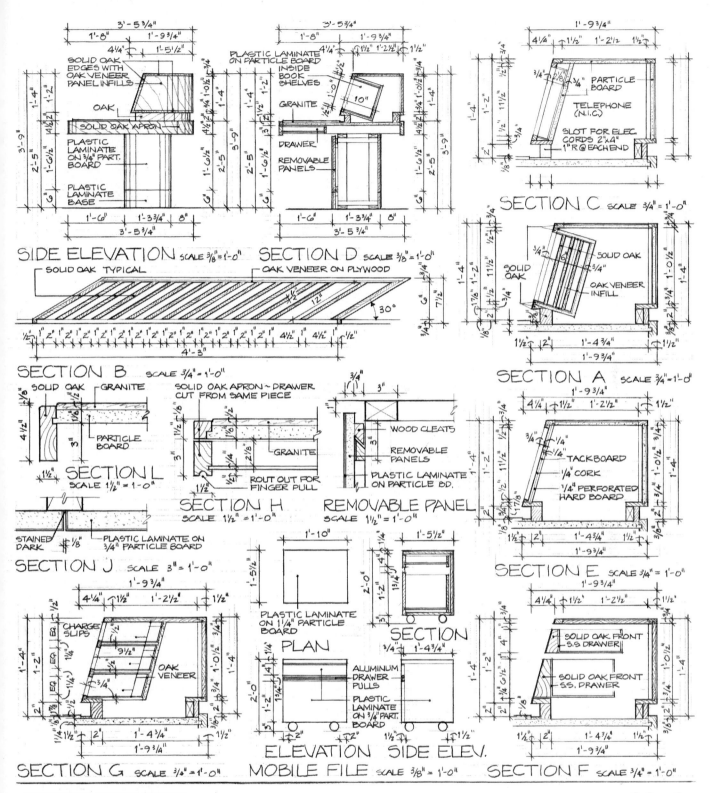

EMERGENCY NURSE'S STATION

These details of Emergency Nurse's Station by Robert D. Lynn Associates, architects and planners, show two variations of an emergency nurse's station. This basic design can be used for various types of nurse's stations just by changing the components which make up the back panel on the nurse's side. Such examples are: inserting a central control, station displays, single and/or multiple drawers, etc., and placing the electrical controls in the base. Thus the basic design can be used for nurse's stations for progressive care, intensive and cardiac care, medical and surgical units, and surgical pulmonary units. In like manner, the basic unit is designed to take care of a video terminal unit. By increasing the width of the supporting base to the face of the apron at each end, a deep drawer with a printer unit can be installed in the end panel. The EKG printer unit is only for cardiac care nurse's stations.

14—4

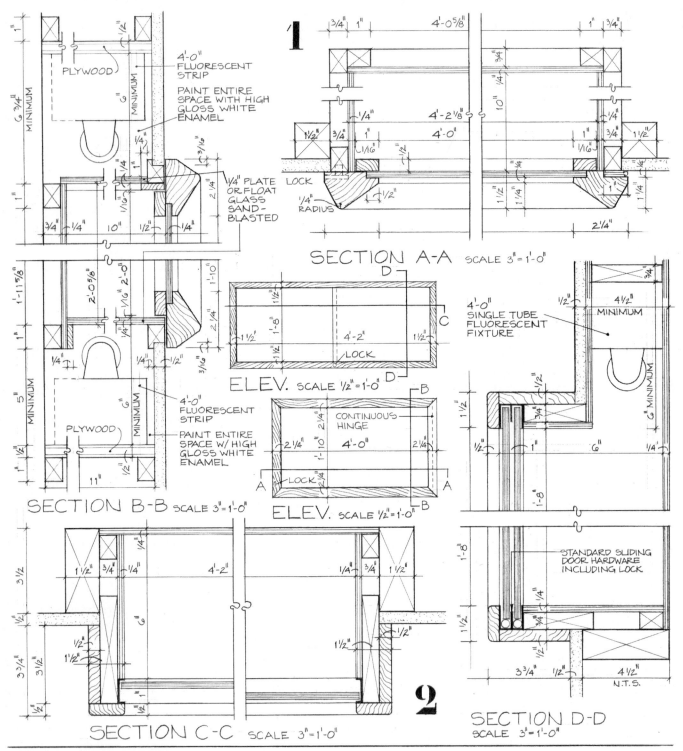

SECTION A-A SCALE 3″=1′-0″

ELEV. SCALE ½″=1′-0″

ELEV. SCALE ½″=1′-0″

SECTION B-B SCALE 3″=1′-0″

SECTION C-C SCALE 3″=1′-0″

SECTION D-D SCALE 3″=1′-0″

N.T.S.

PLYWOOD

4'-0″ FLUORESCENT STRIP

PAINT ENTIRE SPACE WITH HIGH GLOSS WHITE ENAMEL

¼″ PLATE OR FLOAT GLASS SANDBLASTED

LOCK

¼″ RADIUS

4'-0″ SINGLE TUBE FLUORESCENT FIXTURE

CONTINUOUS HINGE

STANDARD SLIDING DOOR HARDWARE INCLUDING LOCK

14—5 **TWO DISPLAY CASES**

These two display cases can be used in any area where an accent is required. The first, a simple display case, uses the trim of the glass door to completely conceal the basic framework of the display case. The installation of 4'-0″ single-tube fluorescent fixtures, located at both top and bottom and concealed by sand-blasted glass, allows for dramatic types of display. The second display case can be used in any existing wood or metal stud wall by simply projecting it 3¾″ or more beyond the existing wall's surface. Here again, a 4'-0″ single-tube fluorescent fixture, sufficiently concealed, is used for down lighting from the top.

The first display case can be electrified with separate switches for each fixture; this would allow for either up or down lighting only. Black light can be used very effectively for special types of displays.

The interiors of either display case can be painted, mirrored or covered with a fabric, synthetic material, or wallpaper, depending on the objects to be displayed and the decorative effect desired.

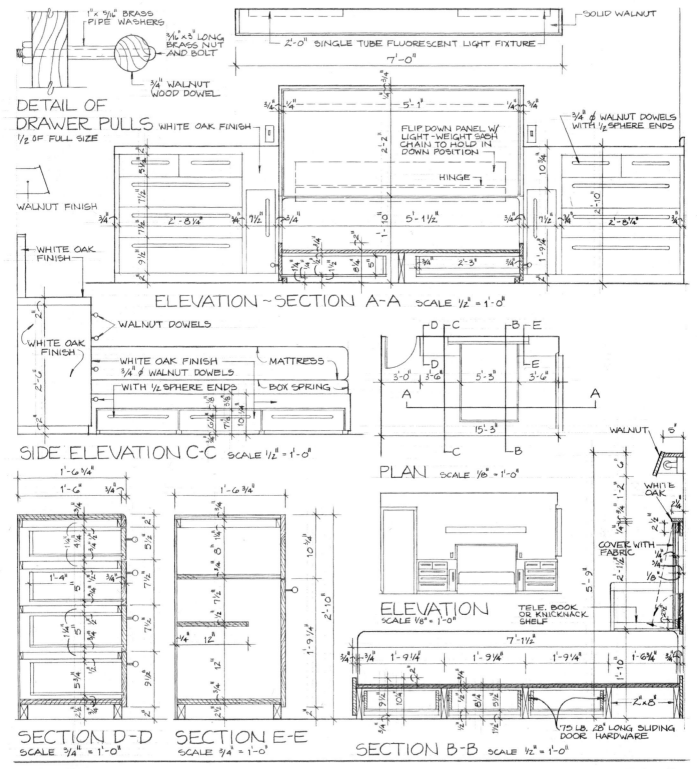

DETAIL OF DRAWER PULLS ½ OF FULL SIZE

1" x 5/16" BRASS PIPE WASHERS
3/16" x 3" LONG BRASS NUT AND BOLT
¾" WALNUT WOOD DOWEL
WHITE OAK FINISH
WALNUT FINISH
WHITE OAK FINISH

SOLID WALNUT
2'-0" SINGLE TUBE FLUORESCENT LIGHT FIXTURE
7'-0"
FLIP DOWN PANEL W/ LIGHT-WEIGHT SASH CHAIN TO HOLD IN DOWN POSITION
HINGE
¾" ∅ WALNUT DOWELS WITH ½ SPHERE ENDS

ELEVATION ~ SECTION A-A SCALE ½" = 1'-0"

WHITE OAK FINISH
WALNUT DOWELS
WHITE OAK FINISH ¾" ∅ WALNUT DOWELS WITH ½ SPHERE ENDS
MATTRESS
BOX SPRING

SIDE ELEVATION C-C SCALE ½" = 1'-0"

PLAN SCALE ⅛" = 1'-0"

WALNUT
WHITE OAK
COVER WITH FABRIC

ELEVATION SCALE ⅛" = 1'-0"

TELE. BOOK OR KNICKNACK SHELF

SECTION D-D SCALE ¾" = 1'-0"

SECTION E-E SCALE ¾" = 1'-0"

SECTION B-B SCALE ½" = 1'-0"

75 LB. 28" LONG SLIDING DOOR HARDWARE

BUILT-IN BED

14—6

The challenge to design a complete built-in bed unit came into the author's office three times in one year. This detail combines all of the important design requirements of such a unit and shows how the problems were solved.

Taking each design problem separately: (1) storage compartments or drawers under the bed; (2) a telephone, book, or knicknack shelf at each side of a double bed; (3) a light with its own switch for each occupant of the bed; (4) a backboard that can be adjusted for reading in bed; and (5) bureau units to supply sufficient drawer space for each. Careful study of the details will show how simply all of these different design problems were answered. Note the use of hardwood dowels for drawer pulls.

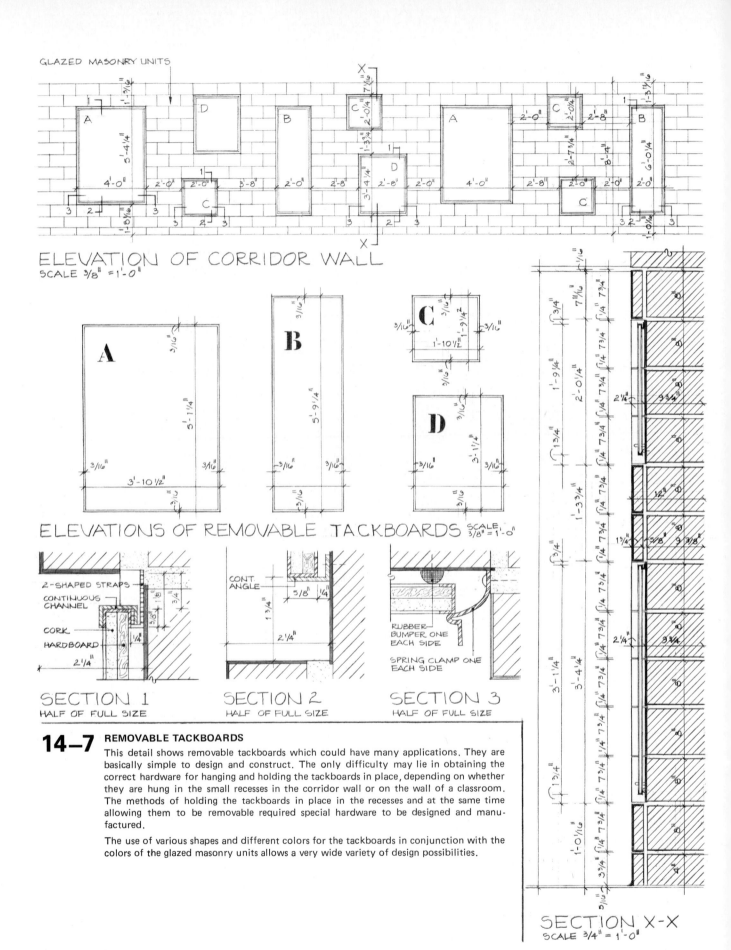

GLAZED MASONRY UNITS

ELEVATION OF CORRIDOR WALL
SCALE 3/8" = 1'-0"

A

B

C

D

ELEVATIONS OF REMOVABLE TACKBOARDS
SCALE 3/8" = 1'-0"

Z-SHAPED STRAPS
CONTINUOUS CHANNEL
CORK
HARDBOARD

CONT. ANGLE

RUBBER BUMPER ONE EACH SIDE
SPRING CLAMP ONE EACH SIDE

SECTION 1
HALF OF FULL SIZE

SECTION 2
HALF OF FULL SIZE

SECTION 3
HALF OF FULL SIZE

14–7 REMOVABLE TACKBOARDS

This detail shows removable tackboards which could have many applications. They are basically simple to design and construct. The only difficulty may lie in obtaining the correct hardware for hanging and holding the tackboards in place, depending on whether they are hung in the small recesses in the corridor wall or on the wall of a classroom. The methods of holding the tackboards in place in the recesses and at the same time allowing them to be removable required special hardware to be designed and manufactured.

The use of various shapes and different colors for the tackboards in conjunction with the colors of the glazed masonry units allows a very wide variety of design possibilities.

SECTION X-X
SCALE 3/4" = 1'-0"

138

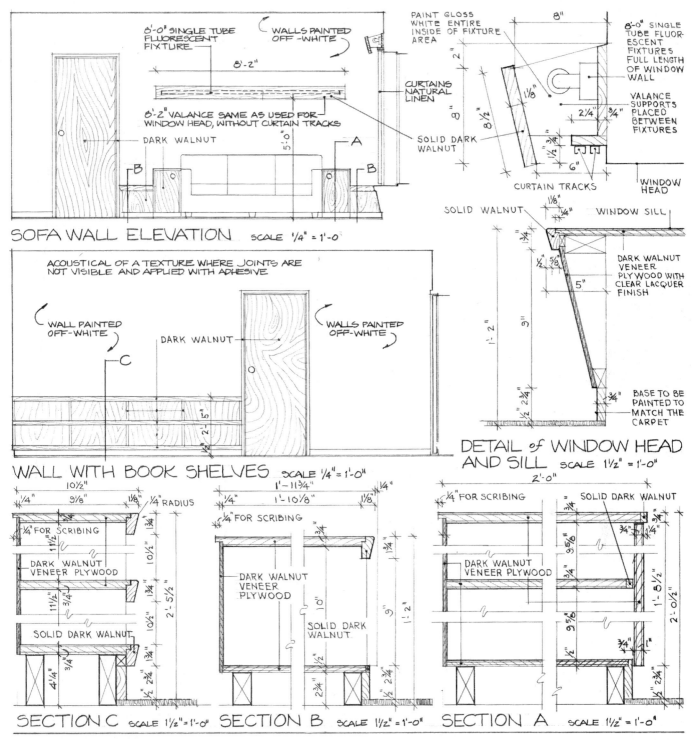

SOFA WALL ELEVATION   SCALE ¼" = 1'-0"

6'-0" SINGLE TUBE FLUORESCENT FIXTURE

WALLS PAINTED OFF-WHITE

8'-2"

8'-2" VALANCE SAME AS USED FOR WINDOW HEAD, WITHOUT CURTAIN TRACKS

DARK WALNUT

5'-0"

A

B

B

PAINT GLOSS WHITE ENTIRE INSIDE OF FIXTURE AREA

8"

8'-0" SINGLE TUBE FLUORESCENT FIXTURES FULL LENGTH OF WINDOW WALL

CURTAINS NATURAL LINEN

VALANCE SUPPORTS PLACED BETWEEN FIXTURES

SOLID DARK WALNUT

2¼"   ¾"

CURTAIN TRACKS

WINDOW HEAD

ACOUSTICAL OF A TEXTURE WHERE JOINTS ARE NOT VISIBLE AND APPLIED WITH ADHESIVE

WALL PAINTED OFF-WHITE

DARK WALNUT

WALLS PAINTED OFF-WHITE

C

WALL WITH BOOK SHELVES   SCALE ¼" = 1'-0"

SOLID WALNUT   1⁄8"   ¼"   WINDOW SILL

DARK WALNUT VENEER PLYWOOD WITH CLEAR LACQUER FINISH

5"

1'-2"   9"

BASE TO BE PAINTED TO MATCH THE CARPET

DETAIL of WINDOW HEAD AND SILL   SCALE 1½" = 1'-0"

10½"
9⅛"   1⁄8"   ¼" RADIUS

¼" FOR SCRIBING

DARK WALNUT VENEER PLYWOOD

11½"   ¾"

SOLID DARK WALNUT

4¼"   ¾"

2-5½"

SECTION C   SCALE 1½" = 1'-0"

1'-11¾"
1'-10⅛"   ¼"   1⁄8"

¼" FOR SCRIBING

¾"

DARK WALNUT VENEER PLYWOOD

SOLID DARK WALNUT

1'-2"   9"

SECTION B   SCALE 1½" = 1'-0"

2'-0"

¼" FOR SCRIBING   SOLID DARK WALNUT

¾"   ¼"

DARK WALNUT VENEER PLYWOOD

9⅝"

1'-8½"   2'-0½"

SECTION A   SCALE 1½" = 1'-0"

BUILT-IN SOFA AND BOOKSHELVES

14—8

This detail shows the simple treatment of a vice-president's office in a rayon and yarn corporation in Mount Vernon, New York. The one wall contains a built-in sofa and shelves and cabinets. The window wall has a valence for continuous indirect lighting and curtain tracks; there is also a continuous window seat. The indirect lighting at the head of the window has a bottom piece of wood which supports the curtain tracks and also blocks off seeing the actual fluorescent tube. The same kind of unit over the sofa has a similar bottom cover piece but a little larger, again to cut off direct view of the fluorescent tube.

The entrance wall has built-in shelves, and the desk, chairs, computer units, and other incidental office furniture are commercial dark walnut units.

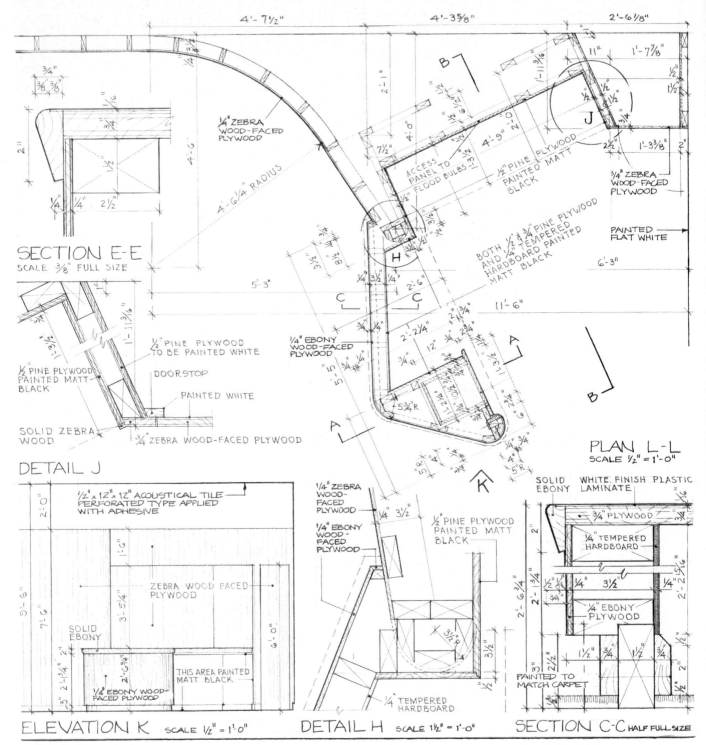

SECTION E-E
SCALE 3/8" FULL SIZE

DETAIL J

ELEVATION K   SCALE 1/2" = 1'-0"

DETAIL H   SCALE 1 1/2" = 1'-0"

SECTION C-C HALF FULL SIZE

PLAN L-L
SCALE 1/2" = 1'-0"

14—9 RECEPTION DESK

These details show a reception desk designed for the first *TV Guide* publishers' main offices in New York City. The detail is updated by adding space for a word processor and printer, as the original had only a telephone switchboard. This design used contrasting woods to create a striking effect. The zebra wood on the floating curved partition leads up to the ebony desk with white matt plastic laminate, which is in front of a white wall. The zebra wood then turns almost at a right angle and envelops the word processor and printer space and continues over the storage closet to stop against the white wall. Note that the 2 1/2" base is painted to match the carpet, and the spaces below the desk top and the word processor and printer space are painted matte black. Section-elevation B-B shows the location of down lights and the shelf where flood bulbs are installed for indirect lighting of the area around the desk.

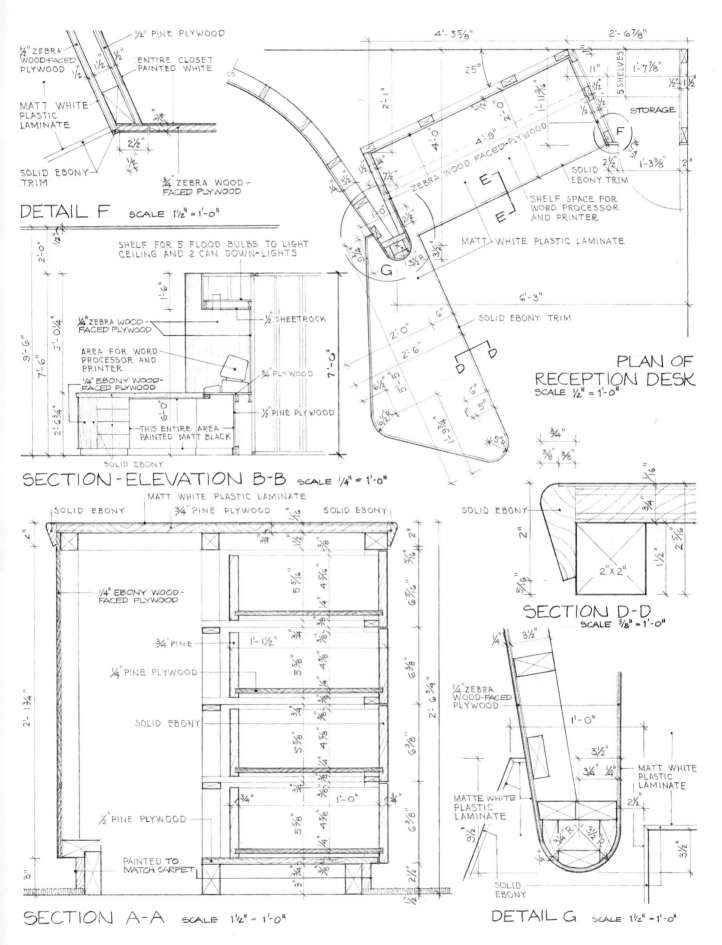

DETAIL F SCALE 1½" = 1'-0"

½" PINE PLYWOOD

½" ZEBRA WOOD-FACED PLYWOOD

ENTIRE CLOSET PAINTED WHITE

MATT WHITE PLASTIC LAMINATE

SOLID EBONY TRIM

¾" ZEBRA WOOD-FACED PLYWOOD

SHELF FOR 5 FLOOD BULBS TO LIGHT CEILING AND 2 CAN DOWN-LIGHTS

¼" ZEBRA WOOD-FACED PLYWOOD

AREA FOR WORD PROCESSOR AND PRINTER

¼" EBONY WOOD-FACED PLYWOOD

½" SHEETROCK

¾" PLYWOOD

½" PINE PLYWOOD

THIS ENTIRE AREA PAINTED MATT BLACK

SOLID EBONY

SECTION-ELEVATION B-B SCALE ¼" = 1'-0"

MATT WHITE PLASTIC LAMINATE

SOLID EBONY

¾" PINE PLYWOOD

SOLID EBONY

¼" EBONY WOOD-FACED PLYWOOD

¾" PINE

¼" PINE PLYWOOD

SOLID EBONY

½" PINE PLYWOOD

PAINTED TO MATCH CARPET

SECTION A-A SCALE 1½" = 1'-0"

STORAGE

5 SHELVES

ZEBRA WOOD FACED-PLYWOOD

SHELF SPACE FOR WORD PROCESSOR AND PRINTER

SOLID EBONY TRIM

MATT WHITE PLASTIC LAMINATE

SOLID EBONY TRIM

PLAN OF RECEPTION DESK
SCALE ½" = 1'-0"

SOLID EBONY

2" X 2"

SECTION D-D
SCALE ⅜" = 1'-0"

¼" ZEBRA WOOD-FACED PLYWOOD

MATT WHITE PLASTIC LAMINATE

MATTE WHITE PLASTIC LAMINATE

SOLID EBONY

DETAIL G SCALE 1½" = 1'-0"

141

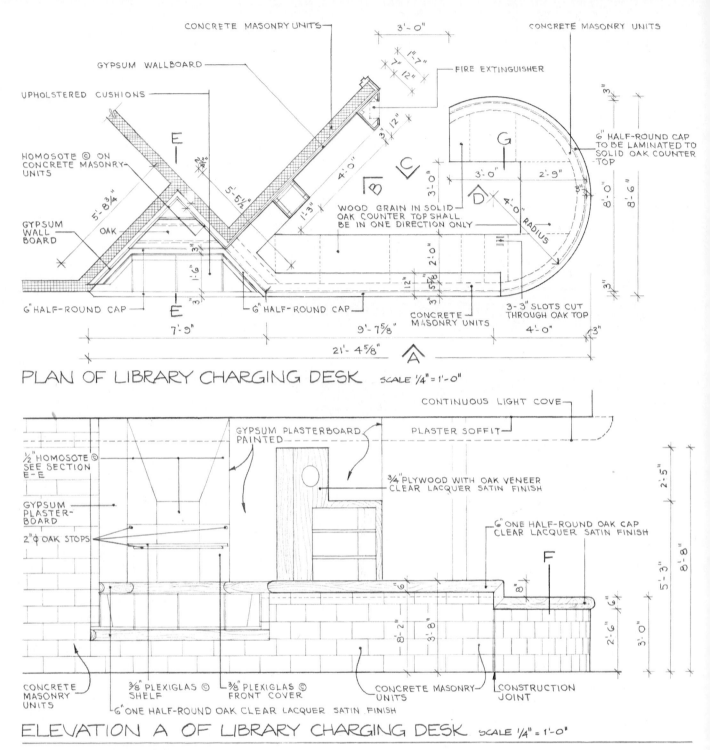

CONCRETE MASONRY UNITS

GYPSUM WALLBOARD

UPHOLSTERED CUSHIONS

3'-0"

1¾"
7" 1'-7"
12"

FIRE EXTINGUISHER

CONCRETE MASONRY UNITS

3"

E

3" 12"

G

C

6" HALF-ROUND CAP TO BE LAMINATED TO SOLID OAK COUNTER TOP

HOMOSOTE © ON CONCRETE MASONRY UNITS

B

4'-0"

3'-0"

D

3'-0"

2'-9"

8'-0"

8'-6"

WOOD GRAIN IN SOLID OAK COUNTER TOP SHALL BE IN ONE DIRECTION ONLY

4'-0" RADIUS

5'-8¾"

5'-5½"

1'-3"

GYPSUM WALL BOARD

OAK

2'-0"

3"

E

6" HALF-ROUND CAP

E

6" HALF-ROUND CAP

CONCRETE MASONRY UNITS

3'-3" SLOTS CUT THROUGH OAK TOP

3"

7'-9"

9'-7⅝"

4'-0"

3"

21'-4⅝"

A

PLAN OF LIBRARY CHARGING DESK   SCALE ¼" = 1'-0"

CONTINUOUS LIGHT COVE

GYPSUM PLASTERBOARD PAINTED

PLASTER SOFFIT

½" HOMOSOTE © SEE SECTION E-E

¾" PLYWOOD WITH OAK VENEER CLEAR LACQUER SATIN FINISH

2'-5"

GYPSUM PLASTERBOARD

6" ONE HALF-ROUND OAK CAP CLEAR LACQUER SATIN FINISH

8'-8"

2"∅ OAK STOPS

F

5'-3"

2'-6"

3'-0"

CONCRETE MASONRY UNITS

3/8" PLEXIGLAS © SHELF

3/8" PLEXIGLAS © FRONT COVER

CONCRETE MASONRY UNITS

CONSTRUCTION JOINT

6" ONE HALF-ROUND OAK CLEAR LACQUER SATIN FINISH

ELEVATION A OF LIBRARY CHARGING DESK   SCALE ¼" = 1'-0"

14—10   LIBRARY CHARGING DESK

The charging desk of the Eastwick Branch Library, Philadelphia, designed by B/JC Knowles, architects/planners, is a very simply designed, elegant unit that incorporates all the special equipment required for a public library charging desk. Adjoining the desk is a small seating area with a display area above it. The concrete masonry units contrasted against the heavy 6" half-round oak cap laminated to the oak desk top, and the oak 8'-8" high bookshleves, storage cabinets, and clock unit combine to produce a balanced, aesthetically satisfying composition. A careful study of all the details of this charging desk unit will show how even the smallest detail has been carefully designed. The Plexiglas® shelves are supported by oak dowels and the removable Plexiglas® front is held in place by the lip of the 6" half-round cap and small 2" round stops.

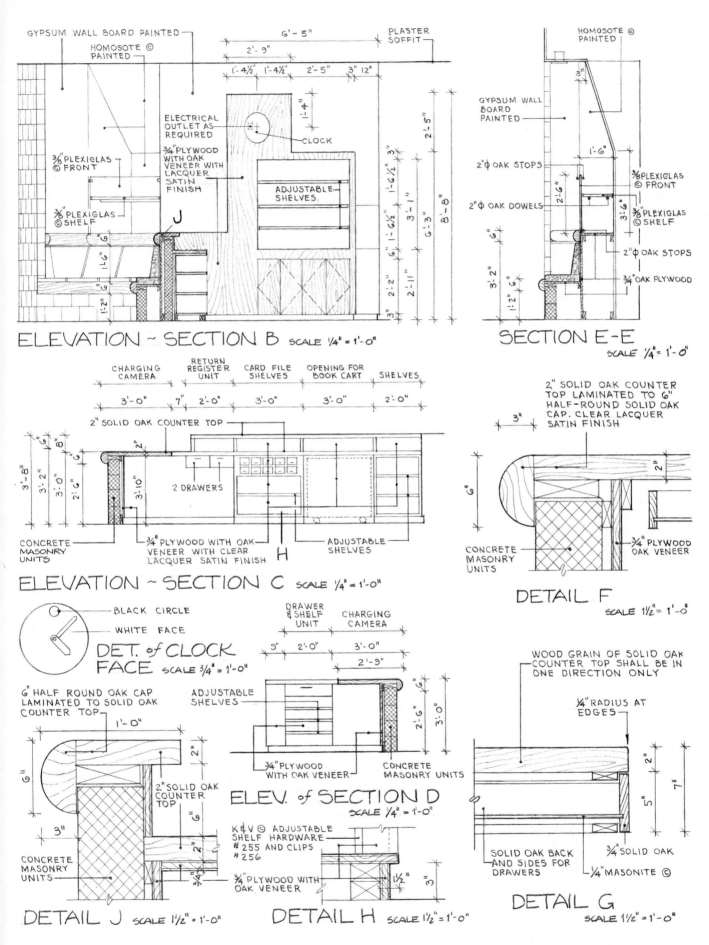

GYPSUM WALL BOARD PAINTED
HOMOSOTE © PAINTED
6'-5"
2'-9"
PLASTER SOFFIT
1'-4½" 1'-4½" 2'-5" 3" 12"
ELECTRICAL OUTLET AS REQUIRED
CLOCK
⅜ PLEXIGLAS © FRONT
¾ PLYWOOD WITH OAK VENEER WITH LACQUER SATIN FINISH
J
ADJUSTABLE SHELVES
⅜ PLEXIGLAS © SHELF

ELEVATION ~ SECTION B SCALE ¼" = 1'-0"

HOMOSOTE © PAINTED
GYPSUM WALL BOARD PAINTED
3"
1'-6"
2" φ OAK STOPS
2" φ OAK DOWELS
⅜ PLEXIGLAS © FRONT
⅜ PLEXIGLAS © SHELF
2" OAK STOPS
¾" OAK PLYWOOD
3'-2"
1'-2" 6"

SECTION E-E
SCALE ¼" = 1'-0"

CHARGING CAMERA
RETURN REGISTER UNIT
CARD FILE SHELVES
OPENING FOR BOOK CART
SHELVES
3'-0"   7" 2'-0"   3'-0"   3'-0"   2'-0"
2" SOLID OAK COUNTER TOP
2"
3'-8" 3'-2" 3'-0" 2'-6"
2 DRAWERS
CONCRETE MASONRY UNITS
¾" PLYWOOD WITH OAK VENEER WITH CLEAR LACQUER SATIN FINISH
H
ADJUSTABLE SHELVES

ELEVATION ~ SECTION C SCALE ¼" = 1'-0"

2" SOLID OAK COUNTER TOP LAMINATED TO 6" HALF-ROUND SOLID OAK CAP. CLEAR LACQUER SATIN FINISH
3"
6"
2"
CONCRETE MASONRY UNITS
¾" PLYWOOD OAK VENEER

DETAIL F
SCALE 1½" = 1'-0"

BLACK CIRCLE
WHITE FACE
DET. of CLOCK FACE SCALE ¾" = 1'-0"

DRAWER & SHELF UNIT
CHARGING CAMERA
3" 2'-0"   3'-0"
2'-9"
ADJUSTABLE SHELVES
2'-6" 3'-0"
¾" PLYWOOD WITH OAK VENEER
CONCRETE MASONRY UNITS

ELEV. of SECTION D
SCALE ¼" = 1'-0"

6" HALF ROUND OAK CAP LAMINATED TO SOLID OAK COUNTER TOP
1'-0"
2"
6"
2" SOLID OAK COUNTER TOP
3"
CONCRETE MASONRY UNITS

DETAIL J SCALE 1½" = 1'-0"

K&V © ADJUSTABLE SHELF HARDWARE #255 AND CLIPS #256
¾" PLYWOOD WITH OAK VENEER
1½"
3"

DETAIL H SCALE 1½" = 1'-0"

WOOD GRAIN OF SOLID OAK COUNTER TOP SHALL BE IN ONE DIRECTION ONLY
¼" RADIUS AT EDGES
2"
5"
7"
SOLID OAK BACK AND SIDES FOR DRAWERS
¾" SOLID OAK
¼" MASONITE ©

DETAIL G
SCALE 1½" = 1'-0"

CROSS-REFERENCES TO *BUILT-INS AND FURNITURE*
IN OTHER CHAPTERS

Chapter Number	Drawing Number	Drawing Title	Described on Page	Drawing on Page
5	5–3	Interior joints for quarter-inch plywood	35	38
	5–4	Cabinet and millwork joints for plywood and solid wood	35	39
15	15–1	Interior planters for residences	147	149
	15–2	Interior planters for buildings	147	150
16	16–2	Kitchen	155	158, 159
	16–3	Bathroom with dressing room	155	160, 161

15

Planters

INTRODUCTION

With the reappearance of the atrium as an important design element in to-day's buildings and with all the planting that must be installed to achieve the desired effect, it is surprising that a wide gamut of articles and books about design and details for planters has not flooded the professional literature.

Planters can vary from a plain shallow pan with simple drainage, filled with gravel at the bottom and pea gravel at the top, in which plants in pots are set in the gravel, to an atrium, where large trees, bushes, shrubs, and even ground cover are installed permanently and require professional maintenance.

The problem of having living plants within or on terraces of buildings, be they only petunias, also can be complex or simple. Is the planting to be permanent (trees and shrubs) or interchangeable? What kind of plant, tree, or shrub with a minimum of sun? What happens when there is air conditioning? How much soil will all the planting require?, and so on. These problems can be answered only by landscape architects and/or plant experts of the firms that supply and maintain the planting material.

The architect faces detailing problems of size and depth of the planting area; if on the interior, what kind of waterproofing is necessary, and how to take care of excess water. On the exterior the same problems exist, but the water problem can cause trouble due to freezing if the planter is not well drained. If special plant-growing lights (bulbs, tubes) are used, they must be taken into consideration and incorporated into the overall design of the planting area and be included in the electrical circuitry.

CHAPTER DETAIL TEXT

15-1 Interior Planters for Residences

DETAIL 1.   This window planter is from the O'Brig residence in Greenwich, Connecticut. Two low planters are located one at each side of a built-in window seat. The planters hold earth (planting medium) so that the plants can be installed and allowed to blossom and continue to grow until a complete renewal is needed or desired.

DETAIL 2.   This is a simple floor planter in which the plants are also semi-permanently installed to grow and blossom. Redwood or cedar chips are placed on top of the earth to a depth that will stop the growth of weeds.

DETAIL 3.   This room divider detail in the Ackermann residence in Southampton, New York, was developed to separate an open entrance stairway from the living room. The method of pitching the entire galvanized steel pan toward one end and thereby catching any excess water in a small container within the unit answered the problem of drainage.

15-2 Interior Planters for Buildings

DETAIL 1.   An interior planter 16'-0" long, in the Politan residence, Riverdale, New York, was located on the south wall of the entrance hall. The fixed insulating glass above the planter was divided into a series of shelves on which Mrs. Politan displayed fine antique crystal, which contrasted well with the various greens, leaf shapes, and flowers of the plants.

DETAIL 2.   This detail is of a planter for a mild climate. It shows the answer to excess water and allows the plants to be permanently installed in the planter. The copper pan in this detail completely answers the requirements of a planter, namely, a waterproof container to hold the topsoil, gravel, enough depth for root development, and drainage.

DETAIL 3.   This is a planter for a store or restaurant, where plants live and grow within the planter more or less permanently. In this type of planter the elimination of excess water and the disposal of the odds and ends dropped into the planter are important.

DETAIL 4.   Detail of a floor planter that has the same problems as any other planter, such as the removal of excess water and the use of a topping to give a color base to the plants, but is adapted to use in a business setting.

15-3 Exterior Planters

DETAIL 1.   This is a simple type of planter for terraces, garage roofs, and roof terraces. All excess water and possible leakage are taken care of by fill, which raises the bottom of the planter above terrace level, and simple tubes take care of drainage from the planter.

DETAIL 2.   Any exterior planter for a terrace, patio, court, etc., is simply answered in this detail. The only difficulty that can arise is in very cold climates, where freezing can occur. In this case planter walls have to be continued down below frost level.

DETAIL 3.   This detail of a square wood planter shows a method of construction wherein the planter is good for at least 15 years. Any planter of this type must be evaluated from the viewpoint of the type of planting material, bush, or tree and its life expectancy before it must be replaced.

DETAIL 4.   An example of a planter on the exterior of a building which is part of the structure. The use of sloping fill answers the drainage problems, and a good waterproof membrane will keep the water from seeping or otherwise getting into the building.

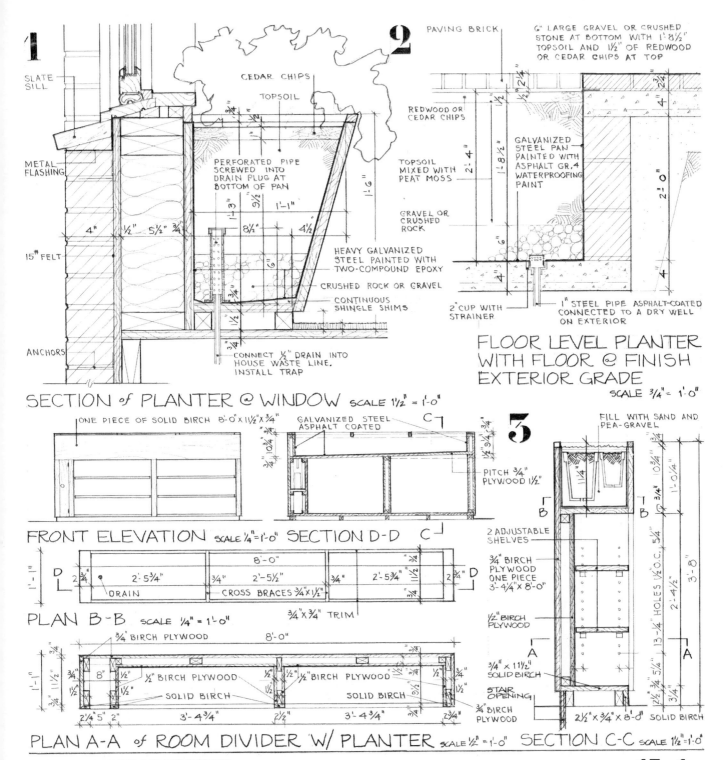

1

SLATE
SILL

METAL
FLASHING

15" FELT

ANCHORS

CEDAR CHIPS

TOPSOIL

PERFORATED PIPE
SCREWED INTO
DRAIN PLUG AT
BOTTOM OF PAN

4" ½" 5½" ¾"

8½" 4½"

HEAVY GALVANIZED
STEEL PAINTED WITH
TWO-COMPOUND EPOXY

CRUSHED ROCK OR GRAVEL

CONTINUOUS
SHINGLE SHIMS

CONNECT ½" DRAIN INTO
HOUSE WASTE LINE.
INSTALL TRAP

SECTION of PLANTER @ WINDOW SCALE 1½" = 1'-0"

2

PAVING BRICK

6" LARGE GRAVEL OR CRUSHED
STONE AT BOTTOM WITH 1'-8½"
TOPSOIL AND 1½" OF REDWOOD
OR CEDAR CHIPS AT TOP

REDWOOD OR
CEDAR CHIPS

TOPSOIL
MIXED WITH
PEAT MOSS

GRAVEL OR
CRUSHED
ROCK

GALVANIZED
STEEL PAN
PAINTED WITH
ASPHALT GR.4
WATERPROOFING
PAINT

2'-0"

2" CUP WITH
STRAINER

1" STEEL PIPE ASPHALT-COATED
CONNECTED TO A DRY WELL
ON EXTERIOR

FLOOR LEVEL PLANTER
WITH FLOOR @ FINISH
EXTERIOR GRADE
SCALE ¾" = 1'-0"

ONE PIECE OF SOLID BIRCH 8'-0" X 1½" X ¾"

GALVANIZED STEEL
ASPHALT COATED

FRONT ELEVATION SCALE ¼"=1'-0"   SECTION D-D

PITCH ¾"
PLYWOOD 1½"

3

FILL WITH SAND AND
PEA-GRAVEL

2 ADJUSTABLE
SHELVES

¾" BIRCH
PLYWOOD
ONE PIECE
3'-4¼" X 8'-0"

½" BIRCH
PLYWOOD

¾" X 11½"
SOLID BIRCH

STAIR
OPENING

¾" BIRCH
PLYWOOD

3'-8"

13 - ¼ HOLES ½" O.C.

2½" X ¾" X 8'-0" SOLID BIRCH

SECTION C-C SCALE 1½"=1'-0"

PLAN B-B SCALE ¼" = 1'-0"

8'-0"

2'-5¾" ¾" 2'-5½" ¾" 2'-5¾"

DRAIN   CROSS BRACES ¾"X1½"

¾" X ¾" TRIM

PLAN A-A of ROOM DIVIDER W/ PLANTER SCALE ½" = 1'-0"

¾" BIRCH PLYWOOD   8'-0"

8"   ½" BIRCH PLYWOOD   ½" BIRCH PLYWOOD

SOLID BIRCH   SOLID BIRCH

2¼" 5" 2"   3'- 4¾"   2½"   3'- 4¾"   2¾"

INTERIOR PLANTERS FOR RESIDENCES

15–1

DETAIL 1: In this window planter, the plants are placed directly in the earth or growing medium filling the planter and continue to grow and blossom there. The entire planter is contained within a galvanized steel pan with drain. The 6" high perforated pipe allows for drainage of excess water over a long period of time before the entire planter has to be cleaned out and started anew.

DETAIL 2: This is a simple floor-level planter where the drainage can easily be connected to the building's drainage system. Here also, plants are installed and grow naturally until a complete planting change is required.

DETAIL 3: A room divider planter for the Ackermann residence, Southampton, New York, consists of a planter-bookcase combination. Here the plants remain in their clay pots and are inserted in the planter with or without gravel or some other type of filler. The entire planter is pitched toward one end, where the drain empties into a small container which catches any extra water.

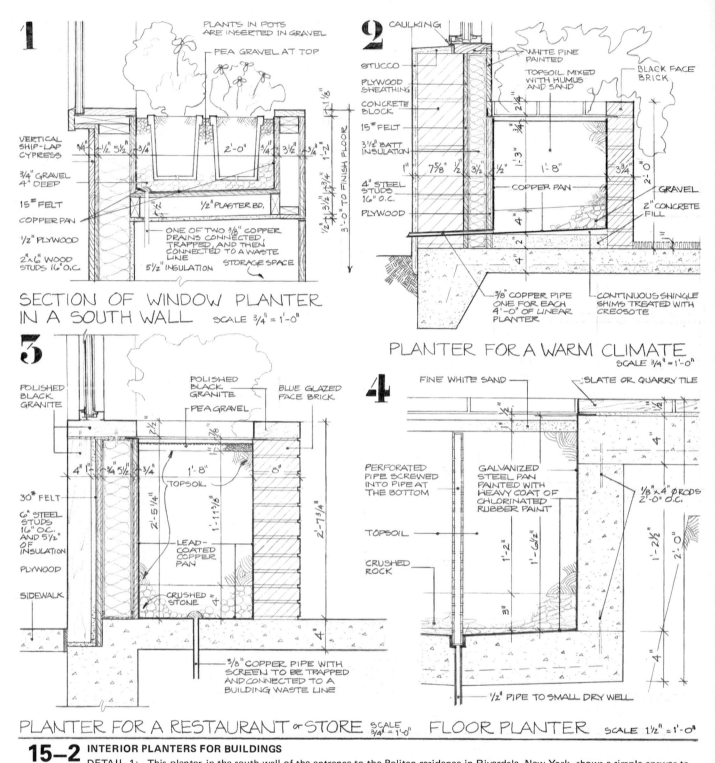

1

PLANTS IN POTS ARE INSERTED IN GRAVEL

PEA GRAVEL AT TOP

VERTICAL SHIP-LAP CYPRESS

3/4" GRAVEL 4" DEEP

15# FELT

COPPER PAN

1/2" PLYWOOD

2"×6" WOOD STUDS 16" O.C.

1/2" PLASTER BD.

ONE OF TWO 3/8" COPPER DRAINS CONNECTED, TRAPPED, AND THEN CONNECTED TO A WASTE LINE

STORAGE SPACE

5 1/2" INSULATION

3'-0" TO FINISH FLOOR

SECTION OF WINDOW PLANTER IN A SOUTH WALL SCALE 3/4" = 1'-0"

2

CAULKING

STUCCO

PLYWOOD SHEATHING

CONCRETE BLOCK

15# FELT

3 1/2" BATT INSULATION

4" STEEL STUDS 16" O.C.

PLYWOOD

WHITE PINE PAINTED

TOPSOIL MIXED WITH HUMUS AND SAND

BLACK FACE BRICK

COPPER PAN

GRAVEL

2" CONCRETE FILL

3/8" COPPER PIPE ONE FOR EACH 4'-0" OF LINEAR PLANTER

CONTINUOUS SHINGLE SHIMS TREATED WITH CREOSOTE

PLANTER FOR A WARM CLIMATE SCALE 3/4" = 1'-0"

3

POLISHED BLACK GRANITE

POLISHED BLACK GRANITE

PEA GRAVEL

BLUE GLAZED FACE BRICK

30# FELT

6" STEEL STUDS 16" O.C. AND 5 1/2" OF INSULATION

PLYWOOD

SIDEWALK

TOPSOIL

LEAD-COATED COPPER PAN

CRUSHED STONE

3/8" COPPER PIPE WITH SCREEN TO BE TRAPPED AND CONNECTED TO A BUILDING WASTE LINE

PLANTER FOR A RESTAURANT or STORE SCALE 3/4" = 1'-0"

4

FINE WHITE SAND

SLATE OR QUARRY TILE

PERFORATED PIPE SCREWED INTO PIPE AT THE BOTTOM

TOPSOIL

CRUSHED ROCK

GALVANIZED STEEL PAN PAINTED WITH HEAVY COAT OF CHLORINATED RUBBER PAINT

1/8"×4" ∅ RODS 2'-0" O.C.

1/2" PIPE TO SMALL DRY WELL

FLOOR PLANTER SCALE 1 1/2" = 1'-0"

15—2 INTERIOR PLANTERS FOR BUILDINGS

DETAIL 1:   This planter in the south wall of the entrance to the Politan residence in Riverdale, New York, shows a simple answer to an interior planter in which the plants remain in their own clay pots. The use of pea gravel at top and only 4" of 3/4" gravel at the bottom permits easy changes of the potted plants. To take care of watering and drainage, the copper pan is simply sloped to one side and two screened drains are connected, trapped, and joined to a waste line. That takes care of any excess water, as it is eliminated by gravity drainage.

DETAIL 2:   This planter is for areas where freezing does not occur, and the drainage of excess water can simply be taken care of by extending small pipes directly to the exterior.

DETAIL 3:   In this planter the plants remain within the planter and excess water is carried off by a screened pipe at the bottom. Pea gravel is used as 1" topping so that odds and ends dropped into the planter can easily be removed.

DETAIL 4:   A planter in a commercial lobby or entrance is shown in this detail. The plants are permanently installed and the tall drainage pipe takes care of any top-applied water. The white sand at the top is to bring contrast to the colors of the plants.

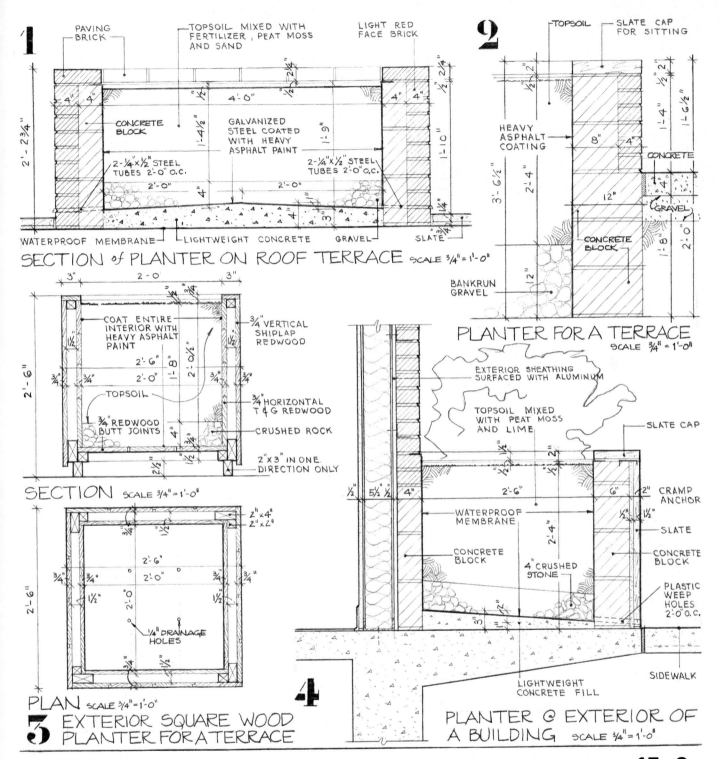

1

PAVING BRICK

TOPSOIL MIXED WITH FERTILIZER, PEAT MOSS AND SAND

LIGHT RED FACE BRICK

2'-2¾"

4" 4"

CONCRETE BLOCK

4'-0"

½ 2¾

1'-4½"

GALVANIZED STEEL COATED WITH HEAVY ASPHALT PAINT

1'-9"

2-¼"x½" STEEL TUBES 2'-0" O.C.

2-¼"x½" STEEL TUBES 2'-0" O.C.

2'-0"

4"

2'-0"

4" 4"

2¾

½

1'-10"

¼

WATERPROOF MEMBRANE

LIGHTWEIGHT CONCRETE

GRAVEL

SLATE

¾

SECTION of PLANTER ON ROOF TERRACE SCALE ¾" = 1'-0"

2

TOPSOIL

SLATE CAP FOR SITTING

½ 2

1'-4"

1'-6½"

HEAVY ASPHALT COATING

8"

4"

CONCRETE

3'-6½"

2'-4"

12"

GRAVEL

CONCRETE BLOCK

1'-8"

2'-0"

12"

BANKRUN GRAVEL

PLANTER FOR A TERRACE SCALE ¾" = 1'-0"

3

3"

2-0

3"

½ 2¾

COAT ENTIRE INTERIOR WITH HEAVY ASPHALT PAINT

¾ VERTICAL SHIPLAP REDWOOD

½

½

2'-6"

2'-0"

8"

2'-0½"

¾

¾ ¾

2'-6"

¾ HORIZONTAL T & G REDWOOD

TOPSOIL

¾ REDWOOD BUTT JOINTS

4"

CRUSHED ROCK

½

2½

2"x3" IN ONE DIRECTION ONLY

SECTION SCALE ¾" = 1'-0"

2"x4"
2"x2"

¾

½

2'-6"

2'-0"

2'-6"

¾ ¾ ¾

1½

2'-0"

1½

¼" DRAINAGE HOLES

¾

½

PLAN SCALE ¾" = 1'-0"

EXTERIOR SQUARE WOOD PLANTER FOR A TERRACE

4

EXTERIOR SHEATHING SURFACED WITH ALUMINUM

TOPSOIL MIXED WITH PEAT MOSS AND LIME

SLATE CAP

½

2"

½ 5½ ½

4"

2'-6"

6"

2"

CRAMP ANCHOR

½

1½

WATERPROOF MEMBRANE

2'-4"

SLATE

CONCRETE BLOCK

4" CRUSHED STONE

CONCRETE BLOCK

PLASTIC WEEP HOLES 2'-0" O.C.

LIGHTWEIGHT CONCRETE FILL

SIDEWALK

PLANTER @ EXTERIOR OF A BUILDING SCALE ¾" = 1'-0"

EXTERIOR PLANTERS

15–3

DETAIL 1: Shown here is a method of installing a planter on roof or terrace so that drainage from the planter of excess water is taken care of. In this planter almost any kind of planting is possible except large trees.

DETAIL 2: The planter enclosure of this exterior terrace planter acts as a seating area. In this type of planter, only the types of plants or trees control the depth of the planter.

DETAIL 3: A simple wood planter for terraces, roofs, patios, etc., is shown in this detail. The construction is simple and can be adapted to any shape of planter not exceeding 4'-0" in any direction.

DETAIL 4: This planter is integrated with the building structure and the use of sloped fill can drain it simply through weepholes.

CROSS-REFERENCES TO *PLANTERS*
IN OTHER CHAPTERS

Chapter Number	Drawing Number	Drawing Title	Described on Page	Described on Page
5	5-2	Exterior internal and external corners for plywood	35	37
	5-3	Interior joints for quarter-inch plywood	35	38
	5-4	Cabinet and millwork joints for plywood and solid wood	35	39

16

Kitchens and Bathrooms

INTRODUCTION

The design concepts for kitchens have shifted for three major reasons. One is the changes in the preparation and storage of food. Another is the appearance, in a constant stream, of new mechanical worksavers. Finally, in many homes the kitchen and laundry are combined in one area or in immediate proximity to each other.

With the introduction of canned, frozen, dehydrated, and semiprepared foods, cooking need no longer be a time-consuming process that requires large areas of space. Fewer pieces of actual kitchen equipment are needed. The old-fashioned pantry which contained cabinets and storage space for liquor, china, glassware, silverware, and trays plus a sink for dishwashing and countertops for the preparation of salads, desserts, cheeses, coffee and tea, served by servants to the dining room, is seldom built today. In many instances it can be condensed into a closet area. Food in quantity is kept in a refrigerator-freezer and often also in a separate freezer. The dishwasher can for practical purposes eliminate the large double sink, and the garbage disposal unit can eliminate disposal of all waste except cans, plastic, and glass containers, newspapers, cardboard, plastic wrap, and the like. Thus many of the complications of preparing food and disposing of waste products can be reduced to almost their ultimate simplicity, except for the gourmet cook.

Stoves have mechanical controls, timing devices, and heat controls and are completely insulated; some are self-cleaning. With the separation of the parts of the stove into stove top burners, separate ovens and separate broiler units with complete controls, and now microwave ovens in a variety of models and functions, kitchens can be planned with complete freedom and flexibility. Cooking odors and excess heat are practically eliminated by fans, filters, and special electric bulbs.

Bathrooms, except in luxurious residences, hotels, and apartments, have become practically a prefabricated unit. Complete prefabricated bathroom units are in common use for less extravagant, more cost-conscious homes, apartments, hotels, and motels. The use of plastics not only as wall materials but also for countertop-sink units, lavatories, bathtubs, complete bathtub wall units, stall showers, and toilets has greatly simplified the designing of bathrooms.

Now one can even obtain prefabricated ceramic tile walls for tub enclosures and stall showers which consist of individual ceramic tile units pasted together with high-strength adhesives that hold the tiles together into a rigid sheet that needs only to be applied to the rough wall with adhesives. Therefore, the actual architectural design of a bathroom generally consists of assembling the prefabricated units.

The only real creative design left in bathrooms is in residential and alteration work, in which there is direct correlation between interesting design and a generous budget. Whenever cost is not a limiting factor, there is such a wide selection of materials, colors, shapes, and types of fixtures, including saunas, steam cabinets, hot tubs, and Jacuzzis®, that there is no limit to creativity in design and detailing.

CHAPTER DETAIL TEXT

16-1 Bathroom Accessories This illustration shows typical locations for all of the numerous bathroom accessories generally required in residential and public bathrooms.

There are also many specialized bathroom accessories for particular building types. Among them are the various combinations of towel dispenser and waste receptacle, the various kinds of soap dispensers (liquid, powder, or flake), and the various types and locations of grab bars and rails used not only in hospitals but also for the handicapped in public buildings.

The different medicine cabinets and mirrors shown include only the more commonly available types and sizes. The basic dimensions that show locations of the accessories can be adapted for almost any bathroom accessory. Depending on the client and the architect, the design of a particular bathroom will govern where each accessory is placed.

16-2 Kitchen An architect's true design strength is brought forth when he or she is faced with how to provide the maximum in a fixed limited space. Architect David Hodges Karp dealt with this problem when he did the alterations for Dr. and Mrs. Steven H. Hammerman, installing a new kitchen in their residence in Philadelphia. The two pages of illustrations show plan, elevations, and sections of the new kitchen. While many of the details have been faced and answered before, here the placement of the countertop gas range as the pivotal unit was done in such a way that, with fold-down sides, a complete working kitchen was created. It made it possible to serve the dining room through a sliding door or the breakfast area, and still have sufficient space for the cook to prepare a meal of any size or number of courses. Once the cooking preparations are completed, the folding sides are raised, and complete movement within the kitchen becomes possible.

16-3 Bathroom with Dressing Room These details are from a major alteration of a very large residence in Garden City, New York, for a sophisticated couple engaged in the high-fashion world. As owners of two exclusive boutiques for tall women, they entertain extensively and use the house as a setting for themselves and the fashion world they are part of.

The bathroom-dressing room shown in the details requires close study to appreciate all the small nuances that this type of design requires. Some examples: the tile niches in the bathtub wall to hold all the various bottles, canisters, flasks, etc., for bathing and beauty care. The installation of a magazine rack in the toilet alcove with its own recessed down light.

Because the existing house had its old steam boiler replaced and the entire system renovated, it was necessary to use radiators for heating. In the bathroom the radiator was recessed and a grille was installed in the bottom of the towel storage cabinet so that in winter all the towels are kept warm.

The entire area was color coordinated to enhance the wife's coloration; white, various tones of gray, and accents of soft orange were used throughout.

16-4 Bathroom Window

This detail shows a single unit which allows a lavatory or a counter lavatory unit to be located on the window wall of a bathroom. It lets in natural light from three sides of the mirror of a medicine cabinet and night lighting on the two sides of the mirror. This unit can be designed to use stock wood or aluminum windows; only the exterior trim will have to be changed.

An important detail to consider is how to take care of the vent pipe for the lavatory. All that is necessary is to install the lavatory trap low enough and to the side so that the vent pipe comes up vertically behind the fluorescent fixture.

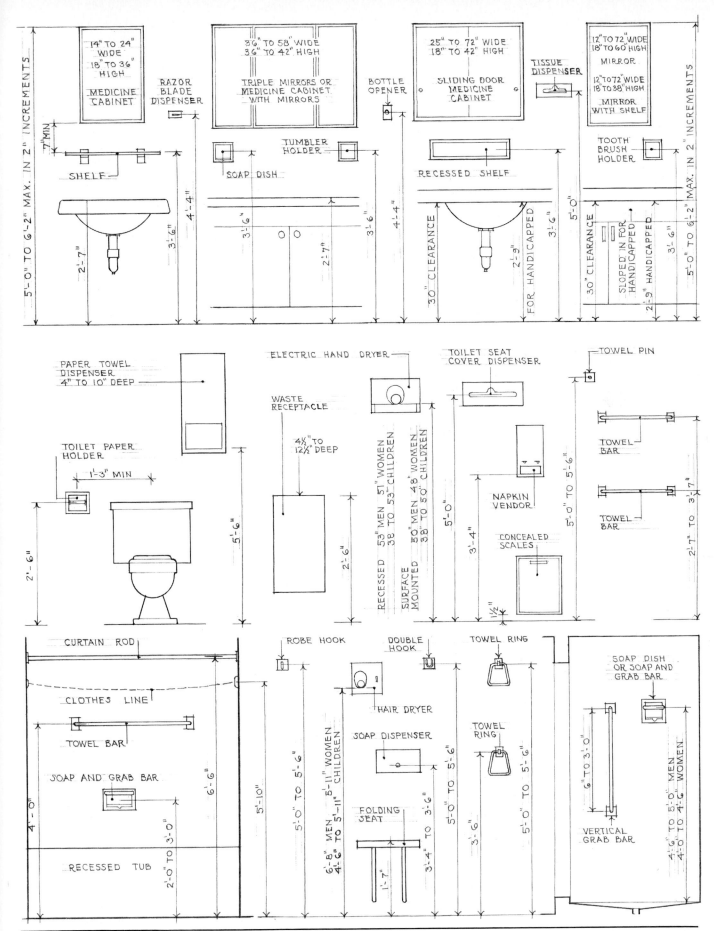

BATHROOM ACCESSORIES

16–1

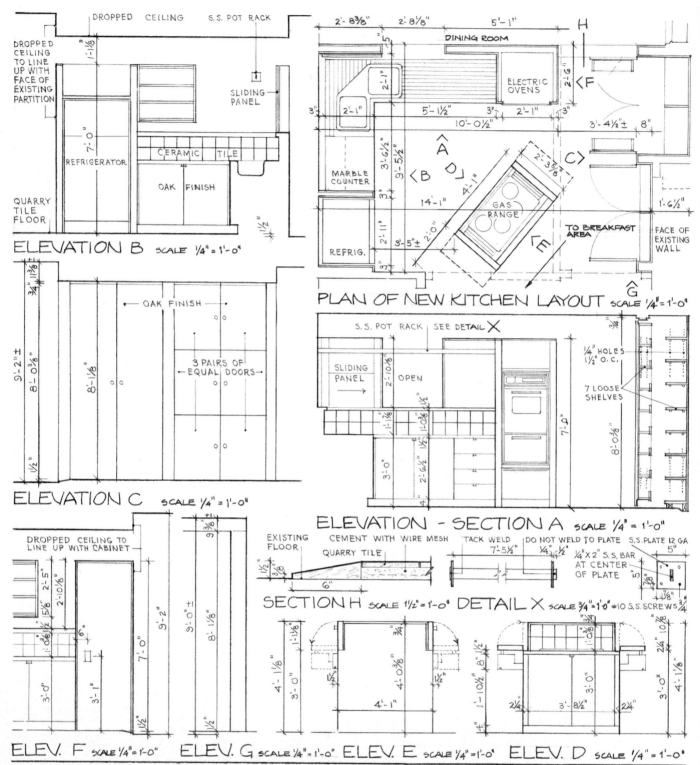

ELEVATION B   SCALE ¼" = 1'-0"

ELEVATION C   SCALE ¼" = 1'-0"

PLAN OF NEW KITCHEN LAYOUT   SCALE ¼" = 1'-0"

ELEVATION - SECTION A   SCALE ¼" = 1'-0"

SECTION H   SCALE 1½" = 1'-0"   DETAIL X   SCALE ¾" = 1'-0"

ELEV. F   SCALE ¼" = 1'-0"   ELEV. G   SCALE ¼" = 1'-0"   ELEV. E   SCALE ¼" = 1'-0"   ELEV. D   SCALE ¼" = 1'-0"

16–2   KITCHEN

These details show how by using ingenuity and creativity, a very small space can become a complete efficient working kitchen. This alteration for Dr. and Mrs. Steven H. Hammerman of Philadelphia by David Hodges Karp, architect, shows how this was accomplished. The key was the use of the countertop gas range unit as the method of creating a highly efficient cooking space but at the same time leaving the entire kitchen with an open aspect. The use of fold-down work areas at each end of the range unit allows for a compact cooking area, and when extra work areas are folded up, freedom of movement within the kitchen is accomplished. Note storage closets and the sliding door for formal service to the dining room. Also note that the range unit does not interrupt passage through the kitchen to the dining room.

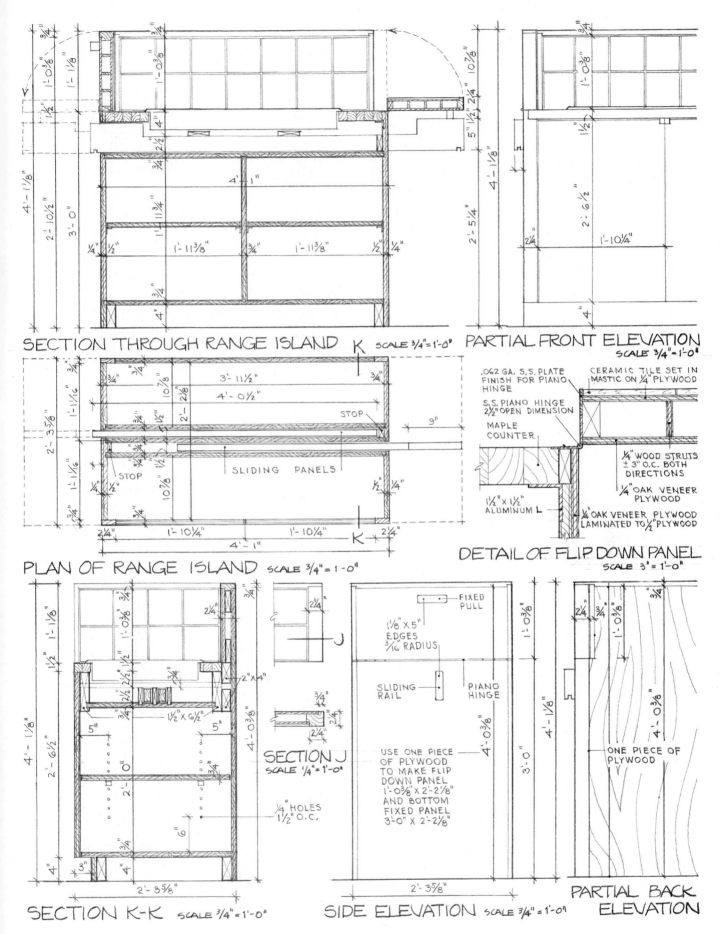

SECTION THROUGH RANGE ISLAND K SCALE 3/4"=1'-0"

4'-1"
1'-11⅜"
1'-11⅜"

PARTIAL FRONT ELEVATION SCALE 3/4"=1'-0"

2'-6½"
1'-10¼"

PLAN OF RANGE ISLAND SCALE 3/4"=1'-0"

3'-11½"
4'-0½"
STOP
9"
STOP
SLIDING PANELS
2'-3⅝"
1-10¼"
1-10¼"
4'-1"

DETAIL OF FLIP DOWN PANEL SCALE 3"=1'-0"

.062 GA. S.S. PLATE FINISH FOR PIANO HINGE
CERAMIC TILE SET IN MASTIC ON ¼" PLYWOOD
S.S. PIANO HINGE 2½" OPEN DIMENSION
MAPLE COUNTER
¼" WOOD STRUTS ± 3" O.C. BOTH DIRECTIONS
¼" OAK VENEER PLYWOOD
1½" X 1½" ALUMINUM L
¼" OAK VENEER PLYWOOD LAMINATED TO ½" PLYWOOD

SECTION K-K SCALE 3/4"=1'-0"

1½" X 6½"
5"
5"
2"X4"
¼" HOLES 1½" O.C.
2'-3⅝"

SECTION J SCALE ¼"=1'-0"

SIDE ELEVATION SCALE 3/4"=1'-0"

FIXED PULL
1⅛" X 5" EDGES 3/16" RADIUS
SLIDING RAIL
PIANO HINGE
USE ONE PIECE OF PLYWOOD TO MAKE FLIP DOWN PANEL 1'-0⅜" X 2'-2⅛" AND BOTTOM FIXED PANEL 3'-0" X 2'-2⅛"
2'-3⅝"

PARTIAL BACK ELEVATION

ONE PIECE OF PLYWOOD

159

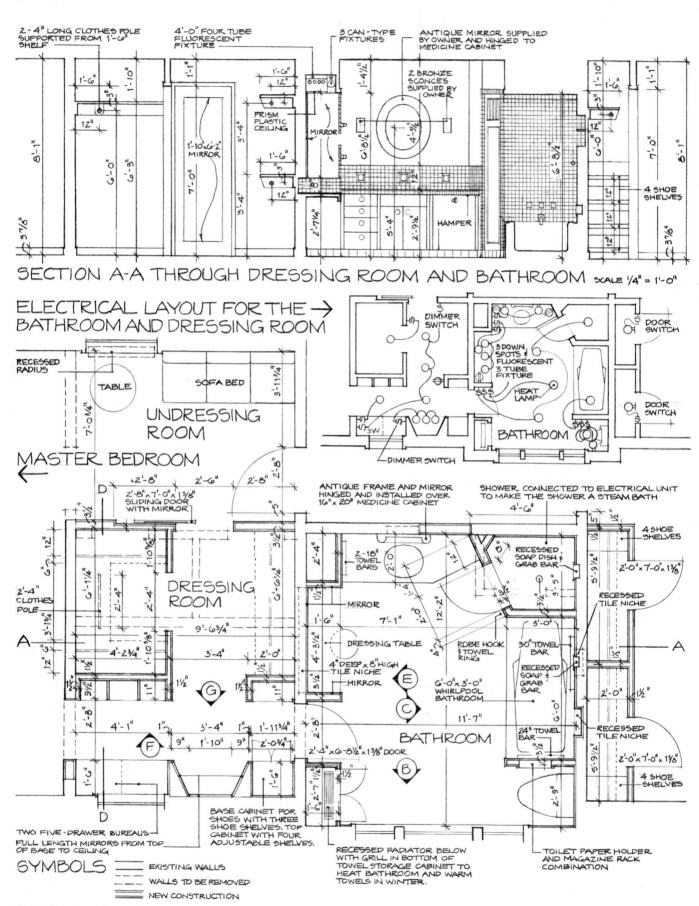

SECTION A-A THROUGH DRESSING ROOM AND BATHROOM SCALE 1/4" = 1'-0"

2-4" LONG CLOTHES POLE SUPPORTED FROM 1'-6" SHELF

4'-0" FOUR TUBE FLUORESCENT FIXTURE

3 CAN-TYPE FIXTURES

ANTIQUE MIRROR SUPPLIED BY OWNER AND HINGED TO MEDICINE CABINET

2 BRONZE SCONCES SUPPLIED BY OWNER

PRISM PLASTIC CEILING

1'-10"x6'-2" MIRROR

MIRROR

HAMPER

4 SHOE SHELVES

ELECTRICAL LAYOUT FOR THE →
BATHROOM AND DRESSING ROOM

RECESSED RADIUS

TABLE

SOFA BED

UNDRESSING ROOM

MASTER BEDROOM

DIMMER SWITCH

DOOR SWITCH

3 DOWN SPOTS & FLUORESCENT 3 TUBE FIXTURE

HEAT LAMP

BATHROOM

DOOR SWITCH

DIMMER SWITCH

2'-8"x7'-0"x1 3/8" SLIDING DOOR WITH MIRROR

DRESSING ROOM

2'-4" CLOTHES POLE

ANTIQUE FRAME AND MIRROR HINGED AND INSTALLED OVER 16"x 20" MEDICINE CABINET

SHOWER CONNECTED TO ELECTRICAL UNIT TO MAKE THE SHOWER A STEAM BATH

4 SHOE SHELVES

2-18" TOWEL BARS

MIRROR

RECESSED SOAP DISH & GRAB BAR

RECESSED TILE NICHE

DRESSING TABLE

4" DEEP x 8" HIGH TILE NICHE

MIRROR

ROBE HOOK & TOWEL RING

30" TOWEL BAR

RECESSED SOAP & GRAB BAR

6'-0"x 3'-0" WHIRLPOOL BATHROOM

BATHROOM

24" TOWEL BAR

RECESSED TILE NICHE

4 SHOE SHELVES

TWO FIVE-DRAWER BUREAUS FULL LENGTH MIRRORS FROM TOP OF BASE TO CEILING

BASE CABINET FOR SHOES WITH THREE SHOE SHELVES. TOP CABINET WITH FOUR ADJUSTABLE SHELVES.

RECESSED RADIATOR BELOW WITH GRILL IN BOTTOM OF TOWEL STORAGE CABINET TO HEAT BATHROOM AND WARM TOWELS IN WINTER.

TOILET PAPER HOLDER AND MAGAZINE RACK COMBINATION

SYMBOLS

——————— EXISTING WALLS

- - - - - - WALLS TO BE REMOVED

≡≡≡≡≡ NEW CONSTRUCTION

DETAIL PLAN OF BATHROOM AND DRESSING ROOM SCALE 1/4" = 1'-0"

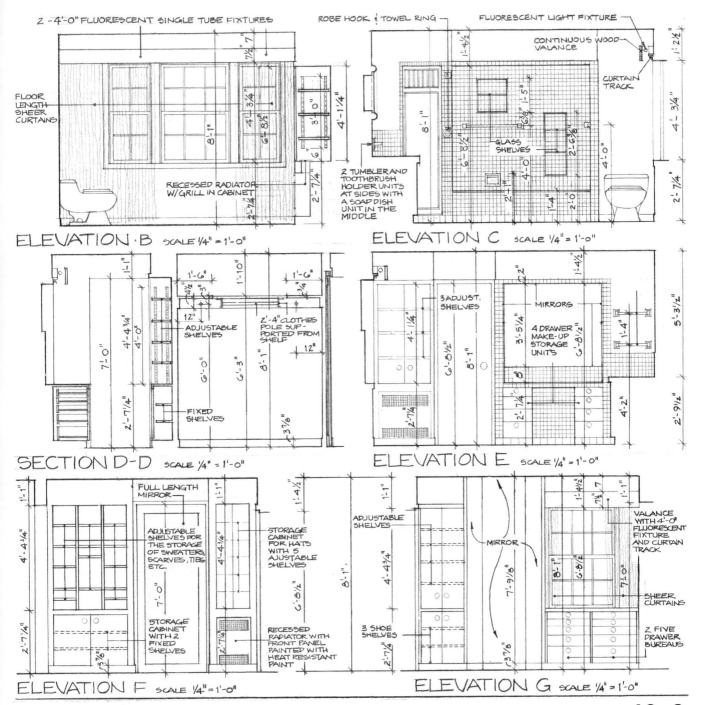

2 -4'-0" FLUORESCENT SINGLE TUBE FIXTURES

ROBE HOOK & TOWEL RING

FLUORESCENT LIGHT FIXTURE

CONTINUOUS WOOD VALANCE

CURTAIN TRACK

FLOOR LENGTH SHEER CURTAINS

RECESSED RADIATOR W/GRILL IN CABINET

GLASS SHELVES

2 TUMBLER AND TOOTHBRUSH HOLDER UNITS AT SIDES WITH A SOAP DISH UNIT IN THE MIDDLE

ELEVATION·B   SCALE ¼" = 1'-0"

ELEVATION C   SCALE ¼" = 1'-0"

ADJUSTABLE SHELVES

2'-4" CLOTHES POLE SUPPORTED FROM SHELF

FIXED SHELVES

SECTION D-D   SCALE ¼" = 1'-0"

3 ADJUST. SHELVES

MIRRORS

4 DRAWER MAKE-UP STORAGE UNITS

ELEVATION E   SCALE ¼" = 1'-0"

FULL LENGTH MIRROR

ADJUSTABLE SHELVES FOR THE STORAGE OF SWEATERS, SCARVES, TIES, ETC.

STORAGE CABINET WITH 2 FIXED SHELVES

STORAGE CABINET FOR HATS WITH 5 ADJUSTABLE SHELVES

RECESSED RADIATOR WITH FRONT PANEL PAINTED WITH HEAT RESISTANT PAINT

ADJUSTABLE SHELVES

MIRROR

3 SHOE SHELVES

VALANCE WITH 4'-0" FLUORESCENT FIXTURE AND CURTAIN TRACK

SHEER CURTAINS

2 FIVE DRAWER BUREAUS

ELEVATION F   SCALE ¼" = 1'-0"

ELEVATION G   SCALE ¼" = 1'-0"

BATHROOM WITH DRESSING ROOM

16–3

This bathroom-dressing room was designed for clients both of whom were over six feet tall and whose business was owning and managing stores for high-style women's clothing. This detail shows the dressing room, the undressing (intimate) room, and the bathroom for the 6'-2" blonde wife. These are directly connected to her own master bedroom, which in turn is adjacent to the husband's bedroom, dressing room, and bathroom.

All countertops and the dressing table tops are extra-high instead of the usual 2'-7" and 2'-5". The dressing room not only had to be carefully planned for all types of dresses, gowns, coats, slacks, blouses, jackets, etc., but it also had to provide storage for sweaters, scarfs, ties, shoes, stockings, and other accessories. Note that the passage in the dressing room which faces the window wall has three full-length angled mirrors and on the back of the sliding door is another full-length mirror, so that she can see herself from all sides to check her total ensemble and makeup. On the electrical plan, note the three down lights in the ceiling within the angular mirror space plus a series of down lights which are installed within the length of the passage so that the effectiveness of her outfit while moving about and walking would be illuminated and could be studied for best results.

The dressing table in the bathroom has three incandescent down lights plus a four-tube fluorescent fixture so that she is able to adjust her makeup and jewelry under either incandescent or fluorescent light alone or under both types of light.

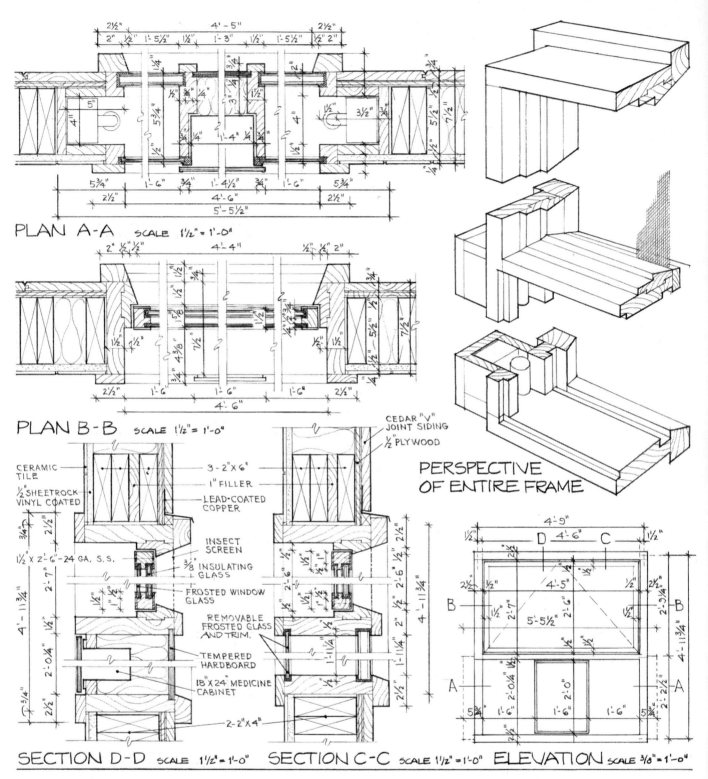

PLAN A-A SCALE 1½" = 1'-0"

PLAN B-B SCALE 1½" = 1'-0"

PERSPECTIVE
OF ENTIRE FRAME

CEDAR "V"
JOINT SIDING
½" PLYWOOD

CERAMIC
TILE
½" SHEETROCK
VINYL COATED

½" X 2'-6"-24 GA. S.S.

3-2" X 6"

1" FILLER

LEAD-COATED
COPPER

INSECT
SCREEN

⅜" INSULATING
GLASS

FROSTED WINDOW
GLASS

REMOVABLE
FROSTED GLASS
AND TRIM.

TEMPERED
HARDBOARD

18" X 24" MEDICINE
CABINET

2-2" X 4"

SECTION D-D SCALE 1½" = 1'-0"   SECTION C-C SCALE 1½" = 1'-0"   ELEVATION SCALE ⅜" = 1'-0"

16–4 BATHROOM WINDOW

One of the problems in bathrooms is how to place fixtures on the wall where windows can be and often are installed. This detail shows the combination of window, medicine cabinet, mirror, and lights all in one unit. This detail was designed for a 18″ X 24″ medicine cabinet with a recess opening 16″ X 22″ X 4″ deep. To fit in any other medicine cabinet, only the two side fixed-glass panes have to change in dimension, and the window height also changes in dimension. This unit was used by the author's office in numerous residential projects with many sizes of medicine cabinets. The entire unit can be manufactured by a kitchen cabinet company or a furniture company in the area where the residence is to be built.

CROSS-REFERENCES TO *KITCHENS AND BATHROOMS*
IN OTHER CHAPTERS

Chapter Number	Drawing Number	Drawing Title	Described on Page	Drawing on Page
5	5-3	Interior joints for plywood quarter-inch	35	38
	5-4	Cabinet and millwork joints for plywood and solid wood	35	39
14	14-1	Executive's desk	127	130, 131
	14-3	Residential bar	127	133
	14-5	Two display cases	127	136
	14-6	Built-in bed	128	137
	14-8	Built-in sofa and bookshelves	128	139
	14-9	Reception desk	128	140, 141
15	15-1	Interior planters for residences	147	149

Index